Sermons by the Reverend and learned Mr. William Wilson, late minister of the Gospel at Perth, viz. I. The Church's extremity ...

William Wilson

Gale ECCO Print Editions

Relive history with *Eighteenth Century Collections Online*, now available in print for the independent historian and collector. This series includes the most significant English-language and foreign-language works printed in Great Britain during the eighteenth century, and is organized in seven different subject areas including literature and language; medicine, science, and technology; and religion and philosophy. The collection also includes thousands of important works from the Americas.

The eighteenth century has been called "The Age of Enlightenment." It was a period of rapid advance in print culture and publishing, in world exploration, and in the rapid growth of science and technology – all of which had a profound impact on the political and cultural landscape. At the end of the century the American Revolution, French Revolution and Industrial Revolution, perhaps three of the most significant events in modern history, set in motion developments that eventually dominated world political, economic, and social life.

In a groundbreaking effort, Gale initiated a revolution of its own: digitization of epic proportions to preserve these invaluable works in the largest online archive of its kind. Contributions from major world libraries constitute over 175,000 original printed works. Scanned images of the actual pages, rather than transcriptions, recreate the works *as they first appeared.*

Now for the first time, these high-quality digital scans of original works are available via print-on-demand, making them readily accessible to libraries, students, independent scholars, and readers of all ages.

For our initial release we have created seven robust collections to form one the world's most comprehensive catalogs of 18th century works.

Initial Gale ECCO Print Editions collections include:

History and Geography
Rich in titles on English life and social history, this collection spans the world as it was known to eighteenth-century historians and explorers. Titles include a wealth of travel accounts and diaries, histories of nations from throughout the world, and maps and charts of a world that was still being discovered. Students of the War of American Independence will find fascinating accounts from the British side of conflict.

Social Science

Delve into what it was like to live during the eighteenth century by reading the first-hand accounts of everyday people, including city dwellers and farmers, businessmen and bankers, artisans and merchants, artists and their patrons, politicians and their constituents. Original texts make the American, French, and Industrial revolutions vividly contemporary.

Medicine, Science and Technology

Medical theory and practice of the 1700s developed rapidly, as is evidenced by the extensive collection, which includes descriptions of diseases, their conditions, and treatments. Books on science and technology, agriculture, military technology, natural philosophy, even cookbooks, are all contained here.

Literature and Language

Western literary study flows out of eighteenth-century works by Alexander Pope, Daniel Defoe, Henry Fielding, Frances Burney, Denis Diderot, Johann Gottfried Herder, Johann Wolfgang von Goethe, and others. Experience the birth of the modern novel, or compare the development of language using dictionaries and grammar discourses.

Religion and Philosophy

The Age of Enlightenment profoundly enriched religious and philosophical understanding and continues to influence present-day thinking. Works collected here include masterpieces by David Hume, Immanuel Kant, and Jean-Jacques Rousseau, as well as religious sermons and moral debates on the issues of the day, such as the slave trade. The Age of Reason saw conflict between Protestantism and Catholicism transformed into one between faith and logic -- a debate that continues in the twenty-first century.

Law and Reference

This collection reveals the history of English common law and Empire law in a vastly changing world of British expansion. Dominating the legal field is the *Commentaries of the Law of England* by Sir William Blackstone, which first appeared in 1765. Reference works such as almanacs and catalogues continue to educate us by revealing the day-to-day workings of society.

Fine Arts

The eighteenth-century fascination with Greek and Roman antiquity followed the systematic excavation of the ruins at Pompeii and Herculaneum in southern Italy; and after 1750 a neoclassical style dominated all artistic fields. The titles here trace developments in mostly English-language works on painting, sculpture, architecture, music, theater, and other disciplines. Instructional works on musical instruments, catalogs of art objects, comic operas, and more are also included.

The BiblioLife Network

This project was made possible in part by the BiblioLife Network (BLN), a project aimed at addressing some of the huge challenges facing book preservationists around the world. The BLN includes libraries, library networks, archives, subject matter experts, online communities and library service providers. We believe every book ever published should be available as a high-quality print reproduction; printed on-demand anywhere in the world. This insures the ongoing accessibility of the content and helps generate sustainable revenue for the libraries and organizations that work to preserve these important materials.

The following book is in the "public domain" and represents an authentic reproduction of the text as printed by the original publisher. While we have attempted to accurately maintain the integrity of the original work, there are sometimes problems with the original work or the micro-film from which the books were digitized. This can result in minor errors in reproduction. Possible imperfections include missing and blurred pages, poor pictures, markings and other reproduction issues beyond our control. Because this work is culturally important, we have made it available as part of our commitment to protecting, preserving, and promoting the world's literature.

GUIDE TO FOLD-OUTS MAPS and OVERSIZED IMAGES

The book you are reading was digitized from microfilm captured over the past thirty to forty years. Years after the creation of the original microfilm, the book was converted to digital files and made available in an online database.

In an online database, page images do not need to conform to the size restrictions found in a printed book. When converting these images back into a printed bound book, the page sizes are standardized in ways that maintain the detail of the original. For large images, such as fold-out maps, the original page image is split into two or more pages

Guidelines used to determine how to split the page image follows:

• Some images are split vertically; large images require vertical and horizontal splits.
• For horizontal splits, the content is split left to right.
• For vertical splits, the content is split from top to bottom.
• For both vertical and horizontal splits, the image is processed from top left to bottom right.

SERMONS

BY THE

Reverend and Learned Mr. *William Wilson*, late Minister of the Gospel at *Perth*, viz.

I The Church's Extremity Chrift's Opportunity.

II. The Lamb's Retinue attending him whitherfoever he goeth.

III. The Father's Promife to the Son, a clear Bow in the Church's darkeft Cloud.

IV. The Watchman's Duty and Defire.

V. Stedfaftnefs in the Faith recommended.

VI. The Bleffednefs loft in the firft *Adam*, to be found in Chrift the fecond *Adam*.

Entred in Stationers-Hall.

E D I N B U R G H,

Printed for *David Duncan* at the Weigh-Houfe in *Edinburgh*, and for *John Henderfon* in *Abernethy:* and fold by the Bookfellers in Town and Country. 1748.

The CHURCH's Extremity, CHRIST's Opportunity.

A

SERMON

Preached upon *Monday*, immediately after the Celebration of the Sacrament of the Lord's Supper at *Abernethy*, *July* 17. 1738.

By the late REVEREND *and* LEARNED *Mr.* WILLIAM WILSON *Minister of the Gospel at* Perth.

Carefully revised by a reverend Member of the Associate Synod.

E D I N B U R G H,

Printed for *David Duncan,* and Sold at his House, opposite to the *Weigh-House*, North Side of the Street. MDCCXLVII.

MICAH iv. 10.

Be in Pain, and labour to bring forth, O Daughter of Zion, like a Woman in Travail, for now shalt thou go forth out of the City, thou shalt dwell in the Field, and thou shalt go even to Babylon, there shalt thou be delivered, there the Lord shall redeem thee from the Hand of thine Enemies.

IT is in the middle Clause of the Verse I design to insist upon, *And thou shalt go even to Babylon, there shalt thou be delivered.*

My Friends, when we are met together about the solemn Worship of God, we are to remember it is a great Point in Worship, to have the solid Faith of the great Object of divine Worship. We are a worshipping Assembly, one of the Assemblies of Mount *Zion,* and, O that we had the lively Impression of that God whom we profess to worship · Without Faith it is impossible to please God : our Worship is but dead Worship without Faith, our Worship is but formal Worship without Faith, yea, let me tell you, our Worship is no Worship at all, in the Sight of God, without Faith. We are one of the Assemblies of Mount *Zion,* of the Gospel Church, met together upon a very solemn Occasion. Yesterday

5

we

we were commemorating the Death of Christ in the Sacrament of the Supper, and we are now assembled this Day to offer up the spiritual Sacrifice of Praise and Thanksgiving unto him, to bless our God aloud   My Friends, have we not much Matter and Ground of Praise? I dare say, that those among you, who are in the darkest Case, in the deadest Case, under the heaviest Complaint with Reference to themselves, with Reference to their own spiritual Case and Condition, have yet Matter and Ground of Praise   Are you saying, *Behold I go forward, but he is not there, and backward, but I cannot perceive him; on the left Hand where he doth work, but I cannot behold him, he hideth himself on the Right-Hand that I cannot see him.* Why, be it so, Sirs, you have yet Matter and Ground of Praise. Have you not Reason to say, *Thou art righteous when thou pleadest with me, when thou hidest thy Face from me, when thou coverest thyself with a Cloud.* Sirs, if there is a Frame of Spirit in you to justify God, and condemn yourselves, it is a good Disposition of Spirit, it is a Bow in your Cloud, when he is hiding his Face from you. Again, is it not Ground and Matter of Praise, that you are not in the bottomless Pit, that you are not in Hell? I am sure, if you are rightly exercised, you will reckon it a Mercy that ye have Access to look towards God's holy Temple, it is a Mercy that the Cup of vindictive Wrath is not put into your Hand. This indeed says, that he hath not dealt with you according to your Sins, nor rewarded you according to your Iniquities. Well, in your lowest Case, may it not be a Note of Praise to you, *He dealt not with us according to your Sins,* &c. In a Word, if you are complaining that you cannot find him in the Sacrament, nor in the Word, ye are just the worst in the

World,

World, ye have the moſt unbelieving Heart, the
moſt obſtinate Heart, the moſt hard Heart, and
the moſt atheiſtical Heart in the World ; ye
are ſaying, There is none like you , ye are
ſaying, It may be there is ſomething peculiar in
your Caſe, that is not to be found in the Caſe
of another, none like you, no Caſe like yours
in this whole Aſſembly . Yet we tell you, there
is ſtill Matter and Ground of Praiſe, that there
is Balm in *Gilead*, and that there is a Phyſician there. It is Matter and Ground of Praiſe to
you, that Chriſt lives ; that tho' he was dead, now
he is alive again, and liveth for evermore, and hath
the Keys of Hell and of Death. It is Matter and
Ground of Praiſe, and that in the very worſt Caſe
amongſt you, the moſt ſingular Caſe out of the bot-
tomleſs Pit, that Chriſt is a Phyſician, that Chriſt
is a Helper in the very greateſt Extremity. Is thy
Caſe a ſingular Caſe ? Chriſt is a ſingular Phyſician, Chriſt is a ſingular Saviour, Chriſt is a ſingular
Remedy, Chriſt is a ſingular Help, a matchleſs and
a none-ſuch Help, whatever your Caſe is. Here
then is Matter and Ground of Praiſe, that the Lord
hath viſited *Adam*'s Family. I remember to have
read in the Diary of an eminent Chriſtian, who,
falling under a Cloud, called all in Queſtion that
ever God had done for him He began to think
God had viſited *Adam*'s Family. There is a
Remnant of *Adam*'s Family that he hath redeemed
to himſelf *I will try to bleſs him*, (ſaid he) *that he
hath redeemed a Company out of* Adam's *Family, tho'
I cannot ſay I am among them*. The honeſt Man
went about to mint at Praiſing, and when he is
doing ſo, it pleaſed the Lord to make him apply
and act Faith upon it as to himſelf, and made him
ſay, *Thou waſt ſlain and haſt redeemed me to God by
thy Blood*. Well, bleſs God that the Day-Spring.

from on high hath visited our Tribe and Family, and perhaps he will lead you on to say he hath visited you, and redeemed you by his Blood. Bless God that he hath made the Light to shine, and sent his Son to bless us, in turning every one of us from our Iniquities. What say you, I cannot bless him, I have neither Heart for Prayer nor Praise? Why, then, you are in the best Tune to go to the Physician. It is best to go poor and empty-handed to Christ. Go, as you are poor and miserable, unable to do any Thing for Christ, or for God Spread the Case out before him who is the Redeemer, come to turn away Ungodliness from *Jacob*. He is a wonderful and only Help, upon whom all our Help is laid. Well, let us have our Eyes to him, and let us essay to give Thanks to him on a Thanksgiving-Day, on a parting Day from this Place, sometimes such a Day has been found a good Day, a convincing Day, a converting Day, a confirming Day, a comforting Day. The Residue of the Spirit is with our Lord, let us have our Eyes to him, that he may send him to bless his own Word we are to deliver to you this Day.

In the first Part of this Chapter where our Text lies, the glorious Advancement and Enlargement of the Church, in New Testament Times, is foretold by the Prophet *Micah*, as in the first Verse, *But in the last Days it shall come to pass, that the Mountain of the House of the Lord shall be established in the Top of the Mountains, and it shall be exalted above the Hills, and People shall flow unto it, and many Nations shall come and say, Come, and let us go up to the Mountain of the Lord, to the House of the God of Jacob, &c.* It is a Prophecy of the Gathering of the Nations to *Shiloh*, of the Gathering of many Nations to the Lord Christ; that Nations shall stir up

up one another to join themſelves unto glorious Chriſt. Alſo, in the latter Part of the Chapter, particularly in the Verſe that I have read, ye have the happy Iſſue of the Church's Trial, the Iſſue of the Trial of the Daughter of *Zion;* tho' ſhe may be brought low. yet ſhe ſhall have a glorious Iſſue to all her ſore Conflicts and Trials. In the Words I have read, the ſore Conflicts of the Church are compared to the Sorrow and Travail of a Woman in Child-bearing. Mark it, they are not like the Agonies of dying Men, but like the Pain and Travail of a Woman, which iſſues in a happy Birth. A Woman, when ſhe is in Travail, ſhe has Sorrow, becauſe her Hour is come, but, as ſoon as ſhe is delivered of the Child, ſhe remembreth no more the Anguiſh, for Joy that a Man-Child is born into the World. But tho' the Church has her ſore Conflicts and Pangs, yet they are promiſing Pangs and Throws, even as the Woman's. They are Pangs that have a promiſing and glorious Iſſue : Therefore, I ſay, the Church being in Pain, labours to bring forth, like a Woman in Travail. Again, in the following Verſe, ye may obſerve, that the Church's Troubles may riſe high, the Floods they may ſwell, the Lord's People (the Daughter of *Zion*) may have Trouble and Trial to the greateſt Extremity meaſured out unto them . *Therefore,* ſaith the Prophet, *thou ſhalt go forth out of the City, and thou ſhalt dwell in the Field.* By theſe ſeveral Expreſſions the Church's extreme Troubles and Trials are held forth by the Prophet There is a gradual Riſe of her Trial ; firſt, *Thou ſhalt go forth out of the City.* By the City we are to underſtand *Jeruſalem. Jeruſalem* was the Place of their ſacred Solemnities, there was the Place of their publick Worſhip ; alſo *Jeruſalem* was the Seat of their
publick

publick Courts of Juftice ; for there are fet Thrones *of Judgment, the Thrones of the Houfe of* David, fays the Pfalmift, *Pfalm* cxxii. 5. *Thou fhalt dwell in the Field;* that is, thou fhalt be ftript naked of all thy fpiritual Privileges in this thy City, and fhalt be even thruft out of thy City. But this is not all, *Thou fhalt even go to* Babylon, thou fhalt fall under the Feet of thine Enemies, the Enemy fhall for a Time get his Will of the Daughter of *Zion, Thou fhalt even go to* Babylon. Ye know, Sirs, what is intended by *Babylon.* That City, the Miftrefs of the then known World, famous for her Tyranny and Oppreffion, in oppreffing the People of God. In the 17th Chapter of the Book of the *Revalaton,* fhe is called, *Myftery,* Babylon *the great, the Mother of Harlots, and Abominations of the Earth*

But again, in the *next* Place, as the Church is brought into thefe Straits, fent out of the City, made to dwell in the Field, brought under the Feet of her Enemies, fo ye may obferve the glorious Deliverance fhe meets with in this Extremity *There fhalt thou be delivered.* Ye would have thought it would been faid, *There fhalt thou be deftroyed, There a full End fhall be made of thee* But, inftead of that, Deliverance is infured unto the Church, it is infured in the Word of Grace and Promife, by the Promife of him who cannot lie. *There fhalt thou be delivered* Ye may notice that the Deliverance is to be given even from *Babylon, There fhalt thou be delivered* The plain Meaning is, juft when thou art brought to the greateft Pinch of Extremity, then in the Mount of the Lord it fhall be feen, then the facred Proverb fhall be verified, JEHOVAH-JIREH, *in the Mount of the Lord it* fhall be feen. *Thou fhalt go even to* Babylon, *and there* fhall *shalt thou be delivered.* When, upon the Matter, all seems to be lost and gone then Deliverance shall come unto thee, *there shalt thou be delivered,* there, in thy utmost Pinch and Strait, Sovereignty shall appear for thee for thy Delivery. Before I pass on to the Doctrine, I observe, by the Way, that the Deliverance from *Babylon,* it is held forth in Scripture under two Things.

1*st.* As a Type of the Redemption of the whole Church and People of God, from the Tyranny and Bondage of Sin and Satan, by the great Redeemer, the Lord Christ. The spiritual Redemption of his People is held forth by the Redemption given by *Joshua,* and by their Deliverance from the Captivity in *Babylon,* at the End of the threescore and ten Years in which he had Indignation. Again,

2*dly.* This Deliverance from *Babylon* is held forth as a Type of that glorious Deliverance that the New Testament Church, in the latter Days, shall obtain from mystical *Babylon,* from Antichristian Tyranny and Idolatry. Hence, in the 18th Chapter of the Book of the *Revelation,* and 2d Verse of that Chapter, *Babylon* the great is said to be fallen, and shall rise no more. But I do not insist farther on any Explication of the Words.

I proceed to draw a plain doctrinal Proposition from them, and in the Prosecution of which I resolve to offer a very few Thoughts.

Doct. *That the greatest Extremity, the Church and People of God may be brought into, makes Way for a glorious Deliverance unto her.* Or thus, *That the Church and People of God are sometimes brought into the greatest Extremity, that her Deliverance may be the more conspicuous and glorious.*

Thou

Thou shalt go even to Babylon, *and there shalt thou be delivered.* The Lord brings his Church and People to very great Extremities, and then just steps in for their Relief and Deliverance, according to that sacred Proverb I cited already, *In the Mount of the Lord it shall be seen* The Scripture is full of Instances of this Kind As for Example, when the Church was in *Egypt,* what a great Extremity was she in ? She cries out under her Bondage, in that 3d Chapter of *Exodus,* and behold, when she is brought into an Extremity, the Lord brings about a wonderful Deliverance for her. In like Manner also, in *Hezekiah's* Days, in the 37th Chapter of the Prophecies of the Prophet *Isaiah,* the Church, in his Time, is brought to such an Extremity, that he cries out, *This Day is a Day of Trouble, and of Rebuke, and of Blasphemy, for the Children are come to the Birth, and there is not Strength to bring forth.* So the Lord makes a surprising Appearance, and works a great Deliverance for his Church and People, even in the Days of this King, when she was so very low. Consider, my Friends what a low Pass the Church was in, when the Prince of Life was lying in the Grave Then the Church was scattered, and brought to the lowest Extremity, yet this did issue in the most glorious Day that ever the Church of Christ did see Then out of *Zion* came forth the Law, and the Word of the Lord from *Jerusalem,* then came the Fountain out from the House of the Lord, and watered the Valley of *Shittim* · That glorious Deliverance is the Foundation of all the after Deliverances to the Church and People of God But, not to insist, all I intend upon the Doctrine, is,

In the *first* Place, to offer some Remarks concerning those extreme Straits that the Church and
People

People of God may be brought into before Deliverance come. 2*dly.* Give the Reasons why the
Church and People of God are brought into such
extreme Straits 3*dly.* Observe some of the remarkable Deliverances the Lord gives to the Daughter of *Zion,* when she is brought to *Babylon,* or to
those extreme Straits or Difficulties And then, in
the 4*th* and *last* Place, make some practical Use and
Improvement of the Subject.

I return then to the *first* of these, *namely,* to offer some Remarks concerning those extreme Straits
that the Church and People of God may be brought
into

In the *first* Place, I remark, that as the Church
may be brought into extreme Straits before Deliverance come, so all the Children that are brought
forth in *Zion,* they are sometimes brought into extreme Straits, as, in the *first* Place, they are brought
into extreme Straits at their Birth, 2*dly.* Sometimes they are brought into extreme Straits after
their Birth

In the *first* Place, I say, they are brought to extreme Straits in their spiritual Birth Those that
are brought forth in *Zion,* the Lord makes a fearful Work in less or more in their Consciences, the
Terror of the Lord takes hold on them, they are
brought to the Foot of Mount *Sinai,* the awful
Thunder of Mount *Sinai* thunders on their Hearts,
and here some of them are kept under the Spirit
of Bondage for a considerable Time. One of which
the Apostle *Paul* seems to have been, he seems to
have had something of this exemplified in himself,
when the Lord appeared to him in his Way to
Damascus. He was struck down to the Ground,
struck blind for some Days, till *Ananias* came to
him with a Message of Deliverance from God It
is ordinary that the Children of God, in such a
Case

Case as this, are under extreme Fears with respect to the Issue of their Distress, they are under extreme Temptations; Satan is permitted to attack the Soul with his fiery Darts, and fiery Temptations, in so much that the Soul, in this, or such a Case as this, is brought to draw the Conclusion, as if their Case were desperate. Sometimes, before the Delivery, the Soul is brought to the very Borders of Desperation. Thus, I say, those who are the Children of *Zion* are brought to an Extremity in their spiritual Bath, before the Lord give a Delivery to them, before the Lord Christ be revealed in them, before the Gospel found in their Hearts. They are brought to Mount *Sinai* before they are brought to Mount *Zion*, and when, in such a Case as this, the Lord is pleased sometimes to appear remarkably for them, in their Straits to scatter their Clouds, and to clear their Sky, by manifesting his Christ unto them, thus they are brought unto *Babylon*, and there they are delivered.

Again, 2*dly.* Those Children that are born in *Zion*, they may have extreme Straits after their spiritual Birth, after they are regenerated. They may fall under extreme Straits, sometimes of one Kind, and sometimes of another, they may, and often do fall into the extreme Strait of the Sense of Distance from God, the extreme Strait of the Fear of eternal Wrath, tho' this is their Sin. Legal Terrors may take hold on their Consciences after Regeneration, as in the Instance of *Heman* in the 88th *Psalm* and 15th Verse, *I am afflicted, and ready to die from my Youth up. While I suffer thy Terrors I am distracted.* The Lord's People, after their spiritual Birth, may be brought under extreme Temptations. The Apostle, in writing to the believing *Ephesians*, exhorting them, Chapter 6th and Verse 11th, to *put on the whole Armour* of God, *that they may be able to stand against the Wiles of the Devil*, gives us to understand, that even Believers themselves, Persons who are born again, may be attacked with the fiery Darts of the Devil. Farther, the Lord's People, after their spiritual Birth, may be brought to the extreme Strait of Desertion, and the hiding of God's Countenance. Our Lord Jesus Christ himself drank deep of this Cup, and that for the Sake of all his little Ones, *Psalm* xxii. 1. compared with *Matthew* xxvii 46. *My God, my God, why hast thou forsaken me ?* Again, the Lord's People, even after Regeneration, may bring themselves into extreme Straits by their Backsliding from the Lord, in so much that they may need a Sight of their first Conversion. Hence we find the Psalmist praying, *Psalm* li 10. *Create in me a clean Heart, O God, and renew a right Spirit within me.* They may be brought into such an extreme Strait, that they may be just withering and dying, just expiring; yea more, they may apprehend themselves dead, cut off for their Parts, as in that 37th Chapter of *Ezekiel*, and 11th Verse, *Behold they say, our Bones are dried, our Hope is lost, we are cut off for our Parts.* To these, and such like extreme Straits, I say, the Lord's People may be brought, even after they are born in *Zion*, and I am much afraid, my Friends, this is in a great Measure your Case. There is Ground to apprehend it is the Case of the Lord's Remnant at this Day, that they are brought to the extreme Strait of Distance from God, in their Apprehension, to the extreme Strait of a slavish and unwarrantable Fear of eternal Wrath; to the extreme Strait of Temptations and Attacks from *Satan*, to the extreme Strait of Desertion and the hiding of God's Countenance, and that they are in

many

many such like Cases. But is there not a Bow in the Cloud ? Why, there is just Help in the Lord for such Extremities. When the Church in general, or a Soul in particular, is brought into the greatest Extremity, then, even then, he gives Enlargement to the Church or to the Soul *Thou shalt go even to Babylon, and there shalt thou be delivered.* To excite your Faith and Hope of this Deliverance, when ye are brought to cry, *Our Bones are dried, our Hope is lost, and we are cut off for our Parts,* consider what you heard on *Saturday,* namely, that Christ is the Resurrection and the Life, and so, of consequence, there is Redemption and Deliverance in him, and in him for you.

But then, again, in the *second* Place, upon this Head, I remark, that sometimes *Zion* has an easy and a gentle Labour, and yet brings forth a numerous and glorious Offspring, a Proof of which you have in the 66th Chapter of the Prophecies of the Prophet *Isaiah,* and the 8th Verse, *Who hath heard such a Thing ? Who hath seen such Things ? Shall the Earth be made to bring forth in one Day ? Or shall a Nation be born at once ? For, assoon as* Zion *travailed, she brought forth her Children* Yea, not only assoon as *Zion* travails does she bring forth her Children, in such a Case as this, but even before Travail a numerous and glorious Offspring is produced from *Zion's* pregnant Womb, as in the 7th Verse of that same 66th of *Isaiah, Before she travailed she brought forth, before her Pain came she was delivered of a Man-Child.* This was immediately verified after the Resurrection of our Lord Christ, on the Day of *Pentecoste,* and I may say it has been verified in a particular Manner even in *Scotland,* our native Land, in her reforming Times, when the

Lord

Lord led our Forefathers by the Hand out of the *E-gypt* of black Popery and Paganifm, even to the Length of a folemn Avouching of him to be their God, and that with uplifted Hands to the moft high God · Then, no fooner did *Zion* travail, but immediately fhe brought forth Children, a numerous and glorious Offspring to the Lord Chrift.

But again, farther, in the *third* Place, upon this Head, we may remark, that, before *Zion* be delivered, fhe may have long Trouble and Pain, fhe may go forth out of the City, fhe may dwell in the Field; yea, more, fhe may go even to *Babylon*, before fhe be delivered   You that are Believers in Chrift, true Church-Members, the genuine Sons and Daughters of *Zion*, you muft be brought from one Strait to another, from one Difficulty to another, one Extremity to another, before you be delivered. *Thou fhalt go forth out of the City, thou fhalt dwell in the Field, yea, thou fhalt go even to* Babylon, *there fhalt thou be delivered.*

There are five Particulars with relation to the extreme Straits the Church and People of God may be brought into before Deliverance come, which I fhall mention on this Remark   And, in the *firft* Place, the Daughter of *Zion* may be brought to this Strait, of being ftript of all her Beauty   You have a Word to this Purpofe in the firft Chapter of the Book of the *Lamentations of* Jeremiah, and there the 6th Verfe, *From the Daughter of* Zion *all her Beauty is departed   All her Beauty is departed.*   What think you is the Beauty of the Daughter of *Zion*, or the Church of Chrift ? Why, it confifts chiefly in thefe two Things, 1ft. In Purity, 2dly. In the fpecial Prefence of God

Firft, I fay, the Beauty of the Daughter of *Zion* confifteth in the Purity of Doctrine, Worfhip, Difcipline and Government. The Beauty of the
Daughter

Daughter of *Zion*, I fay, confifteth in the Purity of the Doctrines of the Gofpel delivered from the Word of Truth in the Church of Chrift, when nothing is taught therein, but what is exactly agreeable to his Mind and Will, and when the Difcipline of his Houfe is managed and difpenfed according to the Rule laid down in the Law and Teftimony, and the Government of his Houfe doth exactly quadrate with the Pattern hewn in the Mount of divine Revelation. But then,

2*dly.* Not only does the Beauty of the Daughter of *Zion* confift in the Beauty of Purity, but alfo in the Beauty of Prefence, in the fpecial Prefence of God in and with his Church and People. Remark it, Sirs, when the Beauty of Purity departs from *Zion*, from the Church, the Beauty of Prefence does not readily continue in her. O what a Beauty is it to *Zion* the Prefence of her God! When the Lord Jefus Chrift, the King of *Zion*, is in the Midft of her, he is her Beauty and Glory, he himfelf is her Dignity and Excellency. To apply as we go along, we may fee what a deplorable Cafe and Condition the Daughter of *Zion*, the New Teftament Church, is in at this Day, when her fpiritual Beauty is, in fuch a great Meafure, departed from her. When God took her by the Hand, and led her out of *Babylon*, fhe was a noble Vine, wholly a right Seed, but, alas, the noble Vine is turned into the degenerate Plant of a ftrange Vine! The Beauty of Purity is in a great Meafure defaced among all the Churches of Chrift, and in the Church of *Scotland* amongft the reft. And as the Beauty is defaced, is not alfo the divine Prefence departed in a great Meafure, in fo much that a Lamentation may be taken up over her, *How is thy Gold become dim! How is the moft fine Gold*
changed!

changel ! How is Error mingled with the pure Doctrines of his Word in this Day of Degeneracy from the Lord ! How is the Light of his Countenance withdrawn in a great Measure ! He hath shut up himself in a Cloud, that we cannot perceive him. It is not with us as in Months past, when the Lord made his Candle to shine upon our Head

A *2d* Particular I shall mention on this Remark, is, That the Church of Christ, the Daughter of *Zion*, may be sent out of the City, to dwell in the Field, *&c* before she be delivered., *that is,* The Church may be brought to a very great Strait, laid under the Feet of her Adversaries, under the Feet of her Enemies Hence the Church cries out, because of Affliction, her Persecutors overtook her. Sometimes this is the Case, her Enemies they overtake her, she is carried Captive by them, carried even to *Babylon* by them, and trodden under Foot by them for some Time

But then, a *3d* Particular I mention, on this Remark, is, That the Church of Christ. before she be delivered, may be brought to this Strait, even to be deprived of her sacred Solemnities. This we see was the Case of the Church here, as is plainly pointed out in the Words read, *Thou shalt go forth out of the City*, *that is,* Thou shall be deprived of thy sacred Solemnities, thou shalt be deprived of thy solemn Feast-Days Hence is that Word, *The Ways to* Zion *languish, the Gates of* Zion *languish, none come to her solemn Feasts.*

A *4th* Particular I mention on this Remark, is, That the Church of Christ, the Daughter of *Zion*, before she be delivered, may be brought to this Strait, that there may be no *publick Testimony* lifted up for the Truth of God, for his declarative

C Glory

Glory amongſt them, as for Inſtance, this way the Caſe of the Church in the 74th *Pſalm*, and there the 9th Verſe, *We ſee not our Signs, there is no more any Prophet, neither is there any among us who knoweth how long* You have alſo a Word in the 11th Chapter of the *Revelation*, and 8th Verſe, which concerneth old *Babylon*, but is typical of the New Teſtament Church, *Then dead Bodies ſhall ly in the Street of the great City, which ſpiritually is called* Sodom *and* Egypt, *where alſo our Lord was crucified.* Whether this Prophecy is fulfilled or not, as yet, I ſhall not determine But it ſpeaks a Falling of the Teſtimony of Chriſt in the Church, and among the People of God, when the Beauty of the Daughter of *Zion* departs from her, and her Enemies have her under their Feet O what an extreme Strait is ſhe in when ſhe comes to be ſtript of her Beauty, held under the Feet of her Adverſaries, deprived of her Solemnities, and when all publick Teſtimony for the Glory of *Immanuel* falls to the Ground ! Theſe indeed are great Extremities, yet,

Laſtly, Upon this Remark, we tell you, ſometimes the Church and People of God, the Daughter of *Zion*, before Deliverance, may be brought to this Extremity, that there is no viſible Outgate for her, no Help, no Deliverance to any human Appearance Thus you ſee it was with the Church and People of God in *Ezekiel's* Days In the 37th Chapter of *Ezekiel* and 11th Verſe, the Church is ſpoken of after this Manner *Then he ſaid unto me, Son of Man theſe Bones are the whole Houſe of Iſrael. Behold, they ſay, Our Bones are dried, and our Hope is loſt we are cut off for our Parts.* Thus far may the Daughter of *Zion* be brought before Deliverance : But it is worthy of our Notice and Obſervation '

Obſervation, that, when ſhe is brought to this Pinch and Strait, juſt when ſhe is ſaying her Bones are dried and her Hope loſt, even then, in that Interim, behold Deliverance comes, as we may ſee in the Verſes immediately following the Church's grievous Complaint, Verſes 12th and 13th, *Therefore prophecy and ſay unto them, Thus ſaith the Lord God, behold, O my People, I will open your Graves, and cauſe you to come up out of your Graves, and bring you into the Land of* Iſrael *, and ye ſhall know that I am the Lord, when I have opened your Graves, O my People, and brought you up out of your Graves!* Agreeable to this Purpoſe alſo, is what we have in the 11th of the *Revelation*, from the 8th to the 12th Verſe of that Chapter. There we ſee the Witneſſes are ſlain, their dead Bodies are laid on the Streets, all ſeems to be loſt and gone, but even this Extremity juſt preceeds a glorious Delivery and Revival to his Church. *And their dead Bodies ſhall ly in the Streets of the great City, which ſpiritually is called* Sodom *and* Egypt*, where alſo our Lord was crucified, and they of the People, and Kinbed, and Tongues, and Nations, ſhall ſee their dead Bodies, three Days and an Half, and ſhall not ſuffer their dead Bodies to be put in Graves,* (ſo great ſhall be their Tyranny and Cruelty) *and they that dwell upon the Earth ſhall rejoice over them, and make merry, and ſhall ſend Gifts one to another, becauſe theſe two Prophets tormented them that dwelt on the Earth.* Note what follows, *And after three Days and an Half, the Spirit of Life from God entred into them, and they ſtood upon their Feet, and great Fear fell upon them which ſaw them.* Here we ſee plainly, when all Hope ſeemed to be loſt and gone, and the *Babylonians* ſeemed to have got all their Will of the Church of God, yet his Thoughts are not their

their Thoughts, for the Spirit of Life from
God enters into them, and then they are set to
their Feet again. This much for the extreme
Straits that the Church and People of God may
be brought unto before Deliverance come, and so
I pass the Remarks, and go on to the

Second general Head which I proposed, *namely,*
To give the Reasons why the Church and People of
God are brought into such extreme Straits before
Deliverance come

There are only these few Reasons following
which I shall assign for it at present In the *first*
Place, the Church and People of God are brought
into extreme Straits before Deliverance, that the
glorious Majesty of God may be proclaimed, that
his infinite Holiness may be published and declared,
that his Hatred and Detestation of Sin may be e-
videnced, for he is a God of purer Eyes than to
behold Iniquity, and cannot look upon Sin. All
the Churches must know, that the Lord search-
eth the Heart and trieth the Reins, if there be
any Sin latent there, behold he will find it out,
and so, when his Church and People backslide
from him, go a-whoring from him, then he will
manifest his infinite Holiness and Hatred of Sin,
in punishing them for their Iniquity, and, in so
doing, he will bring them into extreme Straits,
put them out of the City, make them dwell in the
Field, yea, bring them even to *Babylon* For the
Transgression of Jacob *is all this, and for the Iniquity
of the House of* Israel. But again, in the

2*d* Place, The Church and People of God are
brought into extreme Straits before Deliverance.
Why? For this End, that he may try the Faith and
Patience of his People that he may be glorified in
and by the Faith and Patience of his People. Observe
the

the Expreſſion you have in the 13th Chapter of the
Revelation, and 10th Verſe, *Here is the Faith and
Patience of the Saints ;* that is, Here the Faith and
Patience of the Saints is tried ; here the Faith
and Patience of the Saints is kythed , here God
is glorified in the Faith and Patience of the Saints ,
here the Truth and Reality of the true Religion
of Jeſus is vindicated and aſſerted by the Faith and
Patience of the Saints.   Again,

3dly. The Church and People of God are,
brought into extreme Straits before Deliverance,
for this End alſo, that God's Hand may be ſeen
in giving the Deliverance to his Church and People.
Thou ſhalt even go to Babylon, *and there ſhalt thou be
delivered , there the Lord ſhall redeem thee from the
Hand of thine Enemies.*   I ſay, the Church and
People of God are brought into extreme Straits
before Deliverance, juſt that God himſelf may be
eminently and conſpicuouſly ſeen in giving the Deliverance , that the Love and Pity of God may be
ſeen, in taking Care of his Church and People till
the Deliverance be wrought , that the Power and
Omnipotence of God may be eminently ſeen and
diſplayed in giving the Deliverance , it is juſt,
that *Jehovah* do appear like himſelf, in breaking
the mighty Gates of Braſs, and cutting the Bars
of Iron aſunder .   It is he that ſpeaks of *Cyrus* as a
Type of Chriſt, in the 45th Chapter of *Iſaiah's*
Prophecies, and 2d Verſe   When he is about
to deliver *Zion*, he ſays, *I will go before thee, and
make thy crooked Places ſtreight : I will break in
Pieces the Gates of Braſs, and cut in ſunder the Bars
of Iron , and I will give thee the Treaſures of Darkneſs and hidden Riches of ſecret Places, that thou
mayeſt know that I the Lord, which call thee by thy
Name, am the God of* Iſrael.   Thus, I ſay, he al-
lows

lows the Church and People of God to be brought into extreme Straits before Deliverance, that his Hand may be seen in giving the same, that his glorious Sovereignty may be known, that he may manifest to the World that he is *Israel's* own God, in raising them up when brought low, *for, when the Lord builds up* Zion, *he shall appear in his Glory.*

The 4th and *last* Reason I shall assign, why the Church and People of God are brought into extreme Straits before Deliverance, is, that he may purify and refine the Daughter of *Zion*   She must go even to *Babylon*   Why ? It is just that she may be purified and refined in *Babylon;* that she may be purified in *Babylon,* that her Drofs may be removed in *Babylon*   To this Purpose you have a remarkable Word in the 13th Chapter of the Prophecies of the Prophet *Zechariah,* and there the last Verse, *And I will bring the third Part through the Fire, and will refine them as Silver is refined, and will try them as Gold is tried   They shall call on my Name, and I will hear them   I will say, It is my People, and they shall say, The Lord is my God.* For this End and Purpose, I say, he sees meet to bring his People even to *Babylon;* that he may purify and refine them.   Why, hereby his Church is reformed, and the Drofs separated from the true Metal.   The Lord makes such a Time, and such a Mean, a manifesting Time and Mean. My Friends, there are many of you, who are flocking to Communions now, who, if the Lord bring his Church into *Babylon,* I am afraid there will be sad Difcoveries of you; Chrift, it may be, will have a thin Backing then, in refpect of what is now, tho' Chrift will never want a Backing For these and many fuch Reafons it is, that the Church and People of God, the Daughter of *Zion,*

are

are ordinarily brought into extreme Straits before Deliverance come. But

I proceed to the 3*d* general Head in the Method, which was, to obferve fome of the remarkable Deliverances which the Lord gives to the Daughter of *Zion*, when fhe is brought to *Babylon*, or to thefe extreme Straits and Difficulties

I only offer thefe few Thoughts concerning this Deliverance In the *firft* Place, this Deliverance which he gives to the Daughter of *Zion*, his Church and People, as to its Nature, it is a fpiritual Deliverance, fuch a Deliverance as all who have received the Spirit of Adoption, do look out for, and earneftly defire, and as it is a fpiritual Deliverance as to the Nature of it, fo it is a fpiritual Deliverance in refpect of the Means by which it is brought about. What then are the primary Means by which it is brought about by which the Lord gives it ? Why, it is by the Power and Spirit of Chrift *Not by Might nor by Power, but by my Spirit, faith the Lord of Hofts* When the Lord comes to deliver his Church and People from myftical *Babylon* How fhall the Deliverance be brought about ? Why, you have the Anfwer, 2 *Theff* ii 8. *The Lord fhall confume him with the Spirit of his Mouth, and fhall deftroy him with the Brightnefs of his Coming* With the Spirit of his Mouth, that is, juft the Word of the Gofpel accompanied with his holy Spirit, giving a glorious Manifeftation of the Son of God in a Gofpel-Difpenfation, *With the Brightnefs of his Coming*, that is, there fhall be fuch a bright Manifeftation of the wonderful Perfon of Chrift in the Gofpel Difpenfation, that the blinded Nations fhall give over wondring after the Beaft, and fhall look upon this great Sight with Wonder and Praife There is a Vail drawn over the

the Glory of the Perſon of Chriſt by *Babylon* at this Day, and ſo *Babylon* ſhall be deſtroyed, and the Church and People of God delivered, juſt by a bright ſupernatural Diſplay of the Glory of the Perſon of Chriſt in the Diſpenſation of the Goſpel carried home to Sinners by the holy Spirit. And thus, I ſay, it is a ſpiritual Deliverance, as to the Nature of it, and the Means by which it is brought about.

A 2*d* Thought I offer concerning this Deliverance, which he gives his Church and People when brought to extreme Straits, is, That as it is, as to its Nature, a ſpiritual Deliverance ſo the Way and Manner in which he brings about this Deliverance, is, by pouring out his Spirit upon his Church and People. If it be asked, How long is it till the Daughter of *Zion* be delivered? You have the Anſwer, which alſo points out the Manner of it, *Iſa* xxxii. 15 *Until the Spirit be poured upon us from on high, and the Wilderneſs be a fruitful Field, and the fruitful Field be counted for a Foreſt* The Lord works Deliverance for his Church and People, when the Spirit comes down like Dew upon Mount *Zion*, when that Promiſe hath its Accompliſhment, *Hoſea* xiv 5 *I will be as the Dew to Iſrael, he ſhall grow as the Lilly, and caſt forth his Roots as* Lebanon The Lord works Deliverance for his Church and People, when that Word of Grace, *Iſa* xliv. 3, 4. 5. is accompliſhed, *I will pour Water upon him that is thirſty, I will pour Floods upon the dry Ground, I will pour my Spirit upon thy Seed, and my Bleſſing upon thine Offspring* What ſhall be the Effect? Why, it ſhall be Deliverance to the Daughter of *Zion* For *they ſhall ſpring up as among the Graſs, as Willows by the Water-Courſes. One ſhall ſay, I am the Lord's, and another ſhall call himſelf by the Name of* Jacob, *and* another shall subscribe with his Hand unto the Lord, and surname himself by the Name of Israel. O then, Sirs, when the Spirit is thus poured out from on high, they shall go to Zion, as it is said of the returning Captives, Jer. l. 4, 5 In those Days, and in that Time, saith the Lord, the Children of Israel shall come, they and the Children of Judah together, going and weeping, they shall go and seek the Lord their God, they shall ask the Way to Zion, with their Faces thitherward, &c. The Time of the Church's Deliverance it is a weeping Time, a Time of weeping for the great Dishonours done to the Head of the Church, by the Sins of the Members of the Church, then they look upon him whom they have pierced, and mourn for him, there is a Going, and a Weeping as they go. But as it is a weeping Time, so it is a rejoicing Time. These are not inconsistent, we see it was a rejoicing Time to the returning Captives, as well as a weeping Time to them, Psalm cxxvi. 1, 2, 3. When the Lord turned again the Captivity of Zion, we were like them that dream. Then was our Mouth filled with Laughter, and our Tongue with Singing. Then said they among the Heathen, The Lord hath done great Things for them, the Lord hath done great Things for us, whereof we are glad. But then, as it is a weeping Time, and a rejoicing Time, so a Time of Deliverance to the Daughter of Zion, it is a covenanting Time. When the Daughter of Zion is delivered from Babylon it is a covenanting Time, as in that forecited 50th of Jeremiah, and 5th Verse, Come, (say Israel and Judah) and let us join ourselves to the Lord in a perpetual Covenant, that shall never be forgotten. It is a Time of taking hold of God's Covenant of Grace, of taking hold of the Head of the Covenant of Grace, of taking hold of him who is the All and in all of the Covenant of Grace, who is given to be the Covenant of the People, who is gi-

D   ven

ven to be God's Salvation to the Ends of the Earth; and, in confequence of this taking hold of God's Covenant of Grace, of him who is the Head and Surety of the Covenant of Grace, there is a Joining themfelves to the Lord in a Covenant of Duty, to keep his Judgments and Statutes, and to hearken to his Voice. It is a Time when they vow and fwear Subjection to the King of *Zion*. I might tell you, upon this Head, were I to infift, how that, when the Lord, by Means of the Preaching of the Go-fpel, did deliver the Church of *Scotland* from An-tichriftian *Babylon*, when, by the Blowing of the Sil-ver Trumpet of the glorious Gofpel, he made the Walls of *Babylon* to fall in *Scotland*, juft like the Walls of *Jericho* by the Sounding of Rams Horns, then he fo remarkably appeared againft Antichrift, that he led our Fathers the Length of a folemn A-vouching of the Lord to be their God, fo that that Time of Deliverance was a Time of folemn Cove-nanting. I might alfo fhew that it has been the Practice of the Churches of *Germany*, *France*, and others, in fuch a Time, to devote themfelves to the Lord in a Covenant of Duties. Such a Time has been a Time of thefe Nations faying, *Come, and let us join ourfelves to the Lord in a perpetual Covenant ne-ver to be forgotten ;* wherein the Nations have faid, *Come, and let us go up to the Mountain of the Lord, to the Houfe of the God of* Jacob, *and he will teach us of his Ways, and we will walk in his Paths.* But, not to infift,

In the 3d Place, another Thought I offer, with reference to the Deliverance of his Church and People, when brought into extreme Straits, is, That he delivers her in a moft furprifing Way and Manner: *Thou fhalt even go to* Babylon. Strange! What to do at *Babylon*? Why, *There fhalt thou be delivered.* Who would expect Deliverance in *Babylon*? Well, but there thou fhalt be delivered. This was fur-

prifing

prifing to the Church of old, as is intimated in that forecited 126th *Pfalm*, and 1ſt Verſe, *When the Lord turned again the Captivity of* Zion, *we were like Men that dream.* We could not believe it, we were like to take it for a Dream, it came ſo ſurpriſingly to Hand in ſuch a ſurpriſing Place, even in *Babylon.* As the Lord delivers his Church and People in a ſurpriſing Way and Manner, even in *Babylon* ſo we may notice here, that the Inſtruments the Lord gives the Deliverance by are alſo ſurpriſing. The Lord raiſed up *Cyrus* King of *Perſia,* as an Inſtrument for the Deliverance of his Church from *Babylon* Who would have expected Deliverance from ſuch an Airth? He caſts down the Bomiſh Empire, and ſets up the *Perſian* Why is all this? Juſt for *Jacob* his Servant's Sake, and *Iſrael* his Elect, juſt that *Cyrus* might be the Inſtrument of Deliverance to his People, both in an unlikely Seaſon and by an unlikely Inſtrument, that the Work might be ſeen to be of God. I may tell you here, Sirs, that when God delivered his Church and People in theſe Lands out of Antichriſtian *Babylon,* he did it both in an unlikely Seaſon, and by an unlikely Inſtrument. As to the Time and Seaſon of it, it was juſt when Darkneſs and Tyranny were arrived at their greateſt Height and Degree As to the Inſtrument, why, it was juſt by opening the Eyes of a poor blind Frier, (*Luther*) in ſpiriting him to preach againſt *Babylon,* and ſo, by one Inſtrument after another, he carried on his Work in Spite of all Oppoſition from Hell or Earth Some of you know what a great and extreme Strait this Church was brought into, when God appeared in the Year 1638. and how unexpected the Deliverance was, both as to the Seaſon and Inſtruments, is very well known: By the Inſtrumentality of ſome poor Inſtruments he tumbled

bled down Antichriſtian Prelacy, turned us to himſelf, made us join ourſelves to the Lord by ſolemn
national Engagements, and made Perſons of all
Ranks ſay, *I am the Lord's.* Again, How ſurpriſing
was the Deliverance God wrought for his Church
and People in theſe Lands, when they were brought
to the greateſt Extremity in the Year 1688. fifty
Years ago? If we conſider the Hiſtory of that Time
we will find the Deliverance was moſt ſurpriſing,
both as to the Seaſon when, and Inſtrument by
whom it was brought about. Why, it was in a Time
when theſe Lands were threatned with a Deluge of
Popery, when a Popiſh Sword was drawn, and ready to be ſheathed in the Bowels of the Inhabitants
of theſe Lands · And as to the Inſtrument of that
Deliverance, Who would thought that God ſhould
have ſent to another Land for an Inſtrument, by
whom he would bring back our Captivity, as he
then did, when he brought our late Sovereign King
William from *Holland,* to baniſh a Popiſh Tyrant
from the Throne of *Britain?* Was it not ſurpriſing?
Thus, we ſay, God delivers his Church and People,
when brought into extreme Straits, in a moſt ſurpriſing Way and Manner.

I ſhall only add, on this Head, in the 4*th* and
laſt Place, that the Deliverance he gives to his
Church and People, when brought into extreme
Straits, it is in a Manner becoming the great Deli-
verer, becoming himſelf, it is in ſuch a Manner as
he himſelf will be ſeen in it. I ſhall not here enlarge,
having hinted at this formerly, only, in a Word,
when he delivers the Daughter of *Zion* from the
Daughter of *Babylon* it is in ſuch a Way and Manner, as that it may be ſaid, *That their Sword did
not get them the Land, neither did their Arm ſave them,
but his Right-Hand, and his holy Arm, and the Light of*
his

his Countenance alone, that works the Salvation. It is in a Manner becoming himself.

I shall not insist farther on the doctrinal Part. I come to conclude the whole in an Use of Information, Consolation and Exhortation.

I shall be short, may the Lord assist us in the Use of this Doctrine. It was with Difficulty I entred upon this Subject, but another I could not think upon. Let us then have our Eyes to him in the Use and Improvement of this Doctrine.

Is it so, then, that the Church and People of God are brought into the greatest Extremity, that their Deliverance may be the more conspicuous and glorious? Then, 1*st* for Information. In a short Word, be informed of the present Situation of the Church and People of God. I shall read you a Question upon this Use of the Doctrine, together with its Answer. You have it in the 21st of *Isaiah*, and 11th and 12th Verses of that Chapter, *The Burden of Dumah. He calleth to me out of Seir, Watchman, What of the Night? Watchmen, What of the Night?* If you enquire at me, *Watchman, What of the Night*, I answer unto you just in the Words of the Spirit of God, *The Morning cometh, and also the Night.* The Morning of a Deliverance to his Church shall come, but yet in the mean Time, know that the Night goes before the Morning. We have at this Day, in a great Measure, a Night of it, but the Night will be darker yet, before the Morning come, the Night goes before the Morning. Therefore the Prophet, in this Word gives them to know, that tho' it was Night when the Call was given, What of the Night? Yet it should be darker, for some of it was to come : *The Morning cometh, and also the Night.* And, my Friends, tho' the Night is dark upon the Churches of Christ at present, tho' it be now a Night of

Withering

Withering, a Night of Error, a Night of Back-sliding, a Night of Falling away from the Lord, yet, Sirs, tho' the Night is dark, I am afraid the darkest of the Night is not yet come. Why, say you, Can the Night be darker? Can the Case of the Church be worse than it is just now, under the weary Scatterings there are among the People of God, under the Heart-overwhelming Breakings there are among the People of God, under the sad Witherings and Decays that take Place among the People of God? Yea, Sirs, the Night may be darker yet, the Daughter of *Zion* may not only go out of the City, but dwell in the Field, and go even to *Babylon*, before she be delivered. I think our Text is very expressive of our present Situation in this Land, *Thou shalt go forth out of the City, and thou shalt dwell in the Field, and thou shalt go even to Babylon, &c.* I say, our Text is much expressive of our Case, as for Instance, Are we not made to go out of the City? Are we not cast out of the Bosom of the present established Church by their iniquous Acts and Procedures? But then, tho' we are made to go forth out of the City, we are not yet wholly made to dwell in the Field, not yet deprived of our sacred Solemnities, for we have had Occasion to see, in this Place, the solemn sacred Symbols of our Lord's broken Body and shed Blood set before us, but as this Ordinance has been dispensed in a witnessing Congregation, in a Congregation who are by Profession gone forth out of the City, on their Way to dwell in the Field, why, in so far the Text is expressive of our present Situation, and, before the Deliverance come, we may be deprived of Occasions of this Nature, made to dwell in the Field, yea, brought even to *Babylon*. We are not yet under

under the Feet of an Antichriftian Party in *Baby-lon*, but, ere all be done, we may even go to *Babylon*. We are as yet privileged with the Standard of a *publick Teftimony* for the Doctrine, Worfhip, Difcipline and Government of the Church of *Scotland* · However weak and worthlefs fome of us are to put our Hand to it, yet it is a ftanding Teftimony for the Caufe and Intereft of Chrift, whatever Way a corrupt Generation may look upon it · But, Sirs, before all be done, the Standard of a publick Teftimony may altogether fall to the Ground in this Land. I fhall not determine the Queftion anent that difmal Event we have in the 11th Chapter of the *Revelation*, concerning the Killing of the Witneffes, whether it be paft, or to come. Great Men have differed in their Opinions Some have thought that Event was brought about at the Reformation by *Luther*, they think the Killing of the Witneffes refpected that Time. Others think it will fall in with the laft fatal Stroke that fhall be given unto an Antichriftian Party, which fhall ufher in the Glory of the latter Times ; and that, immediately before that, there fhall be a Deluge of Popery, a general Killing of the Witneffes, a general Falling of a Teftimony for Chrift, I fay, I fhall not determine this Queftion ; I fhall only remark two or three Things farther upon this Ufe, for our Information with reference unto all the Churches of Chrift at this Day, and particularly with reference unto the Church of *Scotland*, which gives Ground to think that we fhall be fent even to *Babylon* before a Deliverance fhall be given unto us.

Firft, I remark, That when an univerfal and general Apoftafy and Tyranny doth prevail in any reformed Church, it threatens we fhall go even to

Babylon

Babylon before we be delivered : And how far this has been and is the Cafe with thefe Churches called *Reformed*, any who are acquainted with the Hiftory of them may judge Why, the *Arian* and *Pelagian* Herefies have fo raged in the Churches abroad, that they juft paved a Way for the Man of Sin and tended to make Antichrift mount the Throne, and fo much do thefe prevail in thofe Churches, which at leaft have the Name of Reformed and Proteftant Churches, together with the prevailing of Antichriftian Tyranny among them, that they bode fair for our going even unto *Babylon*, before a Deliverance come. If any ask the Reafon why the reformed Churches are fo dreadfully fallen under the Feet of Antichriftian Tyranny, the Spirit of God gives the Anfwer of this Queftion, 2 *Theff* 11. 10, 11, 12. *Becaufe they received not the Love of the Truth, that they might be faved · For this Caufe God fhall fend them ftrong Delufion, that they fhould believe a Lie; that they all might be damned who believed not the Truth, but had Pleafure in Unrighteoufnefs* This ufhered in the Revelation of Antichrift, and this paved a Way for that difmal Apoftafy from the Chriftian Faith and Profeffion, which takes Place at this Day in the Churches of Chrift, and in *Scotland* in particular.

In the 2d Place, I remark, That when an univerfal Degeneracy prevails among all the reformed Churches, in Practice as well as in Principle, it threatens that the Daughter of *Zion*, fhall go even to *Babylon* before fhe be delivered How far this is the Cafe with us, let any thinking Perfon judge, the Truth is not received in the Love of it, the Glory of Chrift is darkned and vailed, Men defpife the Grace of God. I think there is nothing

mo

nore threatens us than an Inundation of Popery
it this Day, why, already the Land is overfpread
with a fearful Overflow of Deifm and Atheifm,
and of many corrupt Doctrines fubverfive of the
pure Truths of the Gofpel of Chrift : And does
not this bode an Inundation of Popifh Darknefs,
that we fhall be fent even to *Babylon* before we be
delivered? And withal it bodes very ill, that there
is fuch a Fainting with refpect unto a *publick Teftimony* for Chrift, and the Truths of Chrift Is it
not lamentable and ftrange, we defire to fpeak it
with Grief, that the prefent Church are fo far
from lifting up a particular Teftimony for the
particular Truths that are impugned and denied
in the Day and Time wherein we live, that they
are with Might and Main endeavouring to run
down and oppofe the Teftimony that we have,
under the good Conduct of our God, been directed
to lift up for the Truth of Chrift, and againft a
Deluge of Error and Defection from the Truth
and Caufe of God? Yea, they are come the Length
of flaying and running down fuch as are minting to
own this Mite of a Teftimony for Chrift.   But
what is the Matter of running down us? What
tho' we be run down, providing the Truths of
Chrift, the Rights and Prerogatives of Chrift, were
maintained? Let our Name and Reputation and all
go, but let Chrift's Name and Fame be exalted and
fet on high Sirs, I know not if ever I had Occafion
to fpeak in Chrift's Name to fo many of his fcatter-
ed Flock at once, allow me, for I muft tell you,
that the Daughter of *Zion*, the Church and People
of God, ought not to neglect any publick free
Teftimony for the Truths of Chrift, and againft
the Indignities done to him and his Caufe. I think
it is Matter of Lamentation, and it calls aloud

E   for

for Mourning at this Day, that, when the Banner of a Testimony is lifted up, so few gather to it, and so many are endeavouring to bear it down. It is Matter of Lamentation, and calls aloud for Mourning, Sirs, that the Sins of former Times must be extenuated, covered and palliated. It has a threatning Aspect, that we will not lament our own nor our Fathers Iniquities, and return to the Lord. This would say that we shall go even to *Babylon* before we be delivered. I have observed likeways with Regret how many Professors, through the different Corners of *Scotland*, in the Year 1732 came with their Testimonies before the Church Judicatures of this Land, remonstrating and reclaiming against the violent Intrusions made upon the Heritage of God. They would have been then content to have seen a *publick Testimony* lifted up for Christ, and his Truth and Cause, but, alas, what is become of some of them now! I fear, instead of that former Zeal whereby they were acted, a *Latitudinarian* Principle prevails with them, they have got over their former Strictness, and can fall in with a boundless Toleration for all Sorts of Religion, which will be introductive of of all Sorts of Looseness and Profanity. The Hedge of Government is taken down at this Day, and the Daughter of *Zion* lies open to the wild Boars of the Forest to devour her, and the wild Beast of the Field to waste her. I warn you, in the Name of the Lord, whoever you be that give Countenance and Assistance to the taking down this Hedge, tho' you were the Signet on his right Hand, you shall smart for it, you shall smart for your opposing a Testimony for the Government of Christ's House in this covenanted Land. You are blinded as to the Cause of Christ at this Day;

and

and therefore it is, that you are like the Heath in the Defert, that does not fee when Good comes, and you do not obferve the Operation of his Hand. And is not this a threatning Sign we fhall go even to *Babylon* before we be delivered? I fhall not infift farther upon this Ufe,

But I come, 2*dly.* To drop a few Words by Way of Confolation

If it be fo, as you have heard, that the greateft Extremity of the Church makes Way for a glorious Deliverance unto her, then hence fee for our Comfort a Bow in the Church's darkeft Cloud Tho' the Daughter of *Zion* fhould go forth out of the City, tho' fhe fhould dwell in the Field, tho' fhe fhould go even to *Babylon*, yet there fhall fhe be delivered, there the Lord fhall redeem her from the Hands of her Enemies Tho' fhe fhould be in Pain, and labour to bring forth, like a Woman in Travail, yet all her Pangs and fore Throws, they are all big with a glorious Deliverance, a glorious Deliverance will be the happy Iffue of them all *Therefore fear not, Worm Jacob, and fear not,* Ifrael *my Servant.* Let not the Lord's People be too much caft down, let them not mourn as thofe that have no Hope, faying, *Our Bones are dried, our Hope is loft, and we are cut off for our Parts.* Let Faith fee Comfort to *Zion,* fo long as *Zion*'s King remains Tho' fhe fhould be brought even to *Babylon,* yet there fhe fhall be delivered, her greateft Extremity will make Way for a moft glorious Delivery unto her. Thus we fay there is a Bow in the Church's darkeft Cloud. Hence we find the Prophet faying in the 4th of *Micah,* from the 11th Verfe to the Clofe of the Chapter, *Now alfo many Nations are gathered againft thee, that fay, Let her be defiled, and let our Eye look upon* Zion *, but they know not the Thoughts of the Lord.* Thefe Enemies of *Zion,* they know

not

not the Thoughts of the Lord, what Good the Lord intendeth to bring out of their Ill-will to *Zion*; they know not the Thoughts of the Lord, what the Lord is about to do with *Zion* When *Zion* is brought even to *Babylon*, then *Zion* is looked upon by her Enemies as in a very desperate Case and Condition, then the Daughter of *Babylon* apprehends she hath got her Will of *Zion*. Why, they know not the Thoughts of the Lord, neither understand they his Counsel · Their Design is the Destruction of *Zion*, but the Design of the Lord, in all this, is a most glorious Deliverance to *Zion*, and so it is added in this Place, *Therefore he shall gather them as the Sheaves into the Floor*, namely, the Enemies of *Zion*. What then, *Arise and thresh, O Daughter of Zion, for I will make thine Horn Iron, and I will make thy Hoofs Brass, and thou shalt beat in Pieces many People, and I will consecrate their Gain unto the Lord, and their Substance unto the Lord of the whole Earth* Up your Hearts then, O Friends of *Zion* ! Sirs, I must tell you, they have a terrible Party to deal with who meddle with the Daughter of *Zion* to her Hurt ; for tho' her Husband frown upon her, yet he will return to her with loving Kindness, tho' *Zion's* God should give her the Brim of the Cup to drink, yet her Enemies shall be made to drink the bitter Dregs of that Cup before all be done, yea I say, the Enemies of *Zion* shall drink the very bitter Dregs of the Cup ere all be done. Why then, *Comfort ye, comfort ye my People, saith your God* Speak ye comfortably to Zion. Rejoice in the Lord, ye Righteous; and again, I say, Rejoice.* Surely you have good Reason so to do. It is a noble Ground of Encouragement, that *Zion's* Extremity makes Way for her Delivery, the more her Trouble is increased, the more remarkable will her Deliverance be, the sharper the Shower is, it will be the shorter. *Zion*

in

in this Land, when brought to *Babylon*, will have a sharp Hour, but a short Hour *Thou shalt go even unto* Babylon, *and there shalt thou be delivered* Faint not, then ye Friends of our glorious *Immanuel*, tho' you should go even to *Babylon*. Tho' *Zion*, the Daughter of *Zion*, should go even to *Babylon*, there she shall be delivered Mourn not as those who have no Hope, for *Zion*'s God reigneth *Thy God, O* Zion, *reigneth to all Generations*, and thy God, O *Zion*, will give thee Deliverance when in *Babylon Thou shalt go even to* Babylon, *and there shalt thou be delivered*

I come, 3*dly* to conclude this Subject in a Word of Exhortation

Is it so, as you have been hearing, that the Daughter of *Zion* shall even go to *Babylon*, that the State of the Church is like to be darker yet? Why, then, my first Exhortation to you is, when the Daughter of *Zion* is under a Cloud, and the Night like to be darker and darker, then let me exhort you all to make sure an Interest in Christ, and in that spiritual Redemption from the Tyranny of Sin, Satan and the World, that is purchased by the Lord Christ This is the best Preparative for meeting with the dark and cloudy Day an Interest in Christ, and the Redemption purchased by him from the Bondage and Tyranny of Sin and Satan, every one of us by Nature are under the Bondage and Tyranny of the God of this World, the Prince of the Power of the Air, the Spirit that now worketh in the Children of Disobedience. Ye are every one of you still under the Power of Sin, who are Strangers to Christ, and so consequently under the Curse of the Law, under the Sentence of a broken Covenant of Works. And I must tell you, Sirs, that, in this everlasting Gospel,

spel, Redemption is published, a purchased Redemption is published unto you. I publish and proclaim this Redemption, this spiritual Liberty and Freedom through the Blood of Christ, to every captive Sinner in all this vast Assembly. I publish and proclaim this Redemption and Freedom to every bound Captive hearing me this Day. I tell you, in his Name, it is a Redemption for you, if you be a Captive in Bonds, hear the Proclamation the Spirit of God makes of it in the 61st of *Isaiah* and 1st Verse, *The Spirit of the Lord God is upon me, because the Lord hath anointed me to preach good Tidings to the Meek, he hath sent me to bind up the broken-hearted, to proclaim Liberty to the Captives, and the Opening of the Prison to them that are bound, to proclaim the acceptable Year of the Lord,* &c. O, if the Lord Christ would be pleased to proclaim this Redemption among you this Day, not in Word only, but with Power, and in the holy Ghost, Liberty to the Captives! O captive Sinner, whoever thou art, in thy natural State thou art in Captivity and in Bonds, a Bond Slave to Sin, a Bond Slave to Satan! Why, we tell you good Tidings of great Joy, to you is proclaimed Liberty and Freedom, Redemption is proclaimed unto thee. Thus saith the Lord, To you, O Prisoner, to you, O dark and dead Sinner, go forth and shew yourselves, shew yourselves to be Sinners needing a Saviour, shew yourselves to the Saviour, to the Redeemer, to him who is the mighty God, mighty to save you, the Lord of Hosts able to save you, the merciful God willing to save you · *Thus saith the Lord, I that speak in Righteousness am mighty to save,* Isa lxiii. 1 Mighty to save from the Tyranny and Power of Satan, mighty to save from the Tyranny and Power of Unbelief, mighty to

save

ave from the prevailing Evils in thy Heart, let
them be never fo great, never fo ftrong, he is a
mighty and ftrong Redeemer, a Redeemer not only by Price, but alfo by Power; he paid a Price
of infinite Worth and Value for you, and will
not you come and take Salvation from him? He
is a powerful Redeemer, he hath an Arm that is
full of Power, an omnipotent Arm, that can with
one Stroke (fo to fpeak) break afunder the ftrong-
ft Gates of Brafs, and cut in Pieces the ftrongeft
Bars of Iron. He is not only willing, but *able to*
fave to the uttermoft, all that come to God by him,
feeing he ever liveth to make Interceffion for them.
Behold, Sirs, on this laft Day of the Feaft, our
Lord Jefus ftands and cries, O Prifoners, go forth
and fhew yourfelves ! O Captives, go forth out
of *Babylon* ! Hafte, hafte, hafte, flee out of *Ba-*
bylon, efcape for thy Life, flee out of the *Babylon*
of a natural State, it is the City of Deftruction, hafte, flee for your Lives, flee to a Saviour,
flee to a Redeemer, he is ftanding (fo to fpeak) with
Arms wide open to receive you, the Arms of his
Love are wide open to receive you, the Arms of
his Mercy and Grace are wide open to receive you ;
hafte, flee into the City of Refuge for thy Life :
The Arms of the Saviour are ftretched out to embrace you, with God's Welcome, with the Welcome of God, Father, Son and holy Ghoft O
then, Child of the Devil, come and be the Child
of God ! O Swearer, come and fpeak the Language of *Canaan*, the heavenly Dialect, the pure
Language of the City above ! O Servant of Satan,
come and be the Servant of the living God ! Thou
art yet out of Hell, and whilft thou art out of Hell,
thou haft Accefs to a Saviour, Accefs to a Re-
eemer. O filthy Sinner, come and be wafhed
from

from all thine Idols ; tho' thou haft lien among
the Pots, and be as black as Hell with the Stain
of Sin, yet come, thou fhalt appear *as the Wings
of a Dove, whofe Wings are covered with Silver, and
her Feathers with yellow Gold* What fhould hin
der thy Coming to him, who is a Redeemer by
Price and Power, one that hath infinite Power to
bring thee, to draw thee, to lead thee, to guide
thee ? O who can fpeak forth the Glory of this
Redeemer, the infinite Excellency of this Redeem
er ! O that fome of this Company, that never yet
knew this Redeemer, that are in the *Babylon* of a
natural State, would this Day take hold of his
Grace proclaimed in this Gofpel, and would by
Faith apprehend proclaimed Liberty, Liberty to
Captives, and the Opening of the Prifons to them
that are bound

This Exhortation being to all in general , but to
Strangers, to fuch as have no faving Intereft in
Chrift in particular, I muft therefore add a Word,
by Way of Motive and Excitement, to fall in with
the Word of Exhortation Confider then, O Sinner, to ftir you up to make fure an Intereft in Chrift,
that the Lord is preaching now in a Word of Grace
and Promife to you, but the Lord knows how foon
he may fend the Daughter of *Zion*, his Church and
People, to *Babylon*, and give us a Famine, not of
Bread nor of Water, but of the Word of God,
and O what fhall become of you, in the Day of Vi
fitation, who have no Intereft in Chrift ! O Sirs,
we know not how foon the Lord may be provoked
to fay, *I will whet my glittering Sword, my Hand fhall
take hold of Vengeance, for the Lord hath a Sacrifice.*
Where ? Not in *Bozrah*, not in the Land of *Idumea*,
but in the Church of *Scotland*, among all the Churches, for their woful Apoftafy from God, and in
treacherous

treacherous *Scotland* among the reft, Gofpel-defpi-
fing *Scotland*, finning *Scotland*, Covenant-breaking
Scotland, Chrift-defpifing *Scotland*. O Sirs, how
juftly may he whet his glittering Sword amongft
you, againft you, for your Iniquity? And if he
caufe his Church and People in this Land to go forth
out of the City, and to dwell in the Field, and fend
them even to *Babylon*, O how fad will thy Cafe be,
thou who art a Stranger to Chrift, to have an angry
God, a God out of Chrift meeting thee! O therefore accept of offered Liberty, of an offered Saviour, and offered Salvation through him, as ye were
hearing on *Saturday*! *Now is the accepted Time, now
is the Day of Salvation*: *To-day if ye will hear his Voice,
harden not your Hearts* For to you, even to you, O
Sinner, is the Word of this Salvation fent. Receive it, Sirs, with particular Application, and
Chrift in it, and fo you will have the beft Preparative for, and the beft Prefervative in a ftormy
Day, in the dark and cloudy Day

In the 2*d* Place, let me addrefs myfelf in a Word
of Exhortation, to you, in an efpecial Manner, who
profefs the Name of Chrift, who profefs to be the
Friends and Witneffes of Chrift   And

My Exhortation to you is, O fee to it, and take
care that you be well rooted in Chrift Jefus. Is it
a Time of Darknefs with the Church? Is it Night
with the Church and People of God? And have
we Ground to apprehend that the Night may grow
darker yet before the Morning come? Is the
Church and People of God, the Daughter of
Zion, made to go forth out of the City? Are we
threatned to be made to dwell in the Field, and to
be fent even to *Babylon* before Deliverance come?
Why, then, O Profeffor, be concerned to be well
rooted in Chrift, well rooted in the Truths and

F   Caufe

Caufe of Chrift. We find the Apoftle exhorts to
this Duty in the 2d Chapter of his Epiftle to the
Coloffians, and there the 6th and 7th Verfes of that
Chapter, *As you have therefore received Chrift Jefus
the Lord, fo walk ye in him, rooted and built up in him,
and eftablifhed in the Faith, as ye have been taught,
abounding therein with Thankfgiving.* We exhort
you, take home with you that Word of Exhortation, *Be rooted and built up in Chrift.* It is a great
Matter, Sirs, to be rooted in him; be rooted in
Chrift as the Branch in the Vine, as the Branch is
in the Root. What is that Profeffion of yours,
Man, Woman, w thout this, but an empty Profeffion, an empty Shell without a Kernel, an empty
Shadow without a real Subftance What fignifies
all your publick and glaring Profeffion, if you be
not rooted in Chrift? What fignifies your publick
Religion, Profeffor, who are not rooted in Chrift?
Why, I tell you, it is but a grofs Delufion if you
are not rooted in Chrift. I never like thefe Folks
Religion, Sirs, that begins firft with the Publick.
Be concerned to be firft rooted in Chrift by Faith,
and then a folid Concern for the declarative Glory
of God, the Caufe and Intereft of Chrift, will immediately follow in its due Order. That Concern
for the Glory of God which flows not from Faith's
Views of the Glory of *Immanuel*'s Perfon, is not to
be regarded. Thofe who are concerned in a right
Way and Manner for the Publick, they are fuch
Perfons who have firft come to the Lord Jefus, who
have united with him by Faith, and fo are rooted
in him. Sirs, even tho' there be fome amongft you
who have come the Length of adhering to a publick Teftimony for the born-down Caufe of Chrift
at this Day, yet are you not rooted in Chrift. Why,
Sirs, What will this your Adherence fignify if you
be

be not rooted in Chrift Jefus, by his Spirit taking hold of you, and drawing you to him, and Faith's Outgoing of the Soul from all Things in a World to him alone ? My Friends, try the Matter, then ; Faith in Chrift, and a faithful Witneffing for Chrift, go together : And if any pleafe themfelves with an Adherence to a Teftimony for Chrift and his Caufe, without feeking to be rooted in him, and built up in him, their Naughtinefs may be fhortly difcovered, for all the Length they have gone : You have but gone with the Footmen, how fhall you contend with Horfes ? And what will you do in the Swellings of *Jordan* ? Stay till you come there, which may be fhortly, and then fhall you be difcovered who are not rooted in Chrift. Let none think we fpeak this to difcourage the exercifed Believer, or to difcourage the owning of a Teftimony. This is a plain Duty, which the Lord is calling for at the Hands of all his Servants and People at this Day, whether they will hear, or whether they will forbear. But, Sirs, we want you to own a Teftimony for Chrift, from Faith's Views of the Glory of Chrift. Seek then to be rooted in Chrift. O it is a great Matter to be rooted in Chrift, to be built up and eftablifhed in Chrift. There is a Gathering together among you in praying Societies at this Day, it is well it is fo, it is good for the Lord's People to be thus employed in fuch a Time as this, it is good to be meeting for Prayer and Chriftian Conference ; tho' it is a Practice that is run down by the polite Wits of the Age, yet it is a Duty warranted by the Lord, *Mal.* iii 16. *They that feared the Lord fpake often one to another, and the Lord hearkned and heard it,* &c. Thus the Duty is good, but, Sirs, we would have you to confider, that your being in

a Socia Society will not do the Business, unless you be rooted in Christ For in that Day many will say, Lord, Lord, we have eaten and drunk in thy Presence, and thou haft taught in our Streets, to whom he shall say, I tell you, I know you not whence you are, depart from me all ye Workers of Iniquity No doubt these prayed and also conferred with others about the Matters of God, therefore Professors, Members of Christian Societies study to be rooted in Christ, for Folks to meet together in Societies, and yet to be Strangers to Christ, is dangerous. Study above all to be rooted in Christ, do not sit down upon any profest Adherence unto a Testimony for Christ, do not sit down upon your praying and converfing one with another, seek to be rooted and built up in Christ, otherways, I testify unto you, ye have no Part in Christ, all will be useless to you if ye are not rooted in Christ You will be taken by the great Husbandman and thrown into Hell Fire, as Fuel to the Flame of vindictive Justice, unless you be rooted and built up in Christ.

I shall now conclude this Discourse with a few Directions by Way of Motive to excite you to fall in with the Word of Exhortation

In the *first* Place, study a close, humble and needy Dependence on the Lord Jesus Christ. O be humble ! A humble Christian is a rare Christian. Away with a proud Christian ! Meeknels is among the very first Lessons of Christianity *If any Man will be my Disciple, let him deny himself, and take up his Cross, and follow me,* faith our Lord O feek to be humble and self denied ! Sirs, it is just the Ornament of a Christian to be denied to himself. Again,

In the 2d Place, If you would be rooted in Christ as ye should, study a close, humble and needy Dependence on him in whom all your Springs are

are, so let the Word of Christ dwell in you richly. Hear what he himself adviseth for your Encouragement, John v. 7 *If ye abide in me, and my Words abide in you, ye shall ask what ye will, and it shall be done unto you.* If ye ask, Where is the Word to be found which must abide in you? I answer, It is to be found in the Bible which you have put in your Hands In what Part of it? say you. I answer, In every Part of it, just in all the Bible. What think ye of the Scriptures of the Old Testament? Why, they are just the Word of God, as well as those of the New. The whole Scriptures are given to be the Standard of Truth for the resolving of Controversies, to be the infallible Rule of Faith and Practice to his Church in all Ages and Periods of the same, until Time gives Place to Eternity, when the Church shall be arrived at her triumphant State, and then no more shall the Bible be needful We advise you, then, to abide not only by the Word of the Prophets, but also by the Commandments of the Apostles, as you have it, 2 *Pet.* iii 1, 2 *This second Epistle (Beloved) I now write unto you, in both which I stir up your pure Minds by Way of Remembrance, that ye may be mindful of the Words which were spoken before by the holy Prophets, and of the Commandment of us the Apostles of the Lord and Saviour* What are the Words ye are to be mindful of? You have them in that 2d Verse the Words which were spoken by the holy Prophets under the Old Testament, and the Commandments of the Apostles of Christ under the New. These are the Words of Christ which we are called to lay up in our Hearts, that we may not sin against him

3*dly* If ye would be rooted in Christ, in a shaking Day and Time, I advise you, next to

your

your Bibles, to make Ufe of our Confeffion of
Faith. We have Reafon, Sirs, to blefs God who
fo remarkably directed the Compilers of our excellent Confeffion of Faith. What are Confeffions
of Faith, Sirs ? Why, they are the publick Confeffions of the Churches concerning the divine
Truths they receive and believe, in Oppofition to
the grofs Errors vented in thefe Dregs of Time,
in Oppofition to the Indignities done to the Truth
of God contained in his Word Read our Confeffion of Faith, and there you will fee the Truths
of God drawn out of the Word of God in an orderly and diftinct Manner, for our Inftruction, E-
dification and Eftablifhment in the Truth. Likeways I recommend it to you to read and confider
the Form of Presbyterial Church-Government, Di
rectory for Family-Worfhip, Sum of faving Knowledge, and Books of Difcipline, all which you
have along with the faid Confeffion of Faith. It
hath been obferved of this Country, they can generally fpeak lefs for their Principles than Papifts
can do for theirs. Why, the Reafon is, they are
not concerned to know them, and fo it comes to
pafs that they are fo eafily beaten out of them.
Again,

In the 4*th* Place, If you would be rooted in
Chrift and his Truths, O then pray much for the
Spirit of Chrift, that he may guide you into all
Truth, and that ye may be kept in the High-Way.
Ye know in a dark Night Men commonly lofe their
Way. If it is fo dark a Night, O then pray for
the Leader to break up your Way ! Keep your
Eye upon your Leader, look to him, that he may
lead in a plain Path, becaufe of your Obfervers.

I am afraid I have infifted too long I fhall
only add another Advice, and conclude with it.

If it is so, that the Church's greatest Extremity makes Way for a glorious Deliverance unto her, and that, tho' she should go even to *Babylon*, yet there shall she be delivered, then I will advise you to live in the Faith and Hopes of a glorious Delivery to the Church and People of God. Wait and pray for her Delivery, you have good Ground to hope for that happy Time, because he that has said, *Thou shalt go even to* Babylon, has also said, *There shalt thou be delivered.* What you have so good Ground to hope for, ye should be waiting for, and praying for in a Way of Faith. O cry for his Coming ! Lift up a Prayer for the Remnant that is left ! O cry that he may return in Mercy to *Jerusalem*, that he may hasten a Deliverance to his Church and People, whatever Way he sees meet ! O plead that the Wheel of Providence may move swiftly towards the favouring of *Zion* ! Cry, cry, Let the Time to favour *Zion* come, even the Time that thou hast set ! O cry for a returning God, and a returning Glory ! O cry for his Return to *Scotland* our native Land, for his Return to every one of us ! We are all under sad Symptoms of his Anger at this Day, therefore, O lift up a Prayer for his Return ! For your Encouragement, Sirs, who are concerned for his Return, we tell you, you may die in the hopeful Prospect and Faith of it, tho' you should not live to see it, and it may be, Sirs, you may live to see it · But whether ye live to see it or not, die in the Faith that that Passage of Scripture shall be made out (in this Land) which you have in the 66th of *Isaiah*, from the 10th to the 15th Verse, *Rejoice with* Jerusalem; *and be glad with her, all ye that love her ; rejoice for Joy with her, all ye that mourn for her ; that ye my suck and be satisfied with*

with the Breasts of her Consolations, that ye may milk out and be delighted with the Abundance of her Glory For thus faith the Lord, Behold I will extend Peace to her like a River, and the Glory of the Gentiles like a flowing Stream Then shall ye suck, ye shall be born upon her Sides, and be dandled upon her Knees As one whom his Mother comforteth, so will I comfort you, and ye shall be comforted in Jerusalem. And when ye see this your Heart shall rejoice, and your Bones shall flourish like an Herb, and the Hand of the Lord shall be known towards his Servants, and his Indignation towards his Enemies.

Now, to conclude, O may the Time to favour Zion, the set Time come ' May he build up Zion, and appear in his Glory ' May all his Followers be confirmed and kept in the Way of Truth, led in a plain Path in a dark Day, because of their Enemies, and kept, by the Power of God through Faith unto Salvation.

FINIS.

The Lamb's Retinue attending him whitherſoever he goeth.

Being the Subſtance of

TWO SERMONS,

Preached on *Sabbath* and *Monday*, at the Celebration of the Sacrament of the Lord's Supper at *Orwell, Auguſt* 6. 1738.

UPON

Rev xiv. 4. *Theſe are they which follow the Lamb whitherſoever he goeth*

By the late Revfrfnd and Learned *Mr*. William Wilson *Miniſter of the Goſpel at* Perth

Carefully reviſed by a reverend Member of the Aſſociate Synod.

E D I N B U R G H,

Printed for *David Duncan*, and Sold at his Houſe, oppoſite to the *Weigh-Houſe*, North Side of the Street. MDCCXLVII.

The Lamb's Retinue attending him whitherſoever he goeth.

REV. xiv. 4.

Theſe are they which follow the Lamb whitherſoever he goeth.

MY Friends, we are now aſſembled together, according to an Inſtitution of
divine Appointment, in a publick worſhipping Aſſembly. Let every one of
us endeavour to have the Faith of God's omniſcient
Eye upon us. God is looking upon us at all Times,
and in a more eſpecial Manner his Eye is upon us
when we come before him in the Duties of his Worſhip, when we approach into the Preſence of God
in his Ordinances. I muſt tell you, Sirs, before
we proceed, a great Work is going about in this
Place to day, the greateſt Solemnity that can be
gone about in this Side of Time, the Death of
Chriſt, the worthy Lamb, is celebrating here to-
day, the Ordinance that is diſpenſing in this Place,
it is a Shewing forth the Death of Chriſt, until he
come again Here is an Event that concerns all
this Audience whoever they be, whether deſigned
Communicants or not, the Death of our Lord Chriſt.
If you have no Intereſt in this Death, Sin will be
your Death for ever, it will ruin and undo you
throughout

throughout all Eternity , it is through that Death
that is celebrating in the Sacrament to-day, that ye
muſt have Life, or you can never have it, but muſt
periſh eternally , it is through that Death that you
muſt have Redemption from the Curſe of a broken
Law, Redemption from Wrath to come · If you
have not Redemption through that Death, the Law
Curſe will certainly take hold upon you, vindictive
Juſtice will be execute upon you, the Wrath of God
will come down upon you, and cruſh you down to
the loweſt Hell , it will ſink you down to the bot
tomleſs Pit : That Death, it is a Door of Hope o
pened to periſhing Sinners, opened for the Sins of
Men, for rebellious Men, for ſelf-deſtroying Men ,
a Door of Hope is opened here for Hell-deſerving
Men, for unrighteous Men *For God made him to be
Sin for us, who knew no Sin, that we might be the
Righteouſneſs of God in him.* O, then, is there a
Door of Hope opened for guilty Men, rebellious
Men, and will you not take the Benefit of this Door,
and enter by this Door ? This is the Gate of God,
Redemption through the Blood of Chriſt, through
the Death of Chriſt. This is that Gate by which all
that are juſtified do enter into the Preſence of God ,
by which entring they come to have a ſafe Standing
before God. Sirs, this Death that is commemorating
this Day, in this Place, it is a Door of Hope opened
unto the greateſt Tranſgreſſors amongſt you in all
this Aſſembly. Ye in this Aſſembly have been hear
ing the Word preached, in the other Aſſembly
the Sacrament is diſpenſed Well, Sirs, this is
God's high Market-Day in this Place and Congre
gation , it is not an ordinary Sabbath, it is an high
Sabbath, it is a Communion-Sabbath Ye are come
to God's Market What are you doing in God's
Market ? What are you buying in God's Market ?
It is a rare Market, a Market of Grace, a Market
of

of rich and glorious Grace : It is a none-such Market, the Wares that are at this Market are exceeding great and precious, the Excellency of them cannot be told : If Angels were called to come and tell you the Worth and Excellency of them, they could not do it to the full. If some of the general Assembly of the First-born were sent forth to this Assembly to speak of the Wares which are a selling, or rather a-giving here to-day, they would be so far from fully setting forth the unsearchable Riches of Christ, that they would cry, Come and see, come, taste and see? O Sirs, this will be the best Proof of Christ the worthy Lamb, and of the rich and glorious Commodities in this Gospel-Market, just to come and see. *O taste and see that God is good* Come, partake of that Grace that is in Christ Jesus ' Come,' partake of that unsearchable Riches of Christ, that are exposed in this Market of Grace ' O Sirs, the Market of Grace is a rare Market, the Wares that are therein proclaimed are all given freely *Ho, every one that thirsteth, come ye to the Waters, and he that hath no Money let him come, and buy Wine and Milk without Money and without Price ' Whosoever will, let him take the Waters of Life freely* O come and take freely ' O come and enjoy ' O come and share of the unsearchable Riches of Christ Jesus, the worthy Lamb ' O do not stand all the Day idle in the Market-Place ' Ye are here just in the Market-Place, be not idle in the Market-Place Do not complain you have not wherewith to buy, for the Wares, we tell you, are free, and the great Merchant is saying in this Gospel, *Buy of me Gold tried in the Fire, that ye may be rich, and white Raiment that thou mayest be clothed, that the Shame of thy Nakedness do not appear, and anoint thine Eyes with Eye-Salve, that thou mayest see.* O what think you of it, Sirs,
that

that God hath thus visited us, in rearing up his Tabernacle among Men! Will God in very deed dwell with Men? If we had Eyes to see, and Hearts to understand, we could not but be filled with Amazement at that Grace revealed unto us in this Gospel, at the Condescension of God, the low Stooping of God unto us. God hath reared up his Tabernacle among Men, God hath condescended to dwell in very deed among Men, and said concerning Men, *I will be their God, and they shall be my People* Upon what Foundation? Why, just upon this Foundation, of God's being manifested in the Flesh, the eternal Son of God his taking our Nature, his stooping to marry our Nature, is the Ground-Work of God's dwelling with Men upon Earth.

But, not to insist farther upon an Introduction, this Book of the *Revelation* is ordinarily and justly reckoned to contain deep and mysterious Prophecies, the Things that are contained in this Book will exercise the Skill, Judgment and Faith of the most discerning in the militant Church in all Ages and Generations, until the Prophecy be fully accomplished. But yet it is a just Observation of One, that the holy Scriptures are like a River, wherein there are some shallow Places, that a Lamb may wade, and other Places so deep that an Elephant may swim. I may say of this Book, that it contains mysterious and dark Things, yet there are Truths scattered up and down in it, that may be Food to the weakest of the Flock of Christ. Among other Things, in this Text and Context you have the Flock of Christ characterized and described, they are the Lamb's Retinue and Train, these who are on the Lamb's Side, with the Lamb on the Mount *Zion*, having his Name and his Father's

Name

Name written on their Foreheads. Thus they are
defcribed in our Context; in the Words we have
read they are defigned, Such as follow the Lamb.
*Thefe are they which follow the Lamb whitherfoever he
goeth.*

I had Occafion yefterday to open up and a little
explain thefe Words, and the Doctrine that I obferved from them was this,

> *That all that are with the Lamb, or are on the Lamb's
> Side, they follow the Lamb whitherfoever he
> goeth.*

*Thefe are they which follow the Lamb whitherfoever
he goeth.* In difcourfing from this Doctrine, I propofed,

In the *firft* Place, to fpeak a little concerning the
Lamb, the worthy Lamb, the Leader of this Company.

2dly. To fpeak a little to the Characters given to
the Followers of the Lamb, his Retinue and Train,
in the Text and Context.

3dly. To fhew what is imported in following the
Lamb.

4thly. To fhew how, or by what Means, the
Lamb's Retinue and Train do follow him.

5thly. To fhew where it is they do follow the
Lamb

6thly Give the Reafons of the Doctrine, or
fhew why all thofe who are with the Lamb, do
follow the Lamb whitherfoever he goeth,

Laftly, To apply the Doctrine.

I fpoke to the firft of thefe yefterday, which was
to fpeak a little concerning the worthy Lamb, the
Leader of this happy Company, and fhall not now
infift upon it, only, in a few Words, the Lamb
whom they follow, the worthy Lamb, he is mentioned under the Defignation of a Lamb frequently
by

by this Apoftle and Evangelift. In his Writings,
in the firft Verfe, he is defigned by him as a Lamb
ftanding upon the Mount *Zion, that is,* the Gofpel-
Church, and indeed he is the Glory of the Church,
the Beauty and Excellency of the Church; all the
Church's Beauty is derived from the worthy Lamb,
the Lamb, in the Midft of the Retinue and Train
that follow him, he is their Light, their Life, their
Strength, their Hope, their Glory, their All; the
Leader of the Company is juft their All, and in all
He is the Captain of the Lord's Hoft, that glorious
One whom the glorious Hofts of Heaven do follow
Who can fpeak of him? Who can exprefs his
mighty Works? Who can fhew forth all his Praife?
If we fpeak of the Perfon of the Lamb, it is a
wonderful Perfon   He is *Immanuel,* God with us,
God manifefted in the Flefh, God in our very Nature   Who can fpeak of this Myftery?   Ay the
more the Eye of Faith looks at this Myftery, it
fees ay the more to be wondred at, of aftonifhing
Wifdom, and amazing Grace and Love   The
wonderful Glory and Condefcendency, that is to be
feen in looking at the Perfon of Chrift, cannot be
told, his Glory and Excellency cannot be expreffed.
He is the Lamb of God, the Lamb of God, cho
fen by God to be a propitiatory Sacrifice for the
Expiation of our Guilt, he is the Lamb provided
by God for a Burnt-Offering, he is the Lamb con
fecrated by God, fet apart in the eternal Purpofe
of God, fet apart in the Council of Peace, before
the Foundation of the Earth was laid, fet apart to
be an Offering and Sacrifice to God of a fweet
fmelling Savour, in the Room and Stead of Sin
ners   Accordingly, in the Fulnefs of Time, he was
actually facrificed   *For, when the Fulnefs of Time was
come, God fent forth his Son, made of a Woman, made*
under

under the Law, to redeem them who were under the Law · And being found in Fashion as a Man, he humbled himself, and became obedient unto Death, even the Death of the Cross. He is this Day exhibited in Word and Sacrament, and you are called to behold the Lamb of God. O will you behold the Lamb of God, behold him in the Word, behold him in the Sacrament ! Behold the Lamb of God, that taketh away the Sin of the World!

I proceed to the second general Head which I proposed in the Method, and that is, to speak somewhat of the Characters given to the Lamb's Retinue and Train, in the Text and Context.

There is a particular Emphasis in the Manner of Expression, These are they which follow the Lamb, &c. Now, who are they which follow the Lamb whithersoever he goeth ? There are these four or five Characters of them laid down in the Text and Context, which I shall endeavour to take Notice of.

First, They are designed, such as were redeemed from the Earth, redeemed from among Men. 2dly. They are designed, such as sing a new Song, that none can learn but the Hundred forty and four thousand, the Lamb's Retinue. 3dly. They are designed, such as were not defiled with Women, for they are Virgins. 4thly. They are designed, the first Fruits to God and the Lamb, and, in the last Place, they are designed, Persons whose Mouths are without Guile.

Now, all I intend, at the Time, is just to drop a Word to these Characters given this blessed and happy Company who are on the Lamb's Side.

And, Oh that what we are to say may, through the Lord's Blessing, prove more instructing, convincing and confirming. In the first Place, then

B

the Lamb's Retinue and Train, they are defigned such as were redeemed from the Earth. In the Clofe of the 3d Verfe they are fuch as are redeemed from among Men. Now, there is a twofold Redemption by which they are redeemed In the *firft* Place there is a Redemption by Price, 2*dly*. A Redemption by Power.

In the *firft* Place, I fay, there is a Redemption by Price, by which the Followers of the Lamb are redeemed The Lord Chrift, the worthy Lamb he paid the Price of their Redemption, he hath given his Life a Ranfom for many, and fo all the Lamb's Retinue and Train, they are a People redeemed to God by his Blood, as we have it in the 5th Chapter of this Book of the *Revelation*, and 9th Verfe, *Thou art worthy, for thou waft flain, and haft redeemed us to God by thy Blood, out of every Tongue, Kindred, People, Nation and Language.* Thus you fee the Price he paid for their Redemption; the Price of his Blood : *Redeemed us to God by thy Blood.* A valuable Price, a glorious Price, a coftly Price, a Price like himfelf. *Redeemed us to God by thy Blood*

2*dly* They who are redeemed from the Earth, they are redeemed by Power This I take to be chiefly intended here, when they are faid to be redeemed from the Earth, or from among Men who are fprung of Earth Now they are redeemed from the Earth in the Day of their effectual Calling Even when they are made a willing People in the Day of the Lamb's Power, then they are redeemed from the Earth, from among Men, *that is*, they are juft feparated from the reft of the World, *redeemed from the Earth*, that is, they are redeemed from that reigning Carnality, that earthly Mindednefs that by Nature they themfelves, as well as others

are

ue under. *Redeemed from the Earth*; · from the Love of the Earth and earthly Things, from the Plague of Darkneſs and Blindneſs that overſpreads the whole Earth, Darkneſs covers the Earth, and groſs Darkneſs the People. And, Sirs, thoſe that are with the Lamb, who follow the Lamb, they are redeemed from this Darkneſs that covers the Earth, the Day-Spring from on high hath riſen upon them, the Light of the Knowledge of the Glory of God in the Face of Jeſus Chriſt hath ſhin-ed into our Hearts. The Retinue of the worthy Lamb, they are a People that are called from Darkneſs to the Lord's marvellous Light, as you have it in the firſt Epiſtle of *Peter* 11 9. *Ye are a choſen Generation, a royal Prieſthood, an holy Nation, a peculiar People, that ye ſhould ſhew forth the Praiſes of him who hath called you out of Darkneſs into his marvellous Light* Sirs, thoſe that are with the Lamb, his Retinue and Train, they have other Views of the Majeſty of God than the reſt of the World have, they have other Views of an inviſible God than others about them have. Why, they ſee him, in the Light of his Spirit, a God in Chriſt, a God of Glory and Excellency, ſhining in the Face and Perſon of his incarnate Son. God's Being and Perfec-tion is a Myſtery to all but them that are on the Lamb's Side, and even to them in a great Meaſure, but they ſee the Glory of God in the Face of Jeſus Chriſt, in another Manner than the World about them do, they are enlightned by the Spirit, redeemed from the Earth by the Power of the Redeemer, the worthy Lamb, they are re-deemed from that Enmity that prevails, yea, that reigns in the Earth, in the Hearts of the Men of the Earth.

Sirs,

Sirs, when Sin entred into the World, as Darkness and Death entred by Sin, so Enmity against God entred by Sin, but Redemption by the Power of the Redeemer, it is the Recovery of the Soul of he sinful Man or Woman, from the reigning Power of that Enmity. There is an Enmity in the Heart naturally against God, which deters the proud Heart from submitting to the Righteousness of God, as it is expressed in the 10th Chapter of the Epistle to the *Romans*, and 3d Verse of that Chapter. Where this natural Enmity and Unbelief is still dwelling, the proud Heart will not bow unto the Authority of God, nor stoop to the Law of God Why, the Reason is, *it is Enmity against God, and is not subject to the Law of God, neither indeed can it be :* So till this Redemption by Power take the Field, which only is a conquering of this Enmity, an overcoming of this Enmity , and so soon as the worthy Lamb, the glorious Redeemer, steps in with his Almighty Power, why, then the proud Heart opens to the Son of God, the obstinate Sinner stoops to *Jehovah*, the obstinate Sinner is meekned by Faith's Views of the meek Lamb, the worthy Lamb and so is made to stoop to the Righteousness of God, the Righteousness of the Lamb ; made to stoop to the Way of Salvation through the Lord Jesus Christ the worthy Lamb, the Heart is made to stoop to God's Method of Grace, and Way of recovering Sinners from Sin and Wrath, through the Righteousness of the Lamb, through the Obedience, Death and Resurrection of his own eternal Son, the worthy Lamb. Thus the Lamb's Company, his Retinue and Train, they are redeemed from the Earth, from the Obstinacy that naturally reigns in the Heart against the Grace and Love of Christ, the Lamb of God, the worthy Lamb.

Again,

Again, the Lamb's Company are defigned, *redeem-ed from the Earth*, becaufe by Nature they bear the Image of the firft *Adam*. The firft Man, *Adam*, it is a Word that fignifies *Earth*, *yea Earth*, and all Mankind they bear the Image of this earthly *Adam*; and fo, when the worthy Lamb comes under the Character of a Redeemer, he redeems his Followers from the Earth, from the earthly Image of the firft *Adam*; and by Grace they are made to bear the I-mage of the fecond *Adam*, the fecond Man, who is the Lord from Heaven, and fo all that have Expe-rience of this Redemption (fo to fpeak) they have the Image of the Lamb juft drawn upon them. When Chrift, the worthy Lamb, comes, and firft pays a Vifit unto a Soul, he juft (fo to fpeak) draws his Image and Picture upon the Man or Woman's Heart by that Vifit. The very firft Sight the Soul gets, by Faith, of the worthy Lamb, it juft affi-milates and changes the Sinner into the fame Image with their glorious Head. Hence, faith the Apoftle, *We all, with open Face, beholding as in a Glafs the Glory of God, are changed into the fame Image, from Glory to Glory.* Try it then, Sirs, if ever you got a faving Sight of the glorious Image of the worthy Lamb, there is a Stamp of Chrift left on you. We do not fay it is alike difcernible in all, for in fome it may be but like the bruifed Reed and the fmoking Flax, but where this Image is ftamped, however interceptible it may be, the bruifed Reed he will not break, the fmoking Flax he will not quench; for the firft faving Difcovery the Sinner gets of the Lord Chrift, it leaves fomething of him behind it, that will remain ay till Grace be confum-mate in Glory. Hence farth our Lord, *John* iv. 14. *Whofoever drinketh of the Water that I fhall give him, fhall never thirft, but the Water that I fhall give him,*

him, shall be in him a Well of living Water springing up unto everlasting Life.

It is very like some may be thinking themselves quite scored off by this Manner of speaking. Why, say you, I find nothing but Enmity, Atheism and Unbelief just prevailing and carrying all before them. But may I not appeal to such, Is there not a Party in thy Heart to bear Testimony for Christ, and against Sin, even in thy lowest Case? Is there not a secret Breathing in thy Heart, O for Deliverance from that woful Enmity! O for Deliverance from the Power of this Atheism and Unbelief! Let me ask you, Would you not, when at the very lowest, when Matters are at the very worst with you, would you not rejoice to have your spiritual Fetters broke off? Would you not rejoice to have your Feet set upon the Necks of your spiritual Enemies, Enmity, Atheism, Unbelief, and the like? Let me ask you, When ye are at the lowest, when you begin to reflect upon what has been the Lord's Way with you, is there not a Breathing in you, saying, *O that it were with me as in Months past, as in the Day when God preserved me, when his Candle shined upon my Head,* &c. *O that I knew where I might find him, that I might come even to his Seat!* When these your Enemies are prevailing in or over you, is there not a Kind of Restlesness in you, you cannot find Rest any where until you come anew to Christ? O to be back to my Rest again! I think I will never be right till I see him again! If Matters are so with you, poor Soul, it is an Evidence you are redeemed from the Earth, and if there be really an inward Principle of Grace in thy Heart, there will be less or more of this Exercise in you; for where there is an inward Principle of Grace infused in the Heart of a Sinner, by the Spirit

rit of the Lord Jefus Chrift, it is juft fomething like
the Needle in the Compafs, that, through the Influence of the Load-Stone, turn it where you will,
it never refts until it turn to the Pole. So Believers, however dark, difmal and diftreffing their Cafe
may be, yet the Soul can never have folid Reft, until it be pointed towards the great Pole, Chrift Jefus the worthy Lamb. So much for the firft Character I took notice of, which is given to the Followers of the Lamb, his Retinue and Train. *2dly.*
Another of their Characters who are on the Lamb's
Side, is, *That they fing a new Song, that none can*
learn but the Hundred forty and four thoufand, the
Lamb's Retinue and Train. This indeed is a Song
that none could or can learn, but fuch as are on the
Lamb's Side, they that are with the Lamb. And,
by the Way, this gives us to know, that the whole
of Religion is a Myftery to natural Men; to unrege-
nerate Men, it is all a Myftery to them; they cannot know the Things of the Spirit of God. Chrift
the Lamb is a hid Chrift to them, the Gofpel of
Chrift is a hid Gofpel to them, the Love of Chrift
is hid Love as to them, the Grace of Chrift is vailed
to them. In one Word, all that Good that the
Gofpel reveals is hid from them. And that Word
is true concerning them, *If our Gofpel be hid, it is*
hid to them that are loft, in whom the God of this World
hath blinded the Minds of them which believe not, left
the Light of the glorious Gofpel of Chrift, who is the
Image of God, fhould fhine into their Hearts. Thus
we fay the whole of Religion is a Myftery to natural Men, they know nothing of this Song, this
new Song which is fung by the Lamb's Retinue and
Train.

To be more particular on this Character of the
Lamb's Followers, there are three Things I fhall
a little

a little take notice of in this new Song, that none can learn but the Followers of the Lamb. In the *firſt* Place, there is the glorious Object of the Song, 2*dly.* The Matter ; and, 3*dly.* the Manner of this Song , each of which are Myſteries to all but ſuch as are with the Lamb.

In the *firſt* Place, there is the glorious Object of this new Song ; none can learn the glorious Object of the Song, but ſuch as are with the Lamb. Who then is the Object of the new Song ? Why, the worthy Lamb himſelf is the Object of this Song, he is the Object of the Praiſe and the Wonder of all his Retinue and Train · They ſay concerning him, Thou art our Praiſe , each of them ſays for himſelf, *My Praiſe ſhall he of thee.* If it be asked, How it came about that he is the Object of their Song ? We anſwer, in a Word, He is the Object of their Delight, of their Complaceny, Satisfaction and Delight ; the Object of their Wonder and Admiration, and therefore the Object of their Song, *Worthy is the Laml that was ſlain, to receive Power, Riches, Wiſdom, Strength, Honour, Glory and Bleſſing.* Now, when it is ſaid, none could learn this new Song but the Hundred forty and four Thouſand, the Followers of the Lamb, the Meaning is, none could learn the Object of the Song but them ; nor was it any Thing in them that contributed to their learning the Song, no, they have been all taught of God, they have all got a Leſſon from above, from the worthy Lamb, which has not come in Word only, but in Power and in the Holy Ghoſt. They have been all taught by the Spirit, who convinceth the World of Sin ; they have all known that powerful Iuſtruction, that efficacious Inſtruction, which bows the ſtouteſt Heart, and makes the ſtouteſt Heart yield to the Lord Jeſus Chriſt. And

what

that is the great Lesson which has been taught them? Why, it is Christ himself the worthy Lamb; Christ in his Person, in the infinite Glory of his divine Person: Christ in what he hath done, in what he is doing, in what he will do, is the great Lesson they have been taught, and is the Object of their Song, the great and glorious Object of the new Song, which none can learn or sing but the Lamb's Retinue and Train

But then, in the *second* Place, as the Object of his Song is a Mystery, and what none can learn but the Followers of the Lamb, so the Matter of the Song is also a Mystery, that none can learn but them who are with the Lamb; and as Christ, the Lamb himself, is the glorious Object of this Song, so he is also the great Matter of the Song; it all centres in him as to the Matter of it, it centres in what he has done and suffered, it is a Song of the Death and Resurrection of the Lamb. What is the Matter of the Song? It is a Song of the manifold Wisdom of God shining in the Face of the Lamb. and just beaming forth in what he hath done. What is the Matter of their Song? Why, it is just a Song of the wonderful Love of God displayed in the Person and Undertaking of the worthy Lamb. Hence is that Word, *Rev* 1. 5, 6. *Unto him that loved us, and hath washed us from our Sins in his own Blood, and hath made us Kings and Priests unto God and his Father ; unto him be Glory and Dominion for ever and ever.* Again, What is the Matter of their Song? It is just a Song of the Grace of God manifested and displayed in the Face of Jesus Christ, the worthy Lamb, it is a Song of the Mercy of God venting through the worthy Lamb, it is a Song of Mercy, a Song of the Seasonableness of Mercy, of the Rise and Progress of Mercy. Hence the

G

Church

Church sings, *He remembred us in our low Estate,*
for his Mercy endureth for ever. What is the Matter of their Song? Why, the infinite Holiness of
God, shining forth in the Undertaking and Perfor-
mance of the worthy Lamb, is the subject Matter
of their Song. So, in the Vision which *John* saw,
Rev. iv. 8. the living Creatures, joined with the
redeemed from among Men, rest not Day nor Night,
from saying, or singing, *Holy, holy, holy, Lord God*
Almighty, which was, and is, and is to come. Sirs, it
is a Mark and Character of all who are among the
Lamb's Retinue and Train, they love the Holiness
of God shining in the worthy Lamb, as well as the
Mercy of God through which they are saved;
and this indeed is a Mystery that none can learn
but they who are with the Lamb. Have you then
learned the new Song, the Matter of the Song?
If so be, you can in some Measure give Thanks at
the Remembrance of his Holiness, you love the
Holiness of God, and you celebrate the Holiness of
God, as it shines in the worthy Lamb, as well as
the Mercy of God. You love God because he is
holy, and love to join the Retinue above, saying,
Holy, holy, holy, Lord God Almighty. Thus you have
learned the Matter of the Song At whose Mouth
have you learned this Note, to sing of his infinite
Holiness? Why, just at the Mouth of the worthy
Lamb, who cries out, *Thou art holy, O thou that in-*
habitest the Praises of Israel, Psalm xxii 3. This
is his Cry, and the Faith of this makes all the Lamb's
Followers, his Retinue and Train, cry out, *Holy,*
holy, holy, is the Lord God Almighty.

But then, in the *third* and *last* Place, upon this
Character of the Lamb's Followers, as the Object and
Matter of this new Song which they sing, ar Mysteries which none can learn but the Followers of
the

he Lamb ; so the Manner of the Song is a Mystery
o all but such as are with the Lamb ; none can sing
he Song but they, because the Manner how they
sing it, is what none can learn but his Retinue and
Train. In what Manner then is it his Followers sing
his new Song? Why, as the Song is not a carnal, but
a spiritual Song, so they who sing it, they sing it with
a new Heart and a new Spirit. Such as sing it, they
have got the new Heart and new Spirit ; they are
sanctified by the Spirit of Christ How is this Song
sung? Why, it is sung in Faith, it proceeds from
Faith in the Object of the Song, whom Flesh and
Blood doth not reveal to the Soul, but his Father
which is in Heaven. It is just in a Way of Faith
and Believing that this Song is sung, for Faith is
just a giving Glory and Praise to God, Glory to the
worthy Lamb. Hence it is said of *Abraham, He staggered not at the Promise of God, through Unbelief,
but was strong in the Faith, giving Glory to God.*
Thus, we say, the glorious Object, the Matter, and
the Manner of this new Song, are all Mysteries to
such as are not with the Lamb, but are taught
unto his Retinue and Train.   But

I proceed to a *third* Character I took notice of,
of the Lamb's Retinue and Train, the Followers of
the worthy Lamb, and you have it in the first Part
of the Verse which I have read, where they are designed, Such as were not defiled with Women · *These
are they which are not defiled with Women, for
they are Virgins.* The Expressions are figurative, the
Apostle hath a Commentary upon them in his 2d
Epistle to the *Corinthians,* 11th Chapter and 2d Verse,
I have espoused you to one Husband, (saith he) *that I
may present you as a chaste Virgin to Christ* The Meaning is, This Retinue and Train, the blessed Company
here spoken of, they were chaste unto their Husband
the

the Lord Jesus Christ, in a Day of general Defection and Apostasy from him ; they were chaste unto Him in the Time of the Apostasy and Defection that took Place ; particularly, under the Reign of Antichrist, which is principally intended in this Place, that Remnant were kept chaste and pure from the general Defection and Apostasy that then prevailed. They did not defile themselves with the Sins and Whoredoms of the Day, the Snares of the Time wherein they lived. They are chaste Virgins unto Christ their Husband , they observe the Ordinances and Institutions of their Husband. In Scripture it is called spiritual Whoredom and Idolatry, to corrupt the Ordinances and Institutions of Christ ; and so, when the Members of a visible Church do depart from the Purity of the Ordinances and Institutions of Christ, they are justly chargeable with spiritual Whoredom, and Unchastity to their Husband Christ. It is the special Character of the Retinue of the Lamb, that they are not defiled with Women, for they are Virgins, chaste Virgins, chaste in their Endeavour to keep pure and intire all such religious Worship and Ordinances as he hath appointed in his Word ; chaste in their Obedience unto the Laws and Authority of Christ, as their great Lord and Lawgiver , chaste in their Love to and Esteem of Christ ; chaste in their Affections to and Desires after Christ But, more particularly, those who are with the Lamb, his Retinue and Train, their Chastity may be known, and doth evidence itself, in all these particular Characters following.

In the *first* Place, their Chastity may be known, and doth evidence itself, in their Fear of Sin, and Desire to be kept from sinning, they desire to be kept pure in a sinning Time, in a defiling Age and Time,

Time, in an enfnaring Time; particularly, they defire to be kept from the Sins and Snares that prevail in the Time and Place where they live. They are more afraid of Sin than of any Thing elfe. It was a good Saying of an eminent private Chriftian, who was brought before the Jufticiary in the late Times of Perfecution, when they were defiring him not to lie, he anfwered, *I am more afraid to lie, than to die.* That which the Lord's People count Tendernefs, the World reckons Nicety, Hypocrify and Precifenefs. But, O Sirs, regard them not, it is good to be tender, it is a dangerous Thing to give a fquint Look to Chrift's Rivals, or to give an adulterous Look to Idols.

In the 2d Place, the Chaftity of the Lamb's Retinue may be known, and doth evidence itfelf, in their hearty Concern for, and Regard unto the declarative Glory of the Lamb The Lamb is very jealous of his own Glory; and fo all his Followers, who are taught of him, they mingle Interefts with him, and become alfo jealous of his declarative Glory, and concerned for the Advancement of his declarative Glory, and there are weighty Reafons it fhould be fo, if we confider, that it includes all the pofitive Ordinances and Inftitutions of God, and of the Lamb their Husband; and the fecond Commandment in the Moral Law itfelf, doth fix upon every one of us an Obligation to be tender of all the Ordinances and Inftitutions of Chrift, to be tender of his declarative Glory But, alas, Sirs, tho' all are bound to this Tendernefs by the Law of God, how few know any Thing of it! Many think light of the declarative Glory of the Lamb, think light of his Ordinances and Inftitutions, at this Day. For Inftance, How many think the Government of his Houfe a light Matter, at this Day? Be it known

unto

unto them, who think the Government of Chrift's House a light Matter, and not to be contended for, fo far they are from the Character of the Followers of the Lamb, that they are guilty of fpiritual Fornication and Adultery, whoever they be. Why, fay fome, we ought not to be concerned about the the Government of Chrift's Houfe What have we to do with this? It is not neceffary unto Salvation, it is none of the Effentials of Religion, we will hold by the Effentials, but as for the Government of his Houfe, it is not abfolutely neceffary to Salvation. Oh what a grofs Saying is this! If the Government be thrown afide, I fay, if the Government of the Houfe be caft by, the Ordinances of the Houfe will not ftand long pure. If once the Hedge of Government be taken away, why, then all Paffengers will pluck at the Ordinances and Inftitutions of the Houfe; the very wild Beafts of the Field, and the Boar out of the Wood, will wafte it at their Pleafure Chrift, the worthy Lamb, the Lord of his own Houfe, he is a jealous God, he is very zealous for his own Glory, he will have all Things in his Houfe, to the very leaft Pin, managed according to the Pattern fhewn in the Mount. And truly, Sirs, he who is the chafte Virgin, not defiled with Women, he regardeth all the Ordinances and Inftitutions of Chrift's Houfe, and the Order and Government of his Houfe no lefs. As for that felfifh Spirit of theirs, who pretend a Regard to thofe Things they call Effentials of Religion, I fhall only fay this, their Regard is not much to be regarded, who take upon them to difregard any Part of what relates to the declarative Glory of the Lamb. Such a Temper as this is perilous, and exceeding difpleafing in his Sight; and we may be fure of this one Thing,

that

that where God has reared up his House, made the Land a covenanted Land, and even there Matters come to this sad Pass, of disregarding the Government of his House, as a Thing of no Moment, it is an awful Prelude, that the Lord will shortly plead a Controversy with the Land. Sirs, something might be born with such as have not arrived at the same Degree of Reformation that *Scotland* has arrived at. Let such as make light of these Things take it as they will, God looks upon it as spiritual Adultery, and going a-whoring from the worthy Lamb.

In the 3*d* and *last* Place, the Chastity of the Lamb's Retinue may be known, and doth evidence itself, in their sincere Love and Affection to the worthy Lamb their Husband, and a chaste Love unto the Lord Christ, it very well becomes all his Followers; their Love ought to be chaste and pure, their Affections ought to be chaste and pure; Christ, the worthy Lamb, ought to have the chief Room in their Heart and Affections, and it well becomes him to have it; and it is spiritual Fornication and Adultery, if any Thing beside him have it; if other Things, beside Christ, are entertained before him in any Heart or Affections, it is a sad Sign that Heart is not yet opened to the worthy Lamb. This then is another Character of the Followers of the worthy Lamb, his Retinue and Train, *They are not defiled with Women, for they are Virgins.* They are chaste unto the Lord Christ; chaste in the Hatred of Sin, chaste in their Concern for the declarative Glory of, chaste in their Love and Affections towards the worthy Lamb. But

I proceed to a *fourth* Character of those who follow the Lamb, his Retinue and Train; and you have

have it in the Close of the Verse which I have read, where they are defigned, *the firft Fruits unto God and the Lamb.* Now, if it is inquired, why the Lamb's Retinue are defigned, *the firft Fruits unto God,* I anfwer in thefe two Obfervations. In the *firft* Place, you know, under the old Teftament, the firft Fruits were confecrated unto God, and fo they who follow the Lamb, they are a Company confecrated unto God, they have confecrated and devoted themfelves unto the Lord, and they juft look upon themfelves to be the devoted Thing, which belongs to God as his Due and Right. As the firft ripe Fruits were prefented to the Lord, fo the Lamb's Followers, they anfwer that Exhortation of the Apoftle, *I befeech you, Brethren, by the Mercies of God, that ye prefent your Bodies* (a Part put for the whole Man, by an ufual Figure) *a living Sacrifice, holy and acceptable unto God, which is your reafonable Service.* We fay, they confecrate themfelves wholly unto him, they confecrate and devote their Hearts and Souls unto him, they confecrate and devote their Affections and Love unto him; in a Word, they devote all the Powers and Faculties of their Souls unto him, they devote all the Members of their Bodies unto him, they devote likeways their Wealth and Subftance unto him, all that they can call theirs, they are content it be the Lord's. Thus they are the firft Fruits unto God, and to the Lamb The firft Fruits, you know, are but a fmall Part of the Crop, and fo the Expreffion intimates the Paucity of the Number who are with the Lamb: *Many are called, but few are chofen. Strait is the Gate, and narrow is the Way, that leadeth to Life, and few there be that find it.* There are many Profeffors at this Day, Sirs; but, alas, how few know the Myfteries of the

the Kingdom of God ? How few know the Myſtery of Religion ? *Many are called, but few are choſen.* The Lamb's Retinue and Train, I ſay, are but like the firſt Fruits, which are but a ſmall Part of the Crop · They are ſometimes fewer in one Period than in another, but ſtill, even when they are moſt numerous, they are but like the firſt Fruits, in compariſon of the great Bulk who are not of the Lamb's Retinue and Train Some think the Expreſſion here reſpects ſuch a Time as that, when the Lamb has but a very thin Backing, in compariſon of the Multitude wondring after the Beaſt, and who of conſequence go down the Stream of Defection I remember an Expreſſion of worthy *Rutherford,* in one of his Letters, when Epiſcopacy was like to get the Aſcendant in this Land ; ſaith he, *The Queſtion ſhall be, Few Noblemen, if any, few Barons, if any, few Gentry, if any, to ſtand it out.* It is brought to this with us, Sirs , few Noblemen, if any, few Barons, if any, to take the Cauſe of Chriſt by the Hand in *Scotland* · Few Miniſters and few Commons to take the Cauſe of Chriſt by the Hand, they are comparatively like the firſt ripe Fruits. But,

2*dly* There is another Obſervation I would make on the firſt Fruits The firſt Fruits, you know, are a Token of an approaching Harveſt and ſome think the Expreſſion here points at the Time when there will be a glorious Enlargement of the Church and Kingdom of Chriſt, when the Lord begins the Quarrel againſt Antichriſt. Well, tho' the Followers of the Lamb be but like the firſt Fruits, yet the firſt Fruits to God and to the Lamb, they go before a plentiful Crop and Ingathering under the Lamb's Banner. Sirs, here then is good News. However low the Lamb's Cauſe may be brought,

D however

however few his Retinue and Train may be in certain Periods, yet the Lamb shall be uppermost, the Lamb shall gain the Day, ere all be done, the Lamb shall have a glorious Retinue and Train the Lamb shall have a plentiful Gathering in of Souls to him, the first Fruits secure the Harvest What Trials and Difficulties may be in our Way, in a Way of witnessing for the Lamb, in this Day of backsliding and declining, we know not, however, in the mean Time, Faith may feed upon this that the first Fruits to God and to the Lamb, both proceed and secure a glorious Harvest and Ingathering of Souls to the Lamb's Retinue and Train This is good News, good Food for Faith, and we may believe it shall be so, for *Jehovah* hath said concerning the Lamb's Retinue, *Psalm* lxxii. 16. *There shall be an Handful of Corn in the Earth, on the Top of the Mountain, the Fruit thereof shall shake like Lebanon, and they of the City shall flourish like Grass of the Earth.* And of the Lamb himself, Verse 17 *His Name shall endure for ever, his Name shall be continued as long as the Sun, and Men shall be blessed in him; all Nations shall call him blessed.*

The *5th* and *last* Character I took notice of, which is given to the Followers of the Lamb, his Retinue and Train, you have it in the 5th Verse where they are designed, Persons in whose Mouths is no Guile. *And in their Mouth was found no Guile, for they are without Fault before the Throne of God* The Character of the Lamb's Retinue, we see, is twofold

In the *first* Place, they are said to be without Guile · *In their Mouths was found no Guile,* that is their Heart is with their Mouth they correspond together, the Word of their Mouth is the Thought of their Heart Many dissemble in their Profession concerning the worthy Lamb, they shew much Love in their Profession. With their Mouth and

Lip they profess to draw near to God, but, in the mean Time, their Heart goeth after their Covetousness, and so that is a dissembling Profession. But it is otherways with the Followers of the Lamb, in their Mouth is no Guile, their Heart and their Mouth agree together, their Heart and Profession correspond together. All that are with the Lamb, and follow the Lamb, they are single and true-hearted Men: They that are the Lamb's true Followers, they are single for the Lamb s Glory and Honour; they follow the Lamb whithersoever he goeth. Many take up a Profession of Religion, in a fair Day, and they just lay it down again, when this and the other Temptation or Trial casts in the Way Try your Profession, Sirs. If you be the Lamb's Followers, you will have Mouths this far without Guile, that your Heart and Profession will agree together, and so, when the Heart and Profession do correspond and agree together, then they have the other Part of the Character, as it follows, *they are without Fault before the Throne of God*

If it be asked, How are they without Fault before the Throne of God? I answer, They are without Fault in a two-fold Respect. In the 1*st* Place, They are without Fault in regard of their Justification, 2*dly* In respect of their Sanctification.

In the *first* Place, I say, the Retinue of the Lamb are without Fault in regard of their Justification, *being justified freely by his Grace, through the Redemption that is in Jesus Christ*, Rom iii. 24 When God pardons the Sins of his People in Justification, he just casts them all into the Depths of the Sea, and accepts their Persons as righteous in his Sight, only for the Righteousness of the Lamb, and in this Respect they are all without Fault before the Throne of God, having their Sins washed away

in

in his Blood, and their Perſons accepted through, and covered with the Righteouſneſs of the Lord Jeſus Chriſt, the worthy Lamb.   He is juſt their Clothing, their Ornament, their only Covering be-fore God, and they are all beautified with his Excel lency, and made comely with his Comelineſs And hence it follows that they are without Fault before the Throne of God, in reſpect of their Juſtification But then,

In the 2d Place, the Lamb's Followers are with-out Fault in reſpect of their Sanctification.   Altho' the Work of Sanctification be but imperfect while the Soul is in this World, yet the Work of Sancti fication is a progreſſive Work, it is growing up to Perfection , yea, even in this World it hath a Perfection of Parts, altho' it is not perfect as to its Meaſure and Degree , and this begun Perfection, this Perfection of Parts, is an undoubted Pledge and Evidence of a full Perfection, as to Meaſure and Degree, in due Time , for all that are with the Lamb, who follow the worthy Lamb, they ſhall be preſented before the Throne of God, waſh ed with Water by the Word , ſo ſanctified and cleanſed, that there they ſhall appear, *not having Spot or Wrinkle, or any ſuch Thing , holy and without Blemiſt*, Eph v 26, 27.

Now, Sirs, thus have I ſet before you ſome of the Characters of the Lamb's Retinue and Train, the Followers of the worthy Lamb   Have you been applying as I have been ſpeaking What has been ſaid may be improved, as Marks and Evi dences by which you may try yourſelves, whether you are among the Lamb's Retinue or not.   Try it, then, `Sirs Are you redeemed from the Earth, redeemed from among Men, redeemed by the Price of the Lamb's Blood, and by the Power of his

his Spirit? Are ye among those who have learned the new Song, which none can learn but such as are with the Lamb, and follow the Lamb? Have you ever been taught of God, taught the mysterious Song, which is a Mystery to all but the Lamb's Retinue and Train? Have you learned the Object of the Song, the Matter of the Song, and the Manner of the Song? Again, are you such as are not defiled with Women, who are Virgins? Are you chaste to the worthy Lamb your Husband, chaste in your Hatred of Sin, chaste in your Concern for his declarative Glory, &c? Are you the first Fruits to God, and to the Lamb? And, finally, are you ranked and numbred among those in whose Mouths is no Guile, and who are without Fault before the Throne of God? Does your Heart and your Mouth correspond together? Are you justified by the Righteousness of the Lamb, and sanctified by his Spirit? Why, then you have the Lamb's Call to go to his Table, to take the Seal of his Covenant, the confirming Seal of his Love, to remember him, and what he hath done for you? He hath given himself for you, and go ye, then, and take a View of the worthy Lamb in the Sacrament, in the Ordinance of his Supper. Go, and there behold the Lamb of God

I cannot proceed farther upon this Subject at the Time. The Lord bless his Word, and to his Name be Praise.

ORWELL,

ORWELL, *Monday, 7 August* 1738.

REV. xiv. 4.

Thefe are they which follow the Lamb whitherfoever he goeth.

MY Friends, we are affembled together this Day, to give Thanks unto the Lord, the worthy Lamb, on a Thankf-giving-Day, after a folemn Commun-on-Day: We are affembled together to fing Praifes to our great King, the King of *Zion*, who is gone up with a Shout, as in the *Pfalm* fung in the Entry. He is gone up with a Shout, he hath a-fcended up on high, he hath afcended up with a Shout of Victory over his Enemies, he hath fpoil-ed Principalities and Powers, and made a Shew of them openly upon the Crofs And, upon the Back of his Victory upon the Crofs, he hath gone up with a Shout unto his Throne, to his Crown above, where he reigns and rules, and will do fo until all his Enemies be made his Footftool O Sirs, upon the Back of a folemn Communion-Sabbath, what think you of *Zion's* King, the worthy Lamb? Have you got any Sight of his Beauty, Glory, and tranfcer-dent Excellency? If fo be; what think you of him? What think you of the Prince of the King's of the Earth, the King of Kings, and Lord of Lords? I am fure, my Friends, if you have got any fpiri-tual Views of the Lamb, of the Glory of this great King

King, who is gone up with a Shout, then your Souls have been made to bow unto him, to stoop unto him, to give the Obedience of Faith unto him, and you have been made to say concerning this King. Let him reign over me, let him sway the Sceptre over me, just in my Heart. O let him be great in my Heart, let him be exalted there, let him be all there ' O he is worthy to be exalted, worthy to be honoured, worthy to be glorified, and worthy to be set on high above all , for he is that King, that God who has gone up with a Shout, with a triumphant Shout, with a magnificent Shout, a victorious Shout. And, Sirs, I tell you to-day, that this King, who has gone up with a Shout, will, in like Manner, in a little Time, come down with a Shout. The Lord himself shall descend from Heaven with a Shout, with the Voice of the Archangel, and the Trump of God. O what a Shout will that be ? Why, it shall be heard in all the Ends of the Earth , it will be a Shout that will gather all Nations before him , it will be a Shout that will gather his redeemed and ransomed Ones together before him, to go to Glory with him , it will be a Shout that will gather all his Enemies before him, to receive their final Doom from him. Here is a Mark of the genuine Followers of the Lamb, they long for this Shout. The Old Testament Church longed for the Time when this King should come and finish his Work, and go up with a Shout. The new Testament Church longs for the Time when he shall descend with a Shout. When they think of his descending with a Shout, they cry, *Amen, even so come, Lord Jesus.* Well, his Work is going on, and in a very little his Work will be finished. It is long since he said, *Behold, I come quickly.* And he who said,
Behold,

Behold, I come quickly, he is coming apace, he will come in a little, and gather all his Followers together to be ever with the Lord. We are met together this Day to give Thanks to this King who is gone up with a Shout and, Sirs, in our solemn Affembly a Shout of longing, for his defcending with a Shout, fhould go up to him who is gone up with a Shout. And is there any Longing among you for that Day, that happy Day, that bleffed Day, when the Lamb fhall defcend with a Shout, and when all the Members of his myftical Body fhall be gathered together, with the Lamb at the Head of the Company, and the whole Company of the redeemed from among Men at the Lambs Back, not having Spot or Wrinkle, or any fuch Thing The whole Company with the Lamb, comely through his Comelinefs upon them, the whole Company like unto the Lamb, all fhining with the Glory of the worthy Lamb. O long for that happy Day ! Let every one that is amongft the Lamb's Company, his ranfomed Ones, cry out, *Amen, even fo come, Lord Jefus, come quickly.* Let this be your Language, Sirs, when we are this Day to part one from another We know not what may be before another Seafon of Communions come, but whatever be, my Friends, I tell you good News this Day, *Zion's* King lives, *Zion's* King reigns, the Government is laid upon his Shoulders, and furely the Children of *Zion* have good Reafon to be glad and rejoice in their King What ever dark Things may be in the Womb of Providence, it is good our King lives; our King is and will be exalted, our King will manage all for the real Good of his Subjects Let the Children of *Zion* rejoice in their King, let them glory in their King, let them commit all their Concerns to their King. Let us look

to

to him to give us a parting Blessing with his Word this Day, that ye who know this King may go a-way more confirmed and established, before shaking Winds blow : Indeed shaking Winds are already blowing, but they may blow higher and higher, till a Hurricane of the Lord's Wrath come to a-venge his Quarrel with the Isles of the Sea.   But I proceed.

In the first four or five Verses of this Chapter, which is a Part of the Vision which the Apostle *John*, the Penman of this Book, saw, the Lamb's Retinue and Train are described by several Cha-racters, and, among other distinguishing Charac-ters of them, the Spirit of God takes Notice, that they are such as follow the Lamb whithersoever he goeth . *These are they which follow the Lamb*, &c. I have spoken twice on these Words already upon this Occasion.   After opening up the Words, the Doctrine I offered from them was,

> *That all that are with the Lamb, or are on the Lamb's*
> *Side, they follow the Lamb whithersoever he*
> *goeth.*

These are they which follow the Lamb whithersoever he goeth.   The Method I proposed for discoursing from this Doctrine, was, in the *first* Place, to speak a little concerning the worthy Lamb, the Leader of this Company.

2*dly.* To mention some of the Characters given to the Followers of the Lamb, his Retinue and Train.

3*dly.* To shew what is imported in following the Lamb

4*thly* To shew how, or by what Means, the Lamb's Retinue and Train do follow him.

5*thly.* To shew wherein they do follow the Lamb.

E

6*thly.*

6thly. Give the Reasons of the Doctrine, or shew why all those who are with the Lamb, do follow the Lamb whithersoever he goeth.

And, *lastly*, make Application.

I have already spoken somewhat, 1*st*, concerning the worthy Lamb, and, 2*dly* somewhat of those who follow him, his Retinue and Train. I shall proceed now to the *third* general Head in the Method, which was, to shew what is imported or implied in following the Lamb I shall only offer a few Particulars briefly on this Head.

In the *first* Place, then, to follow the Lamb does import the Knowledge of the Lamb, some Uptaking of and Acquaintance with the Lamb. What we have in the 4th Chapter of *Matthew*, and 20th Verse, is plain to this Purpose. When our Lord made himself known to *Andrew* and *Peter*, then, it is said, they forsook their Nets and followed him. It is just a saving Discovery of the Lamb that draws the Soul after him. They that follow the Lamb, they have got some positive Acquaintance with the Lamb, and this Acquaintance is given to them, *first*, in their effectual Calling, when they are called out of Darkness to the Lord's marvellous Light. When God, who commanded Light to shine out of Darkness, shines into their Hearts, giving the Light of the Knowledge of the Glory of God, in the Face of *Jesus Christ*, then the Face of lowering, cast over all People, is taken off them We say, just when the Lord manifests himself in a saving Manner, then it is they are drawn forth towards the Lamb, then it is they are made to follow the Lamb , then it is they are made to say, *Where thou goest I will go, where thou lodgest I will lodge ; thy People shall be my People, and thy God my God*, as *Ruth* said to *Naomi*. What think you, Sirs, does first effectually draw a

Sinner

Sinner to Chrift? Why, it is juft a faving Difplay of the Glory of Chrift conveying the faving Knowledge of Chrift into the Heart of the Sinner. But then,

In the 2d Place, following the Lamb, it does import and imply a Principle of fpiritual Life. A dead Sinner cannot follow Chrift. It is very true, all the Followers of the Lamb are by Nature dead in Trefpaffes and Sins, as well as others. But the Lamb, he fends forth his quickning Spirit into their Hearts, and fo, in effectual Calling, they are made to hear his quickning Voice. As in the 10th Chapter of *Ezekiel* and 6th Verfe, *I faid unto thee, when thou waft in thy Blood, Live : Yea, I faid unto thee when thou waft in thy Blood, Live* TheLamb makes them hear his Voice, which is a quickning Voice, a Life-giving Voice, and fo, upon hearing the Lamb's Voice, they are immediately led out to follow the Lamb. So, I fay, to follow the Lamb, does imply that there is a Principle of fpiritual Life implanted in them. Again,

In the *third* Place, following the Lamb does import or include in it, the voluntary Subjection of Faith unto the worthy Lamb. Indeed, in that Day when the Lord Jefus Chrift fhines into the Heart of a Sinner, in that Day when he fays unto a dead Sinner, *Live*, then there is the voluntary Subjection of Faith unto him. In the Day of Power, the Day wherein the Obftinacy and Stiffnefs of the Heart is overcome, in that very fame Day the willing People comes unto him and follows him, according to that Word of Promife in the 110th *Pfalm*, and 3d Verfe, *Thy People fhall be willing in the Day of thy Power*. The Day of Power is a Day wherein there is a voluntary Subjection unto the Lamb, to follow the Lamb. We find Unbelief expreft by not

ſubmitting

submitting to the Righteousnesss of God, *Rom.* x. 3.
What is Unbelief? Why, it is just the very opposite
of this voluntary Consent and Subjection of Faith
unto the worthy Lamb It is just the proud Heart re
fusing to stoop to the Righteousness of God, unto the
Righteousness which is by Faith, unto God's Way
of Salvation by rich and free Grace. And, upon the
other Hand, if you ask, What is Faith? Why,
it is just the Heart submitting to the Righteousness
of God, the voluntary Subjection of the Soul unto
the Lord Jesus Christ the worthy Lamb.   In this
Day of his Power, the natural Pride and Obstinacy
of the Heart is broken and brought down, the proud
Heart is brought down, is humbled, and they will
just bow to the Lord Jesus Christ, stoop to the
Righteousness of God which is by Faith in Christ
Jesus, stoop to the Way and Method of Salvation
by Christ Jesus. Faith is just a Sinner's Renoun
cing all Hope of Salvation from the Hills and Mul
titudes of Mountains, and a cheerful submitting un
to Salvation by the free Grace of God through
Christ Jesus It is just a Sinner's subscribing himself
a Debtor unto rich and free Grace, to the Sovereign
Grace of God venting in Christ Jesus the worthy
Lamb And so, we say, in following the Lamb
there is included the voluntary Subjection of Faith
unto him , and in this voluntary Subjection, besides
what we have said, there is a Giving the Lamb his
proper Names and Characters.   The Soul is made
to call him, *Lord,* and this none can do but by the
Spirit of the Lord Christ   And as he gets his pro
per Names, so the Soul, thus subjected to him, it
stoopeth to his Authority and Government It says,
upon the Matter, let him rule over me, let him reign
and rule in and over me, by his Word, by his Grace
and Spirit . Let him sway his Sceptre over me;
let

let all the Powers and Faculties of my Soul be obedient and pay Homage unto him, let his Throne be set up in my Heart, let him alone be enthroned there. But, not to insist,

In the 4*th* Place, following the Lamb, it imports or includes a close Conjunction with the Lamb. All the Followers of the Lamb, so to speak, they are closely conjoined with the Lamb. There is such a close Conjunction between him and them, that they are one Spirit with him. O wonderful is that Oneness that is between the Lamb and all his Followers. They have just one Spirit with the worthy Lamb, that Spirit that rests upon him, that is given unto him without Measure, above all Measure, even that same Spirit takes up his Residence in the Hearts of all the Followers of the Lamb. They are an Habitation of God through the Spirit, they are Temples of the Holy-Ghost, in which he dwells. He takes up his Residence in them, and so, if any Man have not the Spirit of Christ, he is none of his. If any Man have not the Spirit of the Lamb, he is not among the Followers of the Lamb. There is a close Conjunction between the Lamb and all the Followers of the Lamb. The Lamb and his Followers, they have, so to speak, one common Cause, the Cause of the Lamb is the Cause of all his Followers. No sooner does the Sinner take his Standard on the Lamb's Side, but immediately the Lamb's Cause is his Cause. They have one common Cause, and hence, whatever affects the Lamb does likeways, so to speak, affect them. The Dishonours done to the Lamb affect the Followers of the Lamb. The Indignities done to the Lamb affect the Followers of the Lamb. The great Indignities done to the Lamb, they take as done to them, as a great Affront and Indignity done to
them,

them, yea, as the greateſt Hurt that can be done to them. The Lamb and his Followers have ſuch a cloſe Conjunction together, that that which affects him the Head, affects them as his Members, yea, what affects them, does like ways affect him, for, ſaith he, *He that toucheth you, toucheth the Apple of mine Eye* They have juſt common Friends and common Foes. *Pſalm* cxxxiv. 21, 22. *Do not I hate them, O Lord,* (ſaith the Pſal miſt) *that hate thee? And am not I grieved with thoſe that riſe up againſt thee? I hate them with perfect Hatred: I count them mine Enemies.*

But, again, in the *5th* Place, to follow the Lamb, it imports a cloſe Correſpondence with the Lamb All that are with Lamb, and follow the Lamb, they have a cloſe Correſpondence and In timacy with him. The Lamb, ſo to ſpeak, com municates and imparts all his Secrets to them. Ye have a remarkable Word to this Purpoſe in the 15th Chapter of *John*, and 15th Verſe, *Henceforth* (ſaith Chriſt) *I call you no more Servants, for the Servant knoweth not what his Lord doth; but I have called you Friends, for all Things that I have heard of my Father, I have made known unto you.* The Lamb, ſo to ſpeak, imparts to his Followers all the Secrets which his Father has imparted unto him. And what are theſe Secrets, think you, which he imparts to his Followers? Why, he imparts the great Secrets of the Covenant of Grace to them The Secret of the Lord is with them that fear him, and he will ſhew them his Covenant, *Pſalm* xxv. 14 What are the great Secrets he imparts unto them? Why, his Name it is ſecret, and he imparts his Name unto them He juſt imparts himſelf unto them, the Glory of his Perſon unto them. But as, in this cloſe Correſpondence, the Lamb imparts

his

his Secrets to his Followers, fo his Followers, fo
to fpeak, they juft impart their Secrets unto him.
They can freely impart all their Grievances unto
him. They can tell him what they cannot communicate to any Body elfe : They can tell him
what they cannot tell to their neareft Relation upon
Earth. There is a wonderful holy Familiarity between them and the Lamb He juft tells them plainly of the Father, and of himfelf, and even of themfelves He tells them all Things ever they did,
and they tell him all their Heart

I fhall only add, in the *fixth* and *laft* Place, to
follow the Lamb, it imports or implies, that the
Lamb ftands in a manifold Relation to his Followers He ftands in the Relation of a Friend unto
them, *hence he calls them no more Servants, but
Friends*. He ftands in Relation of a Brother unto
them, *wherefore he is not afhamed to call them
Brethren* He ftands in Relation of a Father unto
them. *I will be a Father unto you, and ye fhall be my
Sons and Daughters, faith the Lord Almighty.* At
the laft Day he will prefent them unto the Father,
faying, *Behold, here am I, and the Children whom
thou haft given me* The Lamb's Followers, they
are his fpiritual Seed Again, he ftands in the Relation of an Husband unto them, *Thy Maker is thine
Husband,* &c But when they are defigned, *Thefe
are they which follow the Lamb,* the Expreffion points
at fome particular Relation befides thefe Generals
we have mentioned What then is the particular
Relation pointed at, when they are faid to follow
the Lamb? Why, it points out, or imports, that
he ftands in the Relation and Character of a Leader unto them *Behold, I have given him for a Leader unto the People* He is the great Leader given by
Jehovah the Father unto the People, and all that are

On

on the Lamb's Side, they follow the Lamb as their Leader. They just follow the Lamb, as their Leader, through all the difficult and different Steps of their Wilderness Journey, and they resign themselves wholly to the leading of the Lamb *Thou wilt guide me with thy Counsel while here, and afterwards receive me to Glory.* But not only does this Expression point at the particular Relation of a Leader, but it says also, that the Lamb stands in the particular Relation of a Commander unto his Followers, his Retinue and Train *Jehovah* has not only given him for a Leader, but also for a Commander unto his People All the Armies in Heaven and Earth, who know the Lamb, they follow him as their great Commander All the Armies in Heaven, his Retinue and Train, they follow him in their Robes, which are of fine Linen, clean and white. They follow his Commands and Orders, because he is the blest and only Potentate, the King of Kings, and Lord of Lords, the Prince of the Kings of the Earth And the Truth is, he stands in this Relation to them, of being their King He who is the Captain-General of the Lord's Host, the Captain-General of the Armies in Heaven and Earth, the Captain-General of all the redeemed Company about the Throne, he is their King and rightful Lord, and so it is most fit he should go at their Head, and they at his Back, ready to obey all his Commandments who is their Leader and Commander. But I shall not insist farther upon this Head.

I shall now proceed to the *fourth* general Head in the Method, which was, to shew how and by what Means the Lamb's Retinue and Train do follow him. How then does this happy Company follow the Lamb? I answer, in the *first* Place, they

follow

follow him by frequent Meditations upon him, You have a Word to this Purpose in the 63d *Pſalm*, and 6th Verſe, *When I remember thee upon my Bed, and meditate upon thee in the Night-Watches, my Soul followeth hard after thee* This Company, they love to meditate upon the Lamb, they love to think upon the Lamb, they love to think upon his Undertaking, they love to think upon what he hath done, they love to think upon what he is doing, they love to think upon what he hath promiſed to do, and they love to think upon what he will do, and do for them, yea, they love to think upon the happy Time, when they ſhall be admitted into the immediate Preſence of the Lamb : And thus they follow the Lamb, by frequent Meditations upon the Lamb.

In the 2*d* Place, How do they follow the Lamb ? They do it by their fervent Breathings and Deſires after him, after Acceſs to him, after the Enjoyment of him , they long for Acceſs into his Preſence. O ſay, they *draw me, we will run after thee*, Song i. 4. They follow him by earneſt Longings to be in his Company, to have the Enjoyment of his Preſence for ever Ye find his Followers expreſſing themſelves after this Manner, *Pſalm* ci. 2. *O when wilt thou come unto me ?* And with *Job, O that I knew where I might find him, that I might come even to his Seat ?* What is it that brings them to Ordinances and Inſtitutions of his Appointment? Why, it is juſt this fervent Breathing for him, that there they may find him, draw near unto him, and worſhip him , behold his Beauty, and enquire in his Temple . As in that 27th *Pſalm* and 4th Verſe, *One Thing* (ſays the Pſalmiſt) *have I deſired of the Lord, that will I ſeek after, that I may dwell in the Houſe of the Lord all the Days of my Life, that I may behold the Beauty of the Lord, and to enquire in his*

F

Temple.

Temple. ` Why, Sirs, What is the Reafon the Lamb's Followers love fo well to come to Ordi nances, to Communions ? The Reafon is, they juft want another View of the Glory of the Lamb there, they expect to fee the Glory of the Lamb there, and fo they follow him in the Word, they follow him in the Sacrament, they follow him in fe cret Duties ; in one Word, they follow him in all the Duties of his own Appointment, juft that there they may have Communion with him, that there may have they a Correfpondence with him, that there they may fee his Glory, that there they may hear from him, and that he may fpeak unto them But then, again, in the

3*d* Place, the Lamb's Followers, they follow him by an entire Subjection and Obedience unto him. All that are the true and genuine Followers of the Lamb, they give (fo to exprefs it) an implicite O bedience unto him , but then it is a judicious Obe dience, for it flows from Knowledge of the Lamb. *They follow him whitherfoever he goeth.* When he fays, *Go,* they go , and *Come,* they come They credit his Word, when they cannot tell what is wrapt up in the Word . They credit his Word of Promife, and go forth at his Call, even when they cannot fee his Ways They give an impli cite Obedience unto the Lamb, when, in the mean Time, they know not what their Obedience may coft them You have a memorable Inftance of this in the 11th Chapter to the *Hebrews,* and 8th Verfe, where it is faid concerning *Abraham, That by Faith* ` Abraham, *when he was called to go out into a Place which he fhould after receive for an Inheritance, obeyed, and he went out, not knowing whither he went.* He juft gave implicite Obedience to the Call and Com- mand of God, and he went out, not knowing
whither

whither he went./ So all the true Followers of the Lamb, they so far give implicite Obedience to the Commands of the Lamb, that, even when they cannot see what is in the Womb of Providence, they hearken to his Word of Command, tho' it be never so hard-like or difficult, yea, not only so, but they can credit the Word of God, in Obebience to the Lamb, even when the Providence of God seems quite to contradict the Promise of God, just when Providence seems to fly in the Face of the Promise This likewise is evident in the Case of *Abraham*, in the 4th Chapter of the Epistle to the *Romans*, from the 18th Verse and downward, *Who against Hope believed in Hope, that he might become the Father of many Nations; according to that which was spoken, So shall thy Seed be. And, being not weak in Faith, he considered not his own Body now dead, when he was about an Hundred Years old, neither yet the Deadness of* Sarah's *Womb He staggered not at the Promise of God, through Unbelief, but was strong in the Faith, giving Glory to God, being fully perswaded, that what he had promised he was able also to perform* Thus the Followers of the Lamb, they credit God's naked Word of Promise, even when the Course of his Providence seems directly to contradict the Promise, yea, whatever Difficulties may seem, in their View of Matters, to be in the Way of the Accomplishment of the Promise, they follow the Lamb, by giving Obedience to every one of his Commandments, and that without Exeption to any one of them · They see him to be the only Lawgiver, and so they follow him as their only Lawgiver, saying, *The Lord is our Judge, the Lord is our Lawgiver, the Lord is our King, he will save us.* And so, if the Commands of Men happen to interfere with the Command and Authority of the Lamb,

then

then the Authority of the Lamb will indeed caſt the Balance with all the Followers of the Lamb O for ſome Drops of the Rain of Heaven from him that has the ſeven Spirits of God in his Hand, to make all this Company to liſten to the Command, and Authority of the worthy Lamb, and to follow the Lamb, by giving intire Subjection and Obedience unto him. Again, in the

4th Place, they follow the Lamb by an open Confeſſion of him. Ye ſee it is ſaid of the Followers of the Lamb, in the Beginning of this Chapter, that *they have his Name and his Father's Name written upon their Foreheads.* That imports that they are not aſhamed to make an open Confeſſion and Profeſſion of the Lamb, they are not in the leaſt aſhamed openly to confeſs the worthy Lamb All the Followers of the Lamb, they are Confeſſors of the Lamb, they ought to be ſo, it is a Duty plainly laid down in the Word, *Rom.* x. 3, 10. *If thou ſhalt confeſs with thy Mouth the Lord Jeſus, and ſhalt believe in thine Heart that God has raiſed him from the Dead, thou ſhalt be ſaved : For with the Heart Man believeth unto Righteouſneſs, and with the Mouth Confeſſion is made unto Salvation* All the Followers of the Lamb ought to be Confeſſors of the Lamb before a ſinful and perverſe Generation They ought to confeſs themſelves to be on the Lamb's Side, whatever it may coſt them, and wherever the Lamb ſets up his Standard, there ought they to fix their Station, and deſerve the Character given them, *Iſa* xliii 10. *Ye are my Witneſſes, ſaith the Lord* How ought the Followers of the Lamb to witneſs for him ? Why, every one of them, in their ſeveral Spheres and Stations, ought to witneſs for him as he is pleaſed to give an Opportunity, and ſo, if, in a declining Day, a Teſtimony be lifted up for

the

he Honour and Truth of the Lamb, all his Fol-
lowers ought to espouse that Testimony. And,
Sirs, if the Testimony lifted up at this Day be a
faithful Testimony for the declarative Glory of the
Lamb, for the Truths of the Lamb, (as I make no
Doubt but it is so) then all the Followers of the
Lamb in *Scotland*, they ought to espouse that Testimony, to own that Testimony, whatever it may
cost them. What ever Difficulties may be in the
Way, his Followers must be Confessors, and good
Reason it should be so, good Reason they have to
confess the Lamb, the worthy Lamb, if it is con-
sidered he made a good Confession for them before
Pontius Pilate. No Opposition did hinder his
Confession of them, and so, in like manner, in following the Lamb, he is to be confessed in the Face
of Opposition, let the Opposition be never so great.

In the 5th Place, as the Followers of the Lamb
do follow him by an open Confession of him, so
they ought to follow the Lamb by a constant Cleaving to all the Lamb's Truths, to all his Ordinances
and Institutions The Lamb upon the Mount *Zion*,
he hath given Ordinances to Mount *Zion*, positive
Laws and Institutions to Mount *Zion* The Institutions that the Lamb has given to Mount *Zion*,
they respect the Doctrine of his House, the religious
Worship of his House, the Discipline of his House,
and the Government of his House, and what any
Way concerns any of these, the Followers of the
Lamb they ought all of them to cleave unto them,
they ought to adhere unto them, and in so doing
they own the Lamb to be the Prince of the Kings
of the Earth, the King of Kings and Lord of Lords,
him who only has Right to prescribe Laws and
Rules to Mount *Zion*, our Lord Jesus Christ, the
great King of *Zion*, the King and Head of the
Church,

Church, has not left the New Testament Church without her divine Institutions and Appointments, no more than the Old He has laid down the Doctrine, Worship, Discipline and Government of his Church in his Word, and all the Followers of the Lamb, they ought to follow him by a constant Cleaving unto all the Lamb's Institutions, and particularly, at this Day, the Followers of the Lamb ought to follow him by a faithful Adherence unto the Presbyterial Form of Church-Government, laid down in the Word of God. I shall not enlarge at present upon this Subject, only, with Reference to the Glory of the Lamb's Followers, with Respect unto Presbyterial Church-Government, there are two Things I would say

1st. As our Lord Jesus Christ, the King and only Head of the Church, has committed the Keys of Government unto Office-Bearers, to act in Parity together, without a lordly Prelacy, whereby one ruleth over another, so it is the unquestionable Duty of all the Lamb's Followers, to witness against Prelatists, who maintain the contrary, in as far the Lord is pleased to open up this Truth to every one in their different Stations. I know those who are Favourers of the prelatick Scheme, will tell you, that Opinion of theirs is countenanced in the Word of God, particularly from the Practice of the Apostles, whom they say acted as prelatical Bishops, in a Degree superior to ordinary Pastors. We grant that the Apostles had an extraordinary Mission from Christ, and had no Relation to any particular Place or Charge, but had laid upon them the Care of all the Churches, in that infant State of the Church But then it is to be considered, that that extraordinary Mission was peculiar to the Apostles themselves, and ceased with them: So that no Order of

Church-

Church-Officers above Gospel-Ministers, to whom is committed the Power of Ordination and Government, to act and rule in Parity, as well as Warrant to dispense Word and Sacrament, is acknowledged in the Word of God. Again,

2dly. The Followers of the Lamb, in cleaving to the Government of the Lamb's House, they are to bear Witness with him, against Independents, and all Sectarians, who maintain that our Lord Christ hath committed the Keys of Government unto the Community of the Faithful, and so set up for a popular Government, which is to introduce a plain Confusion. In this Case it is incumbent on all the Lamb's Followers to witness with him, that the Keys of Government are committed to Office-Bearers, to such as are cloathed with official Power and Authority from the King and Head of the Church This Truth we see clearly founded upon the Word of God, as in the 16th of *Matthew* and 16th Verse. There our Lord gives the Keys to *Peter*, in name of the whole Church-Officers, without any Word of the Community of the Faithful. *I will give unto thee the Keys of the Kingdom of Heaven, and whatsoever thou shalt bind on Earth, shall be bound in Heaven; and whatsoever thou shalt loose on Earth shall be loosed in Heaven.* We see also the Spirit of God plainly makes a Difference, in Scripture, between Rulers and Ruled: *They then that have the Rule over you,* &c. It is most reasonable it should be so, for, if all were Rulers, who should be ruled? Thus we see, then, that the Keys of Government are committed to Ministers, to the Office-Bearers of the Lamb's House, who are to manage them, not in a lordly Way and Manner, lording it over the Consciences of Men, but in a ministerial Way and Manner, so as they may thereby edify the Body of Christ, and may contend against

gainſt every Error ſubverſive of the Truths of Chriſt, and ſo as that every Truth of Chriſt may be vindi cated and witneſſed for, and all the Followers of the Lamb are, in their ſeveral Stations, to ſtrength en the Hands of Office Bearers in a Way of vindica ting the Diſcipline and Government of the Lamb's, Houſe. Thus, we ſay, the Followers of the Lamb are to follow him by a conſtant Cleaving to the Diſcipline and Government of the Lamb's Houſe, and as to the Doctrine and Worſhip, and all the Ordinances of his Houſe, they ought to cleave to them, to adhere to them They are to cleave to all the Doctrines of his Word, to all the Truths that are contained in the Lamb's Word, and, in a ſpecial Manner, the Followers of the Lamb, they follow him by cleaving to and witneſſing for what the Spirit of God calls the preſent Truth. There is a Word to this Purpoſe in the 2d Epiſtle of *Peter*, 1ſt Chapter and 12th Verſe, where the Spirit of God ſaith, *Be eſtabliſhed in the preſent Truth*. Now, what is that Truth called the preſent Truth ? Why, Sirs, that Truth that becomes a controverted Truth, that is the preſent Truth, and that is the Truth, in a ſpecial Manner, which the Followers of the Lamb are called to cleave unto, to witneſs for and bear Teſtimony unto Particularly, if the Truth con cerning the Perſon of the Lamb, his being very God and very Man in one Perſon, be attacked, then a Teſtimony is to be given for that Truth by the Lamb's Followers· If the ſupreme Deity of the Lamb be attacked, then a Teſtimony ought to be given for it · If the declarative Glory of God, as the great and ultimate End of all the Followers of the Lamb, be attacked, then a Teſtimony ought to be given for it If any Branch of the Government of Chriſt's Houſe be attacked, then a Teſtimony is

to be given for it: If the Headſhip of the Lamb, his
Sovereignty and Dominion over *Zion* the Hill of his
Holineſs, be attacked, (as it was by the late Act of
Parliament anent Captain *John Porteous*) then a Te-
ſtimony ought to be given for it: If the ſpiritual Privileges and Liberties of the Subjects of the Lamb's
Kingdom are attacked, (as they are manifeſtly at this
Day) then a Teſtimony ought to be given for them:
If the miniſterial Liberty, and Freedom of the Miniſters of Chriſt, either with reſpect to the Doctrine
or Diſcipline of the Houſe of the God of Heaven,
be attacked, then a Teſtimony is to be given for it:
And ſo, by the By, we may ſee the Reaſonableneſs
and Neceſſity of the preſent Teſtimony on the Field,
for theſe Truths, which have been ſo glaringly attacked by the preſent Judicatures of this national
Church. Theſe are, no doubt, ſome good Men and
Miniſters, who have got their Miſſion from Chriſt,
who condemn our preſent Seceſſion from the Judicatures of his Church, as a Thing quite needleſs:
But, when the Truths and Inſtitutions of the Lamb
are ſo manifeſtly attacked as they have been, Is it not
highly reaſonable and neceſſary for all the Followers of the Lamb, to ſide themſelves, and as openly
to give a Teſtimony to theſe Truths and Inſtitutions, as Adverſaries have been open in impugning
the ſame? I ſhall only ſay, if the Banner of a Teſtimony lifted up be againſt the Lamb, I have not
ſeen that, but if it be for the Lamb, and his Truth
and Cauſe, as I doubt not to affirm, then let all the
Friends of the Lamb, who are for cleaving to the
preſent Judicatures, notwithſtanding of all the Height
of Defection and Apoſtaſy from God which they
are arrived at, ſee to their Conduct in this Matter.
As the judicial Teſtimony lifted up, is a free and
faithful Teſtimony for the born-down Cauſe of the

G   worthy

worthy Lamb, and againſt the open Attacks and Diſhonours done to him, then I have no doubt to aſſemble you to that Banner, and where the Lamb lifts up his Standard, all his Followers ought to gather together. Thus, we ſay, the Followers of the Lamb, they follow him by a conſtant Cleaving to all the Lamb's Truths, to all his Ordinances and Inſtitutions, to the Doctrine, Worſhip, Diſcipline, and Government of the Lamb's Houſe.

Again, in the *6th* Place, How do they follow him? They follow him by obſerving the Lamb's Footſteps and Paths, which he takes in the Diſpenſations of his Providence. Sirs, the Providence of God is frequently a Commentary upon the Word of God. The Word of God is the ſtreight Rule and Line by which the Work of Providence is carried on, and will be carried on until the Work of Providence be finiſhed. We ought, then, to obſerve the Operation of his Hand, in following the Lamb. The 107th *Pſalm* is a Summary of many ſpecial Providences, and the Concluſion of it is an encouraging Promiſe to all ſuch as follow the Lamb, by a ſteddy Obſervation of the Lamb's Footſteps and Paths in the Diſpenſation of divine Providence *Whoſo is wiſe, and will obſerve theſe Things, even they ſhall underſtand the loving Kindneſs of the Lord* Sirs, the Lamb is ſpeaking loudly by his Providences at this Day, tho' we are deaf and do not hear. He hath not been ſilent in *Scotland* theſe Years by paſt. as to the Voice of his Providence, yet, alas! this Voice ſeems to be little regarded It is only the ſpiritually wiſe Man that will obſerve theſe Things We need ſpiritual Wiſdom to obſerve the Lamb's Tract and Path in the Diſpenſations of Providence. Many of you think little of the Lamb's Tract and Path with reſpect to the preſent

ent Teſtimony of the Day : But I make no
Doubt to ſay, the Tract and Path of the Lamb
is remarkable, in thruſting out ſome from the
Judicatures of this national Church, and in putting
this Teſtimony in their Hands. We know not
what the Tract and Path of the Lamb is, in putting
it in our Hands. O to be helped to follow the Tract
and Path of the Lamb in this Diſpenſation of his
Providence ! O to be helped to follow his providential Footſteps, according to the Line of his Word ?
I ſhall not enlarge with reſpect to this particular
Providence, in putting a Teſtimony in our Hands at
this Day, I ſhall only ſay, perhaps, in another
Age and Generation, when the Viſion will ſpeak
and be ſeen clearly, then the Lamb's Tract and
Path will, as to this Particular, be more remarkably
ſeen

As the Followers of the Lamb do follow him by
obſerving the Lamb's Footſteps, his Tract and Path,
with reſpect to the Church, ſo they follow the Lamb's
Tract and Path with reſpect to themſelves. You who
are Believers, the true Followers of the Lamb, you
have Reaſon in every Station and Period of your Life,
to remark the Providence of God towards you, to
obſerve his Tract and Path toward you. It was a
juſt Obſerve of one who was a great Obſerver of
Providence, That thoſe that remark Providence,
remarkable Things in Providence will follow them
in Agreeableneſs to the Word Beware of a
ſuperſtitious Regard to any of the Works of God ;
but put the Works and Word of God together, and
obſerve his Providences, ſo as to give Praiſe to the
God of Providence

But then, again, in the 7th and laſt Place, upon
this Head, How do the Followers of the Lamb follow him ? They follow him by imitating and
                                        copying

copying after that Pattern and Example which the worthy Lamb casts before them in his Word, as we see he exhorts in the 11th Chapter of the Gospel according to *Matthew*, the 29th Verse, *Take my Yoke, upon you, and learn of me, for I am meek and lowly in Heart, and ye shall find Rest unto your Souls.* We are frequently called to this Duty, of making Christ the Lamb our Pattern, and copying after him, as in that 5th Chapter of the Epistle to the *Ephesians*, and 1st Verse, *Be ye, therefore, Followers of God, as dear Children* Verse 2. *And walk in Love, as Christ also hath loved us,* &c. And again, *Philip.* ii. 5. *Let this Mind be in you, which was also in Christ Jesus.*

So much for the 4th general Head proposed. I proceed now

To the 5th Thing in the Method, which was, to shew where it is they follow the Lamb It is expressed, in our Text, by a *Following the Lamb whithersoever he goeth*, and truly, Sirs, they follow him through good Report and bad Report, they follow the Lamb in all Cases whatsoever, they follow the Lamb, not only in a sunny Day, but they follow the Lamb in a stormy Day, they follow the Lamb, not only in a Day of Prosperity, but they follow the Lamb in a Day of Adversity But, more particularly, there are three Places I shall touch at, where the Followers of the Lamb do follow him. 1st. When he makes Darkness his secret Place; 2dly. When he goes without the Camp, and, 3dly When he goes to Mount *Calvary* to a suffering Lot.

First, I say, the Followers of the Lamb, they follow him when he makes Darkness his secret Place, when his Pavilion round about him is dark Waters and thick Clouds of the Skies, as in the 18th *Psalm* and 11th Verse, when he wraps up himself

in

in a Cloud, covers himself with a Cloud, that their. Prayers should not pass through, as in the 3d of the *Lamentations*, 44th Verse. Well, if you ask, How do the Followers of the Lamb follow him there, when he sees meet to wrap up himself in a Cloud, and makes Darkness his secret Place? I answer, in the

1*st* Place, They follow him, in such a Case, by lamenting after him When he goes out of Sight, when he covers himself with a Cloud, then they lament after him. Thus, you see, when the Ark of God abode twenty Years in *Kirjath-jearim*, all the House of *Israel* lamented after the Lord, 1 Sam. vii 2. Then, when the Lord was provoked by *Israel*'s Sin, to keep the Ark in a private and obscure Place, and that near the *Philistines*, where many of the *Israelites* neither durst nor could come to it, as when it was in *Shiloh*, What then was the Exercise of the true *Israelites*? Why, they lamented after the Lord Indeed the Majesty of the Lord is provoked, and sees meet to cover himself with a Cloud from all the reformed Churches at this Day No Wonder it be so, for our Iniquities have procured it But what should we be doing? Why, it becomes us, in this Case, to lament after the Lord, to lament over the Grounds of the Quarrel and Controversy. Again, in the

2*d* Place, How do the Followers of the Lamb follow him, when he wraps up himself in a Cloud, and makes Darkness his secret Place? Why, then, and in such a Case, not only do they follow him there, by lamenting after him, but also by waiting for him, waiting upon him We see this expressed by the Prophet *Isaiah* in a like Case, *Isa.* viii. 17 In some preceeding Verses the Lord threatens, that many of Israel and Judah *shall stumble, and fall, and be broken, and be snared, and taken.* Why, then

the

the Proph in Name of the Church, faith, *I will wait upon the Lord, that hideth his Face from the House of* Jacob; *and I will look for him.* Tho' he be a hiding God, yet his true Followers will wait upon him, and look for him   O then, Sirs, tho' at this Day he is a hiding God, wait upon him in the Duty of secret Prayer, wait upon him in the Ordinances of his Inftitution, wait upon him in every Duty   Again, in the

3*d* Place, They follow the Lamb when he wraps up himfelf in a Cloud, and makes Darknefs his fecret Place, by earneft Wreftlings and Expoftulations with him, for his returning and manifefting himfelf   They cry unto him with fuch a Cry as this, *Return, return, for thy Servants Sake, the Tribes of thine Inheritance.* They expoftulate with him by fuch a Cry as this, *O the Hope of* Ifrael, *the Saviour thereof in Time of Trouble, Why fhouldeft thou be as a Stranger in the Land, and as a wayfaring Man that turneth afide to tarry for a Night?* Thus Faith it fees, that tho' he be making Darknefs his fecret Place, yet he gives a Vifit now and then to his People, but they were very fhort, it was but like the Vifit of a Stranger, that ftays but for a Night, and the Followers of the Lamb they want him to abide with them.   It is Ground of Praife, that altho' the Lamb be making Dark nefs his fecret Place at this Day, yet I hope he gives his People now and then a Vifit : But O what a general Reftraint is there of the holy Spirit at this Day? Well, what fhall the Followers of the Lamb do in fuch a Cafe? Why, the beft Way is, juft to fall in with the Exhortation the Spirit of God gives, Ifa lxii. 7 *Give him no Reft till he eftablifh, and till he make* Jerufalem *a Praife in the whole Earth.* Again, in the

4th Place, How do the Followers of the Lamb follow him, when he wraps up himself in a Cloud, and makes Darkness his secret Place ? They follow him, in such a Case, just by trusting him, that he will manifest himself. This was *Job's* Exercise, when the Lamb's Way was very dark to him. *Tho' he slay me, yet will I trust in him.* And we see such as are walking in Darkness, through the Lamb's wraping himself up in a Cloud, are exhorted to this Exercise, *Isa.* l. 10. *Who is among you that feareth the Lord, that obeyeth the Voice of his Servant, that walketh in Darkness, and hath no Light ? Let him trust in the Name of the Lord, and stay upon his God* Take the Exhortation then, and, when he makes Darkness his secret Place, follow him in the Trust and Expectation of Faith that he will return, that he yet will manifest himself, that he will come back , *For the Expectation of the Poor shall not always be forgotten ; it shall not perish for ever.*

2dly. Not only do the Followers of the Lamb, follow him when he wraps up himself in a Cloud, when he makes Darkness his secret Place, but they follow him when he goes without the Camp. If the Lamb sees meet to go without the Camp, there they follow him. Ye have a Word to this Purpose in the 13th Chapter of the Epistle to the *Hebrews,* 12th and 13th Verses, *Wherefore* Jesus *also, that he might sanctify the People with his Blood, suffered without the Gate* What then is the Practice of his Followers in such a Case as this ? We have it in the 13th Verse, *Let us go forth, therefore, unto him without the Camp, bearing his Reproach.* What is that, *without the Camp ?* Without the *Jewish* Church, and all the Privileges that they enjoyed, from *Judaism,* and all its Parts abolished,

and

and all erroneous Doctrines, however numerous and agreeable to Fancy. This lets us see our Duty, when the Lord Christ, the worthy Lamb, is pleased to lift up the Standard of a Testimony without the Camp, without the present legal established Church. *Let us go forth, therefore, unto him without the Camp, bearing his Reproach* The Words plainly insinuate, that the Reproach of Christ, and going forth unto him without the Camp, go together But, even allowing it be so, let us go forth unto him without the Camp, bearing the Reproach of Christ, the Reproach of the Lamb must be born by the Followers of the Lamb· Let us go forth unto him, bearing Reproach for him, Reproach for the Cause of Christ, Reproach for the Testimony of Christ, Reproach for the Name of Christ · Let us go forth unto him without the Camp, bearing his Reproach. The plain Intendment of the Words is, that we ought to abandon all Church-Privileges, from a Church, tho' legally established, when she is become tyrannical in her Government, and erroneous in her Doctrine, which is the Case with the Church of *Scotland*, as represented by the present Judicatures, as has been elsewhere proven at some Length. And when, in Providence, the Standard of a judicial Testimony is lifted up for Christ, his Cause and Truth, without the Camp of the present Establishment, What should be the Language among all the true Followers of the Lamb, but just this, *Let us go forth, therefore, unto him without the Camp, bearing his Reproach?* But again, in the

3*d* and *last* Place upon this Head, the Followers of the Lamb, they follow him when he goes to Mount *Calvary* to a suffering Lot. Not only was the Lamb a Sufferer on Mount *Calvary* in the

Days

Days of the Flesh, but he is a Sufferer to this very
Day in his Members, and so they follow him in
Way of suffering for him, if he calls them to it.
They who follow the Lamb, through his Grace,
will not decline suffering for him at his Call, they
will venture upon it, and prefer it unto the Pro-
its and Pleasures of the World, at the Call of the
Lamb. You have a remarkable Instance of this in
the Case of *Moses*, in the 11th Chapter of the *Hebrews*, 24th, 25th, and 26th Verses, *By Faith Moses, when he was come to Years, refused to be called
the Son of* Pharaoh*'s Daughter, chusing rather to suffer Affliction with the People of God, than to enjoy the
Pleasures of Sin for a Season, esteeming the Reproach
of Christ greater Riches than the Treasures in* Egypt.
Moses was brought up in the Court of a grand *Pharaoh*, and no doubt was trained up in all the Gran-
deur of that Court, but, so soon as *Moses* grew
up, and understood his Relation to the persecuted
and afflicted People of God, why, then he aban-
dones that Court, tho' then the greatest in the
World And why so? Just because he esteemed
the Reproach of Christ greater Riches than the
Treasures in *Egypt*. I might shew that this has
been the Practice of the Lamb's Followers in all
Ages But I now pass this Head, and come to
the

6th and *last* Thing on the doctrinal Part, which
was to give the Reasons of the Doctrine, or shew
why all those who are with the Lamb, do follow
the Lamb whithersoever he goeth

In the 1st Place, then, Why do all those who
are with the Lamb, follow the Lamb, &c They
follow him, because he is excellent and glorious, his
glorious Excellency is the primary Cause of all that
religious Worship, Homage and Obedience that is

H   due

due to him, and that is afcribed to him by all his
Followers. This his Excellency and Glory is proclaimed by the feraphick Tribe, in the 5th Chapter of the *Revelation*, and there the 12th Verle,
*Worthy is the Lamb that was flain, to receive Power,
and Riches, and Wifdom, and Strength, and Honour,
and Glory, and Bleffing.* Why, is all this afcribed
unto him? Juft becaufe he is worthy to receive it
How is it he is worthy to receive all this? Why,
becaufe he is infinitely excellent and glorious. He
is the Brightnefs of the Father's Glory, and the
exprefs Image of his Perfon, and upholdeth all
Things by the Word of his Power. He is the fupreme God, God over all bleffed for ever. He is
the true God, and eternal Life, and for all this
the Followers of the Lamb count him worthy of
Obedience, that he fhould be followed whitherfoever he goeth. But again, in the

2d Place, They follow the Lamb, and that upon
the Account of what the Lamb has done for
them. Tho' this is not the primary Foundation
of their Worfhipping and honouring him, and pay-
ing this Homage unto him, namely, of following
him, yet it is a fecondary Reafon of it, becaufe he
hath redeemed all the ranfomed Company, they
follow him, they throw down their Crowns at his
Feet, and cry, as *Rev.* v 9. *Thou art worthy* ———
*for thou waft flain, and haft redeemed us to God by thy
Blood, out of every Kindred and Tongue, and People,
and Nation* He has done much for them, done
all for them, and therefore they follow him whitherfoever he goeth. Again, in the

3d and *laft* Place, Why do they follow the
Lamb? They follow the Lamb becaufe of the
new Nature given to them in Regeneration. This
new Nature given them by the Lamb, it leads them

to this Work of following the Lamb, just as every Thing points towards its Centre The new Nature it just breathes naturally after the Lamb. Whatever Remains of Corruption be in the best, yet, with Reference unto the renewed Part, it may be said, that there is a Going out after the glorious, worthy and matchless Lamb Wherever the new Nature is implanted, that Soul goes out after the Lamb, follows the Lamb upon the Wings of Faith and Love, mounts upward after him upon the Wings of Faith and Love, tho' many Times born down and retarded in its Motion with a Weight of Unbelief, a Weight of the Body of Sin and Death · But it is remarkable, as to the Followers of the Lamb, when they are disturbed in their Course of following him, by the Weights of Unbelief and the Body of Sin and Death, then it cries out under the Oppression ; it cries out, *O wretched Man that I am, who shall deliver me from the Body of this Death* , from this Clog and the other Clog, that hinders my Motion in following the Lamb , from the Atheism of my Heart, from the Unbelief of my Heart, from the Carnality of my Heart ! Fain would I mount up Heaven-ward after the Lamb, but am born down with these dead Weights ! Fain would I be near the worthy Lamb ! *O set me as a Seal upon thine Heart, as a Seal upon thine Arm, for Love is strong as Death !* &c.

I shall not farther insist upon the doctrinal Part. I come now to make some Application of the Doctrine , and all the Use I design, is, to address myself to three or four Sorts of Persons, in a Word of Exhortation to them severally , and may the Lord himself carry home the Word spoken to their several Hearts !

In

In the 1*st* Place, then, if it is so, that those who are with the Lamb, do follow the Lamb whithersoever he goeth, let me address you that profess to be on the Lamb's Side, who profess to be the Followers of the worthy Lamb, and in this Class I take in all the Communicants that have been in this Place upon this Occasion, and of such there has been a great Number Now, to such there are two or three Things I would offer to your Consideration.

In the *first* Place, let me exhort you to examine your Profession , ye ought to examine yourselve, after a Communion, as well as before it , examine whether your Heart and Profession do agree together or not. If they do not agree together, your Profession is but a hypocritical Profession , you will remember one of the Characters I took notice of, which is given to the Lamb's Followers in the Context, is, *That in their Mouth was found no Guile*, that is, their Heart and Profession agree together If it be not so with you, ye are but hypocritical Professors ; if your Heart and Profession any Way correspond, then your Heart has been made to bow to the worthy Lamb, to stoop to the worthy Lamb Examine your Profession, whether it be a dead or lively Profession, whether you be dead or alive The most Part of the Members of the Church of *Sardis*, they had a Name to live, and were dead. I am afraid many at this Day have a Name to live, and are dead. They may have some Strictness in their Way, and yet dead, yet want a lively Faith in the Lamb , but as, even in *Sardis*, the Lamb had a few Names which had not defiled their Garments, so at this Day he hath yet a few Names, a few who are alive, try if ye be amongst them.   Again, examine whether ye are in the Faith or not, whether Christ be in you the Hope of Glory, or not,

and

and whether you are in him, or not : If you are not in Chrift, and Chrift in you, it is but a hypocritical Profeffion which you are making, and, if Mercy prevent not, your Profeffion will land in Apoftafy from Chrift and his Caufe, and ye will be a Difhonour and Scandal to that Profeffion you now make.

In the 2d Place, I would exhort you, who profefs to be the Followers of the Lamb, to be rooted in the Lamb, to know the Lamb O be concerned to know the worthy Lamb in a faving Manner ! Study to have faving Acquaintance with him ! This, I told you, is included in following of him. Study to know him, not only by the hearing of the Ear, but with the Seeing with the Eye of Faith, with the Believing of the Heart Ye have all heard by the Hearing of the Ear , the outward Report of Chrift hath brought many to the Profeffion of Chrift that have never feen Chrift, never believed in Chrift, and therefore I would exhort you to feek to fee him, not with the natural Eye, not with the Eye that is called natural Reafon, but with Faith which is the Evidence of Things not feen, and the Subftance of Things hoped for It is faid of *Mofes*, Heb xi. 27. *He endured as feeing him who is invifible.* He got a Sight of an invifible God ; he faw him with the Eye of Faith, and that made *Mofes* endure all Hardfhips And, Sirs, we may tell you, whatever your Profeffion is for the prefent, if you get not a Sight of the Lamb by Faith, ye cannot endure Hardfhips, Trials and Sufferings for the Lamb and his Caufe It is only thofe who have feen with the Eye of Faith can endure. *He endured, as feeing him who is invifible* O examine whether you have feen him in Truth, and in Reality,

lity, or not! O be concerned to get the saving Knowledge of him, whom to know is eternal Life! Again,

In the 3d Place, I would exhort you, who profess to be the Followers of the Lamb, to be well acquainted with his Cause and Truths This is needful at all Times, and especially in such a Day as this, when shaking and withering Winds are blowing, Winds of Infidelity and Error are blowing Winds of Neutrality and Indifferency are blowing O, then, be concerned to be rooted in the Lamb, and well acquainted with Christ and the Truths of Christ, that ye may bring forth Fruits unto God, that ye may have the Communication of spiritual Life from this Root Christ, the worthy Lamb, is the Root, and only Spring, in which all his Followers are ingrafted, they are just all rooted in him, as the Branch in the Vine All their Sap comes from him, so that, if you are not rooted in him, you will be sapless, withered, and barren Professors. Be well established in the Truths of Christ, and particularly in the present Truth. As I have exhorted you on other Occasions of this Nature, so I again exhort you, to read your Bible often, and, next to the Bible, your Confession of Faith and Catechisms, and remember it is not an early Reading I am advising you to, but read with Deliberation and Consideration, and if you would be established in the Truth of what you read, and not soon shaken in your Minds then look for the Spirit of Truth to lead and guide you into all Truth, and to settle you in every Truth of God laid down in his Word

In the 4th and last Place, let me exhort you, who are the professed Followers of the Lamb, to lay your Account with this, that your Profession may be tried You have been long warned of Trials a-
coming.

coming. The Lord has exercised long-suffering Patience toward us, yet we have not returned to him with all our Heart, and it is like we will be tried. There are two Things in the Circumstances of the Day that threaten An Inundation of Popery may be our Trial. *First*, There is the close Conjunction of Popish Powers abroad , it hath been rarely seen but their secular Interests have clashed together, whereas, at this Day, there is a close Conjunction, without Clashing of their secular Interests. *Secondl*, There is an universal Formality, Backsliding and Declining, not only of one particular Church, or of some Churches, but of all the Protestant Churches abroad and at home. Now, these two Things, put together, have an awful Aspect If we take a View of our particular Case in *Scotland* at this Day, Have we not Reason to fear we will be tried and punished, as a Nation which has departed from the Lord ? Many Warnings have we got, Yet what Stupidity under them all takes Place with the great Bulk ? Lay your Account, Professors, to have your Profession tried , you may have it throughly tried ere all be done O take heed lest ye be unstable and fickle in your Profession ! I fear there are many Professors like *Reuben*, unstable as Water, which cannot prevail We ought to warn such, that they may meet with shaking Providences to try their Profession It may come to the Time, when some will say, Lo, *here is Christ ! and others, lo, he is there !* I know not what Shakings and Splittings there may be in *Scotland* ere all be done , but I would fain hope the Lord will keep the little Handful he hath brought together to own a Testimony for Christ , that he will keep them together in shaking Days, when some are left to go to great Extreams, some on the Right-Hand, and some on the Left. O be concerned to be established, that you may

not

not be foon shaken in your Minds, that ye may be well fortified againft trying Times! As ye have profeffed to receive Chrift Jefus the Lord, fo walk ye in him, rooted and built up in him, and eftablifhed in the Faith, walk in him as the Lord your Righteoufnefs and Strength, the Glory of your Strength doth only ftand in him, all your Springs are in him. But, not to infift,

There is a *fecond* Sort of Perfons I would addrefs myfelf unto, and that is, not only Profeffors, but fuch as are really with the Lamb, and do follow the Lamb, and of fuch I hope there are a goodly Remnant here. From what I have faid you may know their Character. And try it, Sirs, Are you among the Lamb's Retinue and Train? They who are, they have been quickned by his Spirit, they know what it is to give Obedience to the Lamb, they know what it is to have Correfpondence with the Lamb, they know what it is, in fome Meafure, to be ingrafted in the Lamb. All the Followers of the Lamb, they defire juft to be eternal Debtors to the Lamb, they juft roll themfelves over upon his Righteoufnefs for their Juftification, and upon his Strength for their Sanctification, the Lamb is their Light, the Lamb is their Life, the Lamb is their Leader, the Lamb is their Glory, the Lamb is their Hope, the Lamb is their All, they cannot live without the Lamb. Well, Sirs, if you be amongft the Lamb's Followers, amongft his Retinue and Train, there are a few Words I would fuggeft unto you.

Firft, O keep your Eye upon the worthy Lamb, your glorious Leader, the Captain of your Salvation, who is made perfect through Sufferings: Ye are directed to look unto him, *Heb.* xii. 1. 2. *Wherefore, feeing we alfo are compaffed with fo great*
a Cloud

a Cloud of Witnesses, let us lay aside every Weight, and the Sin which doth so easily beset us, let us run with Patience the Race that is set before us, looking unto Jesus *the Author and Finisher of our Faith.* O, then, keep your Eye upon him, if you lose Sight of him, then you will lose your Way. Look to the glorious Leader, be concerned to keep within Sight of him, look to him just in his Word, and keep Sight of him as he manifests himself in his Word, *looking unto* Jesus *the Author and Finisher of Faith.* Look to him as your Leader, for Conduct, look to him as your Commander and General, for Strength that ye may be strong in the Lord, and in the Power of his Might, mind that all your Strength is in your Leader and Captain, he hath a glorious Magazine in him, all Furniture of Grace in him, Mercy and Grace to help in Time of Need. There is an inexhaustible Treasure of Grace in him, all the Fulness of the Godhead dwells in him. O the glorious Furniture that is in our Captain-General, for the Supply of all his Followers, his Retinue and Train! Look to that inexhaustible Treasure of Grace that is in him for the Supplying all your Wants, for it is just in him for the Behoof and Benefit of his Followers, just in him to be communicated and given forth to all his Followers. But then,

In the 2d Place, Are you among the Followers of the Lamb, his Retinue and Train? Then let me advise you not only to keep your Eye upon your Leader, but also to encourage yourselves in your worthy Leader, in the worthy Lamb, the glorious Leader, in all the Discouragements and Trials that may cast up in your Way. The Lamb's Followers frequently see Temptations cast up that they were not expecting; and it may be, Sirs, when you go home to your Houses, you may

meet

meet with Trials you did not expect, some Loss or another, some Cross or another, some Disappointment or another, may cast up, which you did not expect : But then, let me exhort the Followers of the Lamb, to encourage themselves in the Lamb, under all that casts up. Ye who are the Children of *Zion* have good Reason to encourage yourselves in your King, the glorious and worthy Lamb, to glory in your King whatever befal you. Consider, whatever you meet with, it is all measured out by your King and Leader in infinite Wisdom There is not one Grain Weight of a Cross laid upon you, but what is measured out for you by his own Hand, and he sees it meet for you, needful for you Yea, Sirs, all your Trials are measured out by infinite Wisdom and infinite Love, and therefore you may be assured all is designed for your Good ; there is Good designed in all the hard and trying Providences you meet with, and it will ay be true, *All Things work together for Good to them that love God, to them that are the Called according to his Purpose.* Therefore encourage yourselves in the Lamb, under all your Discouragements outward or inward, and particularly in View of a publick Storm, a general Storm, which is so awfully threatned, and we know not how soon it may blow, yet let the Followers of the Lamb encourage themselves in him. Sirs, you who are the Followers of the worthy Lamb, his Retinue and Train, I would read you a Word that may be Food to your Faith when you go home, yea as long as you live, and ye know not but you may need it very soon in an especial Manner. It is in the 43d Chapter of the Prophecies of *Isaiah,* 1st, 2d, and 3d Verses, *But now, thus saith the Lord that created thee, O Jacob, and he that formed thee, O Israel, Fear not ; for I have*

redeemed

redeemed thee, I have called thee by thy Name, thou art mine When thou paſſeſt through the Waters, I will be with thee, and through the Rivers, they ſhall not overflow thee, when thou walkeſt through the Fire, thou ſhalt not be burnt, neither ſhall the Flame kindle upon thee. For I am the Lord thy God, the holy one of Iſrael, *thy Saviour.* May not this Word of Grace be Food to your Faith while you are in the Wilderneſs? Even tho' a Hurricane of common Calamities ſhould come upon theſe Lands, yea, even tho' you ſhould die in the common Calamity, there is enough here to carry you through all, *I will be with thee.*

But then, again, in the 3*d* Place, Are you among the Followers of the Lamb? Then let me exhort you to be concerned that the Lamb may be honoured and glorified in our Land yet, that the Horn of the Lamb may bud forth pleaſantly yet. The Lamb is repreſented, in Scripture, as having ſeven Horns · It is a figurative Expreſſion, pointing out, that he hath all Power, Glory and Excellency Seven, in Scripture, is reckoned a compleat Number; and ſo the ſeven Horns of the Lamb, points out the Perfection of the Lamb's Power, Glory and Excellency O, then, plead that the Lamb's Horn may bud, his Power, Glory and Excellency may be yet ſeen by all Ranks. That you may be encouraged in your Pleading, there is a Promiſe it ſhall be ſo, in that 132 *Pſalm,* and 17th Verſe, *There will I make the Horn of* David *to bud I have ordained a Lamp for mine Anointed. There will I make the Horn of* David *to bud* If you ask, Where? I anſwer, In the New Teſtament Church, for this is a Promiſe that reſpects the New Teſtament Church, and ſo his Horn it buds forth in the Converſion of Sinners to himſelf, in a Kingdom,

dom, and in a Land. His Horn buds forth, when he appears upon his Mount *Zion*, and makes himself known in accomplishing such a Promise as this. O pray it may be made out more and more ! Pray his Horn may bud forth, that his Glory may be seen yet in our Land and Church. Sirs, his Glory is much vailed at this Day, vailed by Professors, by the untender Lives of Professors, vailed by the Walk, Talk and Conversation of Professors. Pray that the Lamb's Horn may bud forth in the Walk of Professors, when they glorify him in their Walk and Deportment, then his Horn buds forth O pray that his Horn may bud forth yet in *Scotland!* That it may bud forth yet in this covenanted Land ! A Land which the Lamb hath special Interest in, by the special Gift of his Father, and by a voluntary Surrender of themselves unto him. O pray that his Horn may bud forth in *Scotland!* Sometimes his Steps of Majesty have been seen in *Scotland*, in a Work both of the Conversion of Sinners and Confirmation of Saints. O pray that his Name may be yet great in *Scotland!* O cry him back to this Land, to *Scotland!* O plead for his Return ! O that we were exciting and stirring up one another to take hold of him ! This is his Complaint, that there is none that calleth upon his Name, that stirreth up himself to take hold of him It becomes us to use the Means of stirring up ourselves, and of stirring up one another to call upon his Name, and to take hold of him. To us his Voice is, *Ye that make Mention of the Lord, keep not silent, give him no Rest till he establish, and till he make* Jerusalem *a Praise in the whole Earth.* And we exhort you to cry, *Give him no Rest till he establish, and till he make* Jerusalem *a Praise in the whole Earth.* O cry that

he

he may come back to his Mount *Zion* in *Scotland*, where he has had his Dwelling in Times past!

In the 4*th* and *last* Place, let me exhort you, who are the Followers of the Lamb, to follow him fully, *follow him whithersoever he goeth*, as in our Text. You know it is a Commendation given to *Caleb* and *Joshua*, that they followed the Lord fully. Now, to follow the Lord fully, is, 1*st*. to follow all the Orders and Institutions of the Lamb, as you have heard in the former Part of this Discourse, it is to follow all the Truths of the Lamb, to value and esteem every Truth of the Lamb great; their is no Truth little. It is true, some Truths are of greater Importance and Moment than others, but so far is any Truth from being small, that every Point of divine Truth is of greater Moment than Heaven and Earth, of more Value than the whole Creation. Every Point of divine Truth is of more Value than Angels and Men put together. O Sirs, beware of thinking any Truth little! No Truth is little, no Truth is small, not one Hoof of divine Truth is to be parted with by the Followers of the Lamb.

2*dly* To follow him fully, is just to live upon the Lamb. The Lamb is Food to all his Followers, the Lamb is Clothing to all his Followers, the Lamb is just every Thing to all his Followers, that they want and need, for Time and Eternity. The Lamb that is in the Midst of the Throne will lead them to living Fountains of Water, and the Time is coming, Sirs, when the Lamb, with his own Hand, will wipe away all Tears from your Eyes. O then, let the Followers of the Lamb, who have it for their Concern to follow him fully, constantly, and whithersoever he goeth, rejoice and be glad that that Day is a-coming, that there will be

an

an End of the War which they have now with the
Lamb's and their Enemies. The Conflict is but
short, and the Victory is sure, it shall come in a
little. But, as I am afraid I have insisted too long
already, I shall just close with a short Word to the
two last Sorts of Persons I had a View to speak
to Is it so, then, as has been said? Then, from
this Text and Doctrine, I might speak a Word, by
Way of Advice, to such of the Followers of the
worthy Lamb, as for present may be labouring under Doubts and Fears left they be not on the Lamb's
Side. To such I shall say only a Word or two

In the *first* Place, I would exhort and advise you
to mint at a direct Act of Faith on the worthy Lamb
That is a remarkable Word which I cited already
in 50th Chapter of *Isaiah*, and 10th Verse, to such
as are in a dark Case and under Doubts, *Who is a
mong you that feareth the Lord, and obeyeth the Voice of
his Servant, that walketh in Darkness, and hath no
Light? Let him trust in the Name of the Lord, and
stay upon his God* The best Way to get Relief from
thy Doubts and Fears, is just to mint at acting
Faith upon the Promise of God, where it is promised that you shall do it, as in that 48 th Chapter
of *Isaiah*, and 24th Verse, *Surely, shall ne say, in
the Lord have I Righteousness and Strength.* The best
Way to get quite of thy Doubts and Fears, is just
to roll them all over upon the Lord *Cast thy Burden upon the Lord, and he will sustain thee,* cast all
thy Doubts and Fears over upon him, cast all thy
Burdens on him, and act Faith on him that he will
sustain thee.

I shall only say to you 2*dly* Are you under
Doubts and Fears that you are none of the Lamb's
Followers, his Retinue and Train? Then, O wait
upon him! Wait upon a promising God in Christ!

Wait

Wait upon him in the Use of the Means of his own Appointment' *Wait upon the Lord, be of good Courage, and he shall strengthen thine Heart, wait, I say, upon the Lord*

In the 4*th* and *last* Place, I thought to have dropt a Word to all this Assembly, by Way of Exhortation, a Word including all that hear me this Day. And, in a Word, that I may conclude, I would exhort you all, and every one of you, whoever you are, and whatever you are, or have been, to come and follow the Lamb, the worthy Lamb O come ! I call you in his Name to come and follow the worthy Lamb O come, come ! There are a vast Number gathered together here, and I am afraid a great many Strangers to Christ, the worthy Lamb. O Sirs, ye come to Sacraments, ye come to a Communion-Table, ye come to Sermons, but ye never come to Christ, the Lamb of God ! O Sirs, we tell you, the Lamb this Day invites you to come to him, to come and follow him ! This Day you are called and invited in the Word of the Gospel, *Whosoever will, let him come, and take the Water of Life freely* What shall I say ? Does the Lamb invite you, and will you not come? O will you not come upon his Invitation and Call ! What should hinder your Compliance with the Lamb's Call ! ? What tho' you have been bearing Arms against him all your Days to this very Moment, yet, I say unto you, there is Room in the Lamb for you, Room in the Grace of the Lamb for you, Room in the Heart of the Lamb for you, and you are by the Lamb invited this Day to come in Are you a poor graceless Sinner Why, then, I tell you, there is Room in his Grace for you, there are inexhaustible Treasures of Grace in him, and these inexhaustible Treasures of

Grace

Grace are juſt for them that have rebelled and carried Arms againſt the Lamb   O that ye knew and would be perſuaded, that the Lamb hath re ceived Gifts for Men, for ſuch as did rebel, that the Lord God might dwell among them.   O, then be aſſured the inexhauſtible Treaſure of Grace that is in the Lamb, is juſt for you   There is Room in his Grace for you, Treaſures of par doning Mercy and ſanctifying Grace are in him for you.   O come, then, at his Call   Open your Hearts to receive him at his Call   Give Obedience to the Lamb, ſtoop to the Righteouſneſs of the worthy Lamb, be aſſured there is Room in the Righteouſneſs of the Lamb for you,   Room in the Obedience and Death of the Lamb for you whatever thy Guilt is, his Merit is infinite, and in it there is Room for you   O come, then, in under the Shadow of this perfect Righteouſneſs, the Merit and Mediation of the worthy Lamb, with thy guilty Soul, and then, *Tho' ye have lien among the Pots, yet ſhall ye be as the Wings of a Dove, covered with Silver, and her Feathers with yellow Gold*   O come, guilty Sinner   O come, filthy Sinner There is Room in this worthy Lamb for thee Ye were called yeſterday to come under the Lamb's Shadow, and we call you again this Day to come under his Shadow   O, it is a broad Shadow, is a pleaſant Shadow, is a delightſom Shadow. O come under the Shadow of the worthy Lamb O will you part from this Place, and from one another, without coming to the Lord Jeſus Chriſt, the worthy Lamb   O, our Hearts Deſire for you all is, that you may come to the worthy Lamb, that ye may know the worthy Lamb, that you may ſhare of that Grace that is in Chriſt Jeſus the wor thy Lamb, and we are ſure there is enough in him

for you all, whatever you are or have been. O
come to him ! Whatever be thy Case, we assure
you here is something to suit it. Are you full of
Wants ? You will find in him a Supply of all your
Wants. Are you an hungred ? Food is to be
found in him. Are thou thirsty ? Drink is to be
found in him. Are you naked ? Clothing is to be
found in him. Are you poor ? Unsearchable Riches
are to be found in him. Are you blind ? Eye-
Salve is to be found in him. *I counsel thee*, saith
the Lamb, *to buy of me Gold tried in the Fire, that
thou mayest be rich ; and white Raiment, that thou
mayest be clothed, and that the Shame of thy Nakedness do not appear, and anoint thine Eyes with Eye-
Salve, that thou mayest see*, Rev iii 18. O to be
found in the Lamb ! O, are you a poor diseased
Sinner ? Why, then, we tell you, Medicine is to
be found in him for all your Plagues and Maladies,
whatever they are, his Name is *Jehovah Rophi*,
the Lord that healeth thee. Are you an Unbeliever, and cannot trust his Word ? The Spirit of
Faith is in him. Are you dumb, and cannot seek
any Thing from him, lame and cannot come to him ?
Why, *he maketh the lame Man to leap as an Hart,
and the Tongue of the Dumb to sing.* Have you an
obstinate, stubborn and rebellious Heart ? He hath
omnipotent Power to overcome all the Obstinacy
in thy Heart. O, then, come, come to the wor-
ty Lamb, and follow the worthy Lamb whithersoever he goeth ! O that the Spirit of God may
be sent forth into thy Heart ! O that he may be
sent forth as a Spirit of Faith, as a Spirit of Love !
O that he may be sent to take the Face of Covering from every one in all this Company, and manifest the Glory of the worthy Lamb unto us all !
The Lord bless his Word.

F I N I S.

The Father's Promife to the Son, a clear Bow in the Church's darkeft Cloud;

O R,

The fpiritual Seed of Chrift piefcrved in all Ages and amidft all Dangers.

Being the Subftance of feveral

SERMONS

Preached at *Perth*, in the Years 1729. and 1730.

By the late REVEREND *and* LEARNED *Mr.* WILLIAM WILSON *Miniffer of the Gofpel at* PERTH.

2 Sam. iii. 38 *There is* ——— *a great Man fallen in* Ifrael.

Heb. XI. 14. *He being dead yet fpeaketh.*

E D I N B U R G H,
Printed for *David Duncan*, and fold at his Houfe, oppofite to the *Weigh-Houfe*, North-Side of the Street. MCCDXLVII.

ADVERTISEMENT.

THE following Difcourfes were lately found in the Author's Clofet in Manufcript, corrected with his own Hand; an inconteftible Evidence that he defigned the Publication of the fame. So we judge it our Duty to do him the Juftice, and the World the Service of prefenting them with this Part of his Works, whofe Fame is in the Church; and fince a few Sermons are all that Part of this Author's Works the World can be favoured with, it is therefore expected that well-difpofed People will be careful to perufe, and recommend the Perufal of the fame where they can have Influence, which, thro' the Lord's Blefling, will terminate in their Profit.

PSALM lxxxix. 29.

His Seed also will I make to endure for ever.

THIS excellent *Pſalm* was penned by *Ethan* the *Ezrahite*, as the Inſcription bears ; it is probable he is the ſame *Ethan* who was famous in the Days of *Solomon* for Wiſdom together with his Brethren *Heman*, *Chalchol* and *Darda* the Sons of *Macho*, 1 *Kings* iv. 31. It is remarkable, that, in the preceeding *Pſalm*, his Brother *Heman* is under much of a Spirit of Bondage , he cries out, that his Soul is full of Troubles, that the Wrath of the Lord lieth hard upon him, that he is in Darkneſs and in the Deeps, and that he is ready to die from his Youth, and diſtracted with the Terrors of the Lord : But in this Pſalm *Ethan* ſings of the Mercy and Faithfulneſs of God O what adorable Sovereignty is here! Some of the Saints and People of God walk, for the moſt Part of their Time, in Darkneſs and under much Heavineſs and Bondage, while others enjoy a more pleaſant Sun Shine of ſpiritual Light, Joy and Comfort • So it is with *Ethan* in this *Pſalm* , tho' in the Cloſe of it he bewails the Calamity and Diſtreſs that the Church and People of God, in his Day, were brought under, yet he is comforted and encouraged, and his Faith is ſtrengthned and confirmed, from the ſpiritual Diſcoveries that are given him of that rare Superſtructure of Mercy on the Behalf of miſerable Sinners,

and

and also of the solemn Engagement of divine
Faithfulness for the Preservation of Christ's spiritual Seed, according to the Covenant-Transaction
with the Lord Jesus, of whom *David* was an eminent Type ; and therefore, from the Beginning to
the 15th Verse of the *Psalm*, he celebrates, with a
Song of Praise, the Mercy and Faithfulness, the
Sovereignty, Greatness and Power of God manifested in all his Dispensations towards his Church
and People. And, from the 15th to the 19th
Verse, we have some of the special Characters,
with the peculiar Blessings of all such who are
Christ's spiritual Seed, and Heirs of the Promise,
from the 19th Verse and downward, the new Co
venant-Transaction is farther laid open in some
Account of the wonderful Person who has the
first Room and Place in this excellent Bargain, and
who bears all the Weight and Burden of the
whole Building of Mercy, as also of his Furniture
for his Work and his glorious Success in it Who
is he then on whom the Help of self-destroying *Is*
rael is laid ? He is *David Jehovah*'s Servant, 20th
Verse. Surely a greater than *David* the King of
Judah and *Israel* is here, for he is one that is
mighty, 19th Verse. He is indeed the mighty
God, the everlasting Father, who is able to save
unto the uttermost all that come unto God through
him, he is also one chosen out of the People, he
is God in our Nature, or *Immanuel*, God with us.
This is he with whom the Covenant of Grace
stands fast, 28th Verse He is designed the First-
born, 27th Verse *I will make him my First born.*
And so, *Rom.* viii. 29. he is called the First-born a
mong many Brethren, and, *Col* i 15 18 *The*
First-born of every Creature, and the First-born from
the Dead, that in all Things he might have the Pre-
eminence.

eminence. The Right of the Firſt-born is in t Perſon of the Lord Jeſus the ſecond *Adam*, he is the Head of the new Covenant, the glorious Heir of all Things, and unto him all the Promiſes of Grace and Glory are given in the firſt Inſtance, and in him they are made ſure unto all his ſpiritual Seed. With reſpect unto his Furniture for his Work he was anointed with the Oyl of Holineſs, that is, with the holy Spirit in a ſuper-abundant Meaſure, whereby he was furniſhed and ſtrengthned for the Diſchaige of the great Work and Truſt committed unto him in the 20th and 21ſt Verſes. And as for his Succeſs in his Work, he hath trampled under Foot the ſtrong Powers of Darkneſs, Sin and *Satan*, the World, Death, Hell and the Grave, 22d and 23d Verſes And being now exalted into the Throne of his Glory, he ſtretcheth out his omnipotent Arm in the Diſpenſation of the Word of the Goſpel, the Rod of his Strength, by which he makes a Conqueſt of Grace in the Iſlands of the Sea, and alſo in the Continent amongſt the Rivers, 25th Verſe. And unto him it is promiſed, in the Words of our Text, that his Seed ſhall endure for ever, that is, he ſhall have a ſpiritual Seed and Offspring upon this Earth as long as the Sun and Moon do endure *His Seed I will make to endure.* Whatever Oppoſition may be made by Men or Devils unto Chriſt's Cauſe and People, yet that Day ſhall never dawn wherein it can be ſaid that Chriſt's ſpiritual Seed do altogether fail, nay, in all Ages and Generations he ſhall have a Seed to do him Service, a People to honour him, and Subjects to yield Obedience unto him, for his Throne ſhall be as the Days of Heaven. The doctrinal Propoſition I lay before you is almoſt in the Words of the Text, *namely, That Chriſt's ſpiritual Seed*

ſhall

shall endure for ever. The same Thing is promised in the 4th and 36th Verses of the *Psalm,* and the Promise is ratified and confirmed by the Oath of God, in the 3d and 4th Verses *I have sworn unto* David *my Servant, thy Seed will I establish for ever.* And in the 35th and 36th Verses, *Once have I sworn by my Holiness, that I will not lie unto* David *, His Seed shall endure for ever.* The frequent Repetition of this Promise, and with such a Solemnity, shews us of what Importance and Weight this Subject is, and truly it is of great Use, to support and confirm the Faith of Believers in Christ under all shaking and trying Dispensations of divine Providence towards the Church and People of God, and particularly under the sad Thoughts of Heart that we may have from the low State and Condition of the Churches of Christ at this Day. It is also very useful to quicken and encourage us to our Duty, therefore I shall insist a little upon it, and, in discoursing it, I shall endeavour, *first,* to shew you whom we are to understand by Christ's Seed. 2*dly.* Why they are called his Seed. 3*dly* How or by what Means they have been preserved in all Ages and Generations 4*thly* I shall lay before you some few Considerations for confirming you in the Faith of this important Truth. 5*thly* I shall shew you why it is that Christ's spiritual Seed must endure for ever. And, in the *last* Place, I shall make some practical Use and Improvement of this Subject

The first Thing proposed is, to shew who are meant by Christ's Seed

First, All that are ordained unto eternal Life are Christ's spiritual Seed, there is a Remnant, according unto the Election of Grace, even a goodly Number of the apostate and lost Race of Mankind,

Mankind, who were chosen unto eternal Life before the Foundations of the World were laid,
Rom. viii. 29. *Eph.* i. 4. All those are Chrift's
fpiritual Seed, they are his Seed in the Purpose and
in the Decree of God, they are his Seed by the
Father's Gift and Grant unto him; they are the
Men who were given unto Chrift out of the
World, *John* xvii. 6. They are his Seed in refpect of his Undertaking for them; he undertook
from all Eternity to pay the Price of their Redemption from Sin and Wrath, and to bring in a
Law-biding Righteoufnefs for their Juftification.
As all the Pofterity of the firft *Adam* were in him,
as their common Head and Reprefentatives, when
the Covenant of Works was tranfacted with him,
fo all the Elect was in Chrift the fecond *Adam*, as
their common Head and Reprefentative, when
God tranfacted with him, and, in this eternal
Tranfaction, not only was all needful Furniture
promifed unto the Redeemer, to enable him to
difcharge the Work and Truft undertaken by him,
but alfo the Promife of Life, forfeited by the A-
poftafy of the firft *Adam*, is given unto him as
the fecond *Adam*, the Head of the new Family, and
the Heir of all Things. Hence, *Tit* i. 2. it is
faid, *In Hope of eternal Life, which God that cannot lie promifed before the World began.* Yea,
all the Grace defigned for the Veffels of Mercy
in Time, is laid up in the fecond *Adam* as the common Treafury and Store-Houfe : *For in him are
hid all the Treafures of Wifdom and Knowledge,*
Col. ii. 3 And it is *of his Fulnefs that we receive,
and Grace for Grace,* John i. 16. And all the
Grace wherewith the Veffels of Mercy are filled
in Time, is given them in Chrift Jefus before the
World began, 2 *Tim.* i. 9. All this is very well expreffed

preſſed, in a very few Words, in the Anſwer to that Queſtion in our larger Catechiſm, *With whom was the Covenant of Grace made?* The Anſwer is, *The Covenant of Grace was made with Chriſt as the ſecond Adam, and in him with all the Elect as his Seed,* Gal. iii. 16. Rom. v. 15.

Secondly, All who are effectually called are Chriſt's ſpiritual Seed. The Elect, in effectual Calling, are united unto the Lord Jeſus Chriſt, and are made joint Heirs with him unto the Promiſes, *Gal.* iii. 29. And, if ye be Chriſt's, then are ye *Abraham's* Seed, and Heirs according unto the Promiſe. It is in their effectual Calling that the Elect obtain an actual Intereſt in the Promiſes. For clearing this Matter a little, you may obſerve, that tho' all the Poſterity of the firſt *Adam* were in him as their common Head and Repreſentative, when he ſinned and fell, yet they have no actual Communion with him in his Sin, till once they have a Being in him by natural Generation ; then it is that his Sin is imputed unto them, and then it is that they derive a corrupted and depraved Nature from him, *Rom* v. 12, 14, 15, 16 Even ſo, tho' all the Elect were virtually in the ſecond *Adam* as their Head and Repreſentative, yet they have not actual Communion with him in his Grace, till the Day of their myſtical Union with him, when they are apprehended by the Spirit, ſent down from the living and Life giving Head, and are enabled by a lively Faith to apprehend him ; then it is that his Righteouſneſs is imputed unto them, and the Promiſe of eternal Life does then become theirs in their own Perſons. In a Word, then it is that they receive the Remiſſion of Sins, *and an Inheritance among them which are ſanctified by Faith that is in him,* Acts xxvi. 18. It is of the E-

lect

lest converted, or of such who truly believe in the Lord Jesus, that I understand the Promise in in our Text. *His Seed also will I make to endure for ever;* that is, such as really believe in him shall never altogether fail from off the Earth; he shall have some such in all Ages and Generations upon the Earth.

I proceed to the *second* Thing proposed, *namely,* To shew you why Believers in Christ are called his Seed

First, They all spring from him, they are his genuine Issue and Offspring, *Isa* xxii. 24. *And they shall hang upon him all the Glory of his Father's House, the Offspring and the Issue.* They spring from the Sufferings and Death of Christ, *Isa* liii. 10. *When thou shalt make his Soul an Offering for Sin, he shall see his Seed* They are the Travail of Christ's Soul, *Isa.* liii. 11. *In his State of Humiliation he travailed to bring forth many Children to God.* They spring from his Resurrection from the Dead, 1 *Pet.* 1. 3 *He hath begotten us again unto a lively Hope, by the Resurrection of Jesus Christ from the Dead.* They spring from the Covenant-Transaction with him, this glorious Bargain is laid open in the Word and Promises of the Gospel, and by the Word of Truth they are begotten unto him, *James* 1 18 *Of his own Will begat he us with the Word of Truth.* They are born of the incorruptible Seed of the Word, 1 *Pet* i 23. They are brought forth and nourished by the Means of the Word of Promise, therefore they are called the Children of Promise, *Gal* iv 28. They all descend from him as their Father, and are born of his Spirit, *John* iii. 5, 6.

2*dly.* Believers in Christ are called his Seed, because they have all their spiritual Being from him;

him : As Children have their natural Being from their Parents, ſo Believers have a ſpiritual Being from Chriſt , whatever they have as they are Believers, they have it from him · They have all their ſpiritual Life from him, for he quickens them when they are dead in Treſpaſſes and Sins, *Eph.* ii 1, 4, 5. They have that Faith, from which they are denominated Believers, from him, for it is the Faith of his Operation, *Col* ii. 12. They have that Righteouſneſs, whereby they are juſtified in the Sight of God, only from him, *Iſa* liv. 17 *Their Righteouſneſs is of me, ſaith the Lord.* Alſo they have all their Sanctification from him ; for he is made of God unto them Sanctification, 1 *Cor.* i. 30. In a Word, they have all Grace and Glory from him, *for he giveth both Grace and Glory,* Pſalm lxxxiv. 11

3*dly*. Believers in Chriſt are called his Seed, becauſe of that Reſemblance that they bear unto the Lord Jeſus , as Children reſemble their Parents, ſo all Chriſt's ſpiritual Seed reſemble himſelf. 1*ſt* They reſemble him in the new Nature that is given unto him, as Children have the ſame Nature with their Parents, ſo Believers in Chriſt are Partakers in the divine Nature, 2 *Pet* 1 4. The divine Nature, in which they are ſaid to partake, is their Renovation in the Spirit of their Minds, or the new Man, *which after God is created in Righteouſneſs and true Holineſs,* Eph iv 23, 24. 2*dly*. They reſemble Chriſt in the Spirit that is given unto them, the ſame Spirit that is in Chriſt, is alſo given unto every Believer. The Holy Ghoſt was indeed given to him above Meaſure, but he is given unto every one of them according to their Meaſure yet he is the ſame Spirit both in the Head and in all the Members of

the

the myſtical Body. The Holy Ghoſt did reſt upon the Head, as a Spirit of Wiſdom and Knowledge, and he is given unto all his Members, as the Spirit of Wiſdom and Revelation in the Knowledge of Chriſt, *Iſa.* xi. 2 *Eph.* i. 17. The holy Spirit did reſt upon Chriſt as the Spirit of Might, and all his ſpiritual Seed are ſtrengthned with Might by his Spirit in the inner Man, *Eph.* iii. 16. The Spirit deſcended upon the Head as the Spirit of Holineſs, and he is given unto every one that believes as the Spirit of Sanctification. 1 *Cor.* vi. 11. The Spirit did likeways reſt upon the Head as a Spirit of Supplications, for in the Days of his Fleſh he offered up Prayers and Supplications with ſtrong Crying and Tears, *Heb.* v. 7. and he is promiſed and given as the Spirit of Grace and Supplication unto all his ſpiritual Seed, *Zech.* xii. 10. He is in them the Spirit of Adoption *whereby they cry Abba, Father*, Rom viii 15. 3dly. Believers in Chriſt reſemble him in their Graces, ſuch as Faith, Love, Zeal, and the like. The Head and Captain of Salvation was eminent for his Faith and Truſt in God, *Heb.* ii 13 for Love to and Zeal for his Father's Honour and Glory , *The Zeal of thy Houſe did eat me up.* Likeways for his Humility and Meekneſs, *Matth.* xi. 29. *Learn of me, for I am meek and lowly in Heart*, and all Chriſt's ſpiritual Seed bear ſome Reſemblance and Likeneſs to him in theſe , they are a People that put their Truſt in the Lord, *Pſalm* ix 10. It is a Character of them, that they love him, 1 *Pet.* i. 8. they are the Meek of the Earth, *Pſalm* xxv 9

4thly Believers in Chriſt are called his Seed becauſe of his tender Care and Concern about them. As Parents are naturally careful of their Children, ſo the Lord Chriſt has the Heart of a

Father

Father towards his People, and the Care and Concern of a Father for them 1*st*. He loveth them as a
Father loveth his Children.   The Love of a Parent
to his Children is a tender Love, a great Love, a
compassionate and sympathizing Love , so is the
Love of Christ unto his People : He loveth them
with a tender Love.   As the affectionate Parent
carries the little Child in his Arms, and lays it in
his Bosom, so it is said of Christ, that *he gathereth*
his Lambs with his Arm, and carries them in his Bo-
som, Isa. xl. 11. Likeways the Love of Christ unto
his People is a very great Love.   Parents will
readily expose themselves to very great Dangers
for the Sake of their Children , but the Love of
Christ excels in Greatness , he exposed himself to
the greatest of all Dangers, for the Sake of all his
spiritual Seed, even to the Wrath of a Sin-revenging God, and to Death armed with its direful
Sting, *Eph.* v 2. *Christ also hath loved us, and*
given himself for us.   Also the Love of Christ
unto his People is a compassionate and sympathizing Love, *Psalm* ciii 13 *Like as a Father pitieth*
his Children, so the Lord pitieth them that fear him.
Who can express the Pity, Sympathy, the Year-
nings of Bowels that are in a tender-hearted Parent towards his Child, especially in its Affliction
and Distress ? Yet this is but a faint Emblem
and Shadow of that Pity and Sympathy that is
with the Lord Jesus towards his People, such as
a Sympathy with them, that *in all their Afflictions*
he is afflicted, Isa lxiii. 19. and whoever toucheth them, toucheth him in the most tender and
sensible Part, *Zech.* ii 8 *For he that toucheth you,*
toucheth the Apple of his Eye

2*dly.* Parents are careful to provide for their
Children, even so Christ has made a liberal
and

and large Provifion for all his fpiritual Seed, he hath provided a goodly Heritage for them, even the Inheritance incorruptible, undefiled, that fadeth not away, and unto the Hope of this Inheritance they are begotten, 1 *Pet.* 1. 3, 4. He has made Provifion of all fpiritual Bleffings for them, he will give them both Grace and Glory, *Pfalm* lxxxiv 11. and whatever temporal Bleffings are needful for them, thefe are provided in the Covenant likeways, *Ifa* xxxiii. 16. *Then Bread fhall be given them, and then Water fhall be fure* 3*dly.* He corrects them as a Father doth his Children, the Duty of a Parent is carefully to correct the Child when the Rod is needful, and when the Lord fees the Rod to be needful for his Children, he will not fpare it. *Rev* iii. 19 *As many as I love I rebuke and chaften,* Heb. xii 8 *If ye be without Chaftifement, whereof all are Partakers, then are ye Baftards, and not Sons.* And in the Verfes following our Text, 30, 31, 32. *If his Children forfake my Law———Then will I vifit their Tranfgreffions with the Rod*

5*thly* Believers in Chrift are called his Seed, becaufe in him they have a Right and Title unto all Things. All are yours, and ye are Chrift's, 1 *Cor* iii 22. The Head of the Family, as we have obferved already, is the Heir of all Things, *Heb* 1 2 and all Children of the Family are joint Heirs with him, *Rom.* viii 17. All the Promifes are given unto Chrift in the firft Inftance, *Gal* iii 16 *Now to Abraham and his Seed were the Promifes made. He faith not, and to Seeds, as of many, but as of one, and to thy Seed, which is Chrift.* And in him all the Promifes of Grace and Glory are *Yea,* and *Amen,* unto all his fpiritual Seed. The Head of the Family has the firft Right and

Title to plead the Covenant-Relation. In the 26th Verſe of this *Pſalm, He ſhall cry unto me, Thou art my Father, thou art my God, and the Rock of my Salvation*: And it is in him, even under the Shadow of his Wings, that all the Children of the Family may with the Boldneſs of Faith cry unto him, *Thou art my Father, my God, and the Rock of my Salvation*. It is in him that they may plead the Relation; therefore he ſays, *John* xx. 17. *I aſcend unto my Father and your Father, to my God and your God*. Chriſt the Head of the Family has the firſt Right and Title to the Kingdom, to the Glory, and to the Throne; and in him all his ſpiritual Seed have a Right and Title unto the Kingdom, *I appoint unto you a Kingdom, as my Father hath appointed unto me;* yea, in him they have a Right and Title unto his Glory, and unto his Throne, *John* xvii. 22. *And the Glory which thou gaveſt me I have given them,* Rev. iii 21 *To him that overcometh will I grant to ſit with me on my Throne, even as I alſo overcame, and am ſet down with my Father on his Throne.*

I proceed to the third Thing propoſed, *namely,* To ſhew you, how or by what Means Chriſt's ſpiritual Seed have been preſerved in all Ages and Generations.

I anſwer, 1*ſt* By the Miniſtry of the Word.

2*dly.* By the Concurrence of the Spirit of God with the Word.

3*dly.* By the Church's wreſtling with God in Prayer

4*thly.* By the Word of their Teſtimony. And,

5*thly* By remarkable Appearances of the Lord amongſt them and for them.

I ſhall upon each of theſe Heads give you ſome
particular

particular Inftances with reference to the Lord's Church and People in this Land.

In the *firft* Place, Chrift's fpiritual Seed have been preferved in all Ages by the Miniftry of the Word. This is the great outward Mean that the Lord hath made Ufe, and doth ftill make Ufe of for bringing forth a Seed unto himfelf, it is the Rod of his Strength, by which his People are made willing in the Day of his Power, *Pfalm* cx. 2, 3. The Word of the Gofpel was firft preached in Paradife by the Angel of the Covenant, to our firft Parents immediately after their difmal Apoftafy in that Promife, *Gen* iii. 15. *I will put Enmity between thee and the Woman, and between thy Seed and her Seed,* &c. We have no Ground to doubt of the Succefs of this Preaching, and from it we may date the bringing forth of a fpiritual Offspring unto the Lord Jefus, which have continued ever fince, and will continue to the End of Time. The fame Word of the Gofpel was preached unto *Abraham, Gal.* iii 8 compared with *Gen.* xii. 3 And it was believed by him, *Rom* iv. 3. Abraham *believed God, and it was counted to him for Righteoufnefs,* This Word was given by the Lord to the whole Church of *Ifrael*, and great was the Company of thofe that publifhed it, *Pfalm* lxviii 11. The Apoftles were alfo commanded to preach the Word of the Gofpel, firft at *Jerufalem*, and then among the Nations, *Luke* xxiv. 47. The preaching of the Gofpel was the great Mean by which the Kingdom of *Pagan* Darknefs was firft fhaken, and afterwards gradually deftroyed, throughout the *Roman* Empire, even in the *Apoftolick* Age, *their Sound went unto all the Earth, and their Words to the Ends of the World,* Rom. x. 18. The Sound of the Gofpel went at

that

that Time, not only through the *Roman* Empire, but also to thefe Places of the Earth into which the *Roman* Arms had not then penetrated : And it is very probable, that our barbarous Forefathers in *Scotland* were early enlightned by the Word of the Gofpel, if not in the Apoftolick Age, yet in the Beginning of the next. Thus, as the Walls of *Jericho* did fall before the Blowing of Rams Horns, fo was *Pagan* Idolatry deftroyed by the Blowing of the great Trumpet of the Gofpel. Again, when grofs Antichriftian Darknefs had covered the Chriftian World, it pleafed the Lord, by the pure Preaching of the Word of the Gofpel, to fhake the Kingdom of Antichrift. By this glorious Mean, whole Nations and Provinces were brought off from their blind Subjection to Antichrift ; and, amongft others, *Scotland*, being covered with Popifh Darknefs, was, in the Century preceeding the laft, again illuminated by the Miniftry of a *Hamilton*, *Wifhart* and *Knox*, who may be juftly reckoned amongft the firft three, and, by their Miniftry, a numerous Seed was brought forth to the Lord Jefus, which have been preferved in *Scotland* by the preaching of the Word, even when the Church of Chrift in this Land has been brought very low   As for Inftance, in the late cruel perfecuting Days, it was by a preached Gofpel in Corners and in the Defarts, that a fpiritual Seed were preferved unto the Lord Jefus

2*dly*. Chrift's fpiritual Seed have endured in all Ages by the Concurrence of the Holy Spirit with the Word ‧ The Word is only a Mean, it has no Efficacy of itfelf, all the Efficacy depends upon the Energy of the Holy Ghoft, it is through the Power of the Spirit, accompanying the Word, that it has done fuch great Things upon the
Earth.

Earth. The Word in the Hand of the Spirit of God has prevailed over the strong Powers of Darknes, it has overcome Nations and Provinces, and brought many of Christ's Enemies unto a professed outward Subjection, and others unto a real and cordial Subjection unto him. *The Arrows of the Word, when directed by the Spirit of God, is sharp in the Hearts of the King's Enemies,* Psalm xlv. 5 The Old Testament Believers had the Spirit of Faith given unto them, and the same Spirit of Faith is given under the New Testament Dispensation, I *Cor* iv. 13 only, under the New Testament Dispensation, there is a more plentiful and more extensive Effusion of the Holy Spirit, the Success that the Gospel had in the Apostles Days, and also in our reforming Days, was wholly owing to the Concurrence of the Spirit with the Word, and by this Means Christ's spiritual Seed have been preserved to this very Day, according to that Promise, *Isa* lix 21. *My Spirit that is upon thee, and my Words that I have put in thy Mouth, shall not depart out of thy Mouth, nor out of the Mouth of thy Seed's Seed, saith the Lord, from henceforth and for ever* I might here condescend upon some particular Instances of a more than ordinary Down-pouring of the Spirit accompanying the Word, but I will have Occasion to mention these afterwards.

3*dly.* The Lord Christ's spiritual Seed have been preserved by wrestling with God in Prayer, this is a Mean the Church and People of God have tried with good Success, when they have been brought very low, and frequently, when the Lord is about to give any great Deliverance to his Church and People, he pours out a Spirit of Prayer: When the Children of *Israel* were sighing

C

under

under their Bondage in *Egypt*, they cried unto the Lord, and their Cry came up unto him, and he heard their Groaning, and remembred his Covenant, *Exod.* ii 23, 24. When the Church was in great Danger in *Esther's* Days, she fasted and prayed, and appointed *Mordecai* and the rest of the *Jews* at *Shushan* to do so, *Esther* iv. 15, 16 and the Lord answered their Prayers, by giving them a wonderful Deliverance Likeways the Members of the infant primitive Church, *Acts* i 14. were all with one Accord in Prayer and Supplication, before that remarkable Down-pouring of the Spirit on the Day of *Pentecoste* We have had a great Company of Ministers and Christians in *Scotland* who have had Power with God, and have prevailed in Prayer, their Prayers have sometimes been a Terror to their very Enemies. When Queen *Mary* heard of Mr. *Knox* and the Congregation then Fasting and Praying, she declared she was more afraid of their Prayers than of ten thousand Men in Arms. And the History bears, that the Lord gave a remarkable Return to their Prayer. Amongst many others that might be named, Mr *Wishart* one of the first three, after more than ordinary Nearness to God in Prayer, expressed himself in this Manner ' This Realm ' shall be illuminated with the Light of Christ's Go ' spel, as clearly as ever any Realm since the Days ' of the Apostles, the House of God shall be builded in it, yea, it shall not lack, (said he) till that ' the Glory of God shall evidently appear, and shall ' once triumph in Despite of *Satan* But, alas ! if ' the People shall be after unthankful, then fearful ' and terrible shall be the Plagues that shall follow '. Famous Mr *Welsh*, who ordinarily spent eight Hours of the four and twenty in Prayer, was overheard expressing himself after this Manner:

ner : O Lord, wilt thou not give me *Scotland* ! And
he lived and died in the Faith of it, that the Lord
would preserve a Remnant in *Scotland* ! Likeways
great Mr *Robert Bruce*, after some Time spent
in Fasting and Prayer for the Church of Christ in
Scotland, at that Time groaning under Prelatick
Tyranny and Oppression, expressed his Hopes of
that glorious Deliverance which was afterwards given unto this Church in the Year 1638 But particular Instances of this Nature are so many, that I
must stop, and not launch forth into them . I shall
only observe, upon this Head, that the Wrestlers
in Prayer for the Church of Christ in this Land,
have found Footing for Faith and Hope in that
Promise, *Psalm* ii 8 *I will give thee the Heathen
for thine Inheritance, and the utmost Ends of the Earth
for thy Possession.*

4*thly.* Christ's spiritual Seed have been preserved
by the Word of their Testimony This is another
notable Mean by which a Seed have endured to
the Lord in all Ages and Generations By this
Mean they were preserved, under hot Persecution,
from *Rome Pagan* and *Antichristian* Hence, *Rev.*
xii 11. it is said, *They overcame by the Blood of the
Lamb, and by the Word of their Testimony*, they did
bear Witness to the Truth in Face of the greatest
Opposition. They did confess and own the Truths
of Christ, when these were either openly born down
by violent Persecutors, or secretly undermined
by cunning Seducers, and, in doing so, they did
prevail and overcome , and truly this is a special
Mean by which the Truths of Christ have been
transmitted in their Purity from one Generation
to another I shall notice three Ways by which
the Word of the Church's Testimony has been given, particularly in *Scotland*. In the *first* Place,
by

by publick Confeſſions. Theſe have been, and are
the Church's Teſtimony unto the Truths of Chriſt
againſt riſing and prevailing Errors; they are
publick Declarations to the World, what Things
are received and believed by the Church as the
Truths of God agreeable to the Holy Scriptures,
the only infallible Rule of Faith, and what is
rejected by the Church as contrary thereunto,
or of what the Church believes to be Truth, and
condemns as Errors Our Confeſſions of Faith in
the Church of *Scotland* have been bleſſed Means
for preſerving Purity, Harmony and Unity in the
Faith amongſt us Our firſt Confeſſion of Faith is
that which was received and approven by this
Church in the Year 1560. and it contains this
Church's Teſtimony unto the Truths of Chriſt,
given in a ſpecial Manner in Oppoſition to the
Errors of the Church of *Rome* Our laſt Confeſſion of Faith, compiled by that learned and grave
Aſſembly at *Weſtminſter*, and received by this
Church *anno* 1647 is in many Things more full
than our firſt, and contains the Words of this
Church's Teſtimony to the Truths of Chriſt, both
in Oppoſition to the Errors of Popery, and alſo
unto many other Errors that had ſprung up in
the Church ſince the Reformation Our national
Covenant doth alſo bear the Title of the Con
feſſion of Faith of all Ranks in *Scotland*, and truly
our national Covenants were a more ſolemn avouch
ing of the Truth, and particularly of thoſe that
were then moſt oppoſed, and a more ſolemn en
gaging againſt Sin and Errors that the Church was
then moſt in Danger of All Confeſſions of Faith
are now cried down by ſome in this Age, as an
Impoſition upon the Conſciences of Men, and as
an Incroachment upon our Chriſtian Liberty; but
that

that Liberty which those Men would have, it is a Liberty to vent and propagate Error and Heresy, to the Dishonour of God, and the Ruining of the Souls of others. Our national Covenants are undervalued and despised by others, not only by a Set of Men who have, ever since the Reformation, declared their Enmity at the Work of God in this Land, I mean the Popish and Prelatick Party, but there are some lately sprung up amongst us, who, pretending to more Strictness, cry down all national Covenanting, as not warranted under the New Testament Dispensation, but, as national Covenanting was no Part of *the Law of Commandments contained in Ordinances,* (which is now indeed abrogated by the Coming of Christ in the Flesh) so it has been a blessed Mean in the Hand of the Lord, for preserving and transmitting to us the Doctrine, Worship, Government, and Discipline of the Lord's House, pure and free from antichristian Errors and Superstition. 2*dly.* The Word of the Church's Testimony is given by her Office-Bearers, particularly her Ministers in the preaching of the Word. The faithful Ministers of the Church do, in their publick Preachings, bear Testimony unto Truth, and against the Errors and Evils of their Day and Time This Church has been blessed with a great Cloud of such Witnesses, who have preached down every Thing contrary unto the covenanted Doctrine, Worship, and Government of Christ's House in this Land and they have overcome by *the Word of their Testimony:* And if we are enabled to use this Mean honestly and faithfully, we have Ground to hope we shall overcome the rising and prevailing Evils of our Day and Time. 3*dly* The Word of the Church's Testimony is given, by owning and confessing the Truths in Face of the

greatest

greateſt Danger. Chriſt has had, in all Ages, his Witneſſes, who have *not loved their Lives unto Death*,
who have *reſiſted unto Blood, ſtriving againſt Sin*,
and his ſpiritual Seed have been rather increaſed
than diminiſhed by all the ſad Sufferings they have
been expoſed unto, as it was with *Iſrael* in *Egypt*,
ſo it has been with them in all Ages, *the more they
were afflicted the more they grew*. The Church's
ſuffering Times have been her moſt thriving Times.
The Church of *Scotland* has likeways given her
Teſtimony unto the Truths of Chriſt, by ſore and
ſharp Sufferings, before the Reformation was eſtabliſhed, the Word of her Teſtimony was given
and ſealed by the Blood of ſeveral againſt the Ido
latry and Tyranny of the Church of *Rome*, and,
ſince the Reformation, the Word of her Teſti
mony has been ſtated for the Royal Power and
Authority of the Lord Jeſus in his own Houſe,
and for that Government which he hath appointed in it : Theſe two Points are a notable
Branch of the covenanted Teſtimony of the Church
of *Scotland*, to which a great Number have born
Witneſs *even unto Death*, particularly in the late
perſecuting Times, and *they overcame by the Blood of
the Lamb, and the Word of their Teſtimony*

5thly Chriſt's ſpiritual Seed have been preſerved
by remarkable Appearances of the Lord amongſt
them To ſpeak of the great Appearances of God
in Behalf of his Church is a large Subject I ſhall
confine myſelf to few particular Heads, and give
ſome particular Inſtances under each of them In
the

Firſt Place, The Lord has appeared in his Church
by raiſing up eminent Inſtruments, fitted and qualifi-
ed for diſcharging the Duties they were called to,
and encountring the Difficulties that were in their
Way

Way · Thus *Moses* and *Aaron* were raised up to be the Instruments of the Church's Deliverance from the Oppression and Bondage they were under in *Egypt*, likeways, when the Church and People of God were in Captivity in *Babylon*, the Lord stirred up the Spirit of *Cyrus* King of *Persia* to give Liberty to the captive *Jews* to return, and raised up *Zerubbabel* and others to bring them back from *Babylon*, *Ezek* 1 5. and 11 2. Also the Apostles were indued with *Power from on high* for preaching the Gospel, and laying the Foundation of the New Testament. In like Manner, when the Lord was about to bring his Church and People of *Scotland* out of antichristian Bondage and Darkness, he raised up his *Zerubbabels*, who laid the Foundation of a glorious Work of Reformation The first three that I have already named were eminently fitted for the Duties and Difficulties of their Day; the Lord also stirred up the Spirits of some of the first Rank in the Land to put to their Hands to his own Work, and as in that Period, so in after Periods since that Time, he has raised up Instruments fitted for the Dangers and Difficulties in which the Church has been.

2*dly* The Lord has appeared amongst his Church and People, by pouring down his Spirit in a remarkable Way and Manner. The Spirit of the Lord was promised to the Children of *Israel* and *Judah*, at their Return from the *Babylonish* Captivity, *Jer* l. 4, 5 *The Children of* Israel *shall come, they and the Children of* Judah *together, going and weeping, —— saying, Come, and let us join our selves to the Lord in a perpetual Covenant that shall not be forgotten.* Likeways, on the Day of Pentecoste, *Acts* 11 the Holy Ghost was poured down in an extraordinary Manner, and 3000 were born at once

in

in *Zion*, by such remarkable Showers of the Spirit a spiritual Seed have been brought forth, and preserved to the Lord Jesus I shall upon this Head confine myself to a few particular Instances of this Kind in the Church of *Scotland*

1*st.* At the Beginning of the Reformation, the Word of the Gospel had such wonderful Success, that, in a short Time the whole Body of the Nation made a professed Subjection unto the Lord Jesus Christ. In 1560. the first Confession of Faith was approven in Parliament, and the Pope's Authority in *Scotland* was abolished when a very few Years before that antichristian Darkness was over the whole Land. Such marvellous Success had the Word of the Gospel, that it might be said a whole Nation was born at once. That Prophecy was remarkably accomplished in *Scotland*, Isa. lxvi 8 *Who hath heard such a Thing ? who hath seen such Things ? Shall the Earth be made to bring forth in one Day ? or shall a Nation be born at once ? For as soon as Zion travailed she brought forth her Children* This great Work was wrought by a more than ordinary Concurrence of the Spirit of God with the Word.

A *second* Instance is, that remarkable Event * in the Year 1596 The General Assembly of this Church, being conveened at *Edinburgh*, did meet by themselves the 30th of *March*, at nine of the Clock, in the little Church of *Edinburgh*, for solemn Humiliation on Account of their own Sins and the Sins of the Land ; and there being assembled together about 400 Ministers, Elders, and select Christians, there was an extraordinary Down pouring of the Spirit upon them, and such deep Humiliation and Mourning amongst

* *Fulfilling of the Scripture, Part III. Page* 164

mongst them, as that the Place where they were met together might be called a *Bochim;* and before they parted every one of them lifted up their Hands to the Lord, and sware to pursue personal and national Reformation , the like of that Day had not been seen in *Scotland* since the Reformation This same Practice was, by Order of the Assembly, followed in all the Synods of this Church, and afterwards in Presbyteries, and in the several particular Congregations through the Land. This solemn Renovation of Covenant-Engagements unto the Lord, was the Fruit of a Shower of the Spirit of God that did at that Time go through the whole Land.

† A *third* remarkable Instance is in the Year 1625. when the Church was under a dark Cloud, and the Persecution very hot from the Prelatick Party , about that Time there was an extraordinary Out letting of the Spirit of God, a great Spring-Tide of the Gospel, and that for some Years Continuance, in the West of *Scotland,* in so much that the Power of Godliness did advance from one Place to another, and a marvellous Lustre was to be seen on those Parts of the Country. There is one remarkable Appearance of God under this Period, that deserves particularly to be remembred, namely, that solemn Communion at the *Kirk of Shots, June* 20 1630. where there was a great Down-pouring of the Spirit accompanying the Ordinances, especially the *Monday's* Sermon, that it was reckoned near five hundred had a discernible Change wrought on them at that Time , many of whom could date their Conversion, and others some remarkable Confirmation from that Day. At this

D   Time

† *Fulfilling of the Scripture, Part I. Page* 416.

Time a numerous Seed were brought forth to the Lord Jesus Christ, and a People prepared for the Coming of the Lord, in that glorious Work which he wrought *anno* 1638. which leads me to a

Fourth Inftance ; and it is that great Down-pouring of the Spirit upon all Ranks of Perfons in the faid Year 1638. when the whole Land did fhake off the Yoke of Prelacy, and did return by folemn national Covenanting unto the Lord. Famous Mr. *Livingftoun* tells us, in his Life written by himfelf, that he has feen a Thoufand lifting up their Hands to the Lord at once, and not a dry Face amongft them : He obferves likeways, that the whole Land went in moft willingly to the Oath of God , furely there was no Force, no Compulfion here : Yea, a General Affembly of the Church of *Scotland* teftifies with what Joy the Land entred into the Oath of God. In the Act of Affembly 1648. approving the Solemn League and Covenant, we find thefe remarkable Words, ' And having taken the fame, (*viz.*
' the Solemn League and Covenant) as a Matter
' of fo publick Concern doth require, into their
' graveft Confideration, did with all their Hearts,
' and with the Beginnings of the Feelings of that
' Joy which they did find in fo great Meafure up-
' on the Renovation of the National Covenant of
' this Kirk and Kingdom, all with one Voice ap-
' prove and embrace the fame. ' The Solemn League and Covenant was alfo fworn with much Cheerfulnefs and Joy in *Scotland* and *England*, *anno* 1643. and renewed again in *Scotland*, with a folemn Acknowledgment of Sin and Engagement to Duty, *anno* 1648. In thefe covenanting Times there was plentiful Effufion of the Spirit of God upon all Ranks, and many were turned unto the Lord, though, no doubt, there were not a few that were

only

only brought under some common Influences and Impressions, as their after Apostasy and Defection from the Covenant and the Oath of God made too evident to the World, yet saving Knowledge and the Things of God, and Acquaintance with the Power of Godliness, did increase, the sealing Comforts of the Spirit of God were bestowed upon many, some of whom did afterwards *resist unto Blood, striving against Sin.* I shall only add upon this Head, whatever Contempt some Men may cast upon national Covenanting, and our solemn national Covenants, yet *Scotland*'s covenanting Days were amongst her best Days, for the Life and Power of Religion and Godliness, and national Covenanting, have been signally owned and countenanced of the Lord. *5thly* I may add likeways, that very discernible Influences of the Spirit did accompany a preached Gospel in the late persecuting Times. All the Violence and Rage of wicked Persecutors could not hinder Multitudes from resorting unto a preached Gospel in the Fields and in Deserts, and the Lord accompanied his own Word with such Light, Life and Power, that many were brought in to the Lord Jesus, and others were confirmed and established, and so were fitted and prepared to suffer, for the Truths of Christ, unto Imprisonment and Banishment, yea, even unto Death itself. The most Part of that Generation are now gone off the Stage, but some of you are yet alive, and hearing me, who felt the warm Influences of Heaven under a preached Gospel at that Time.

3dly Christ's spiritual Seed have been preserved by remarkable Deliverances given them, when they have been in the greatest Danger, the Lord has often appeared gloriously, when Men have appointed them to Ruin and Destruction, and all outward

Ap-

Appearance of Help and Relief has failed them; as in *Esther's* Days, when the whole Church was in Danger of Destruction, what a wonderful and unexpected Deliverance did the Lord give them, and truly the Church of *Scotland* has Reason to say, *Had not the Lord been on our Side, when Men rose up against us, they had swallowed us up quick, when their Wrath was kindled against us* The remarkable Deliverances the Lord has given to his Church in this Land, in the Day of our Strait and Danger, are so many, that I can scarce venture to descend into Particulars. I shall only mention two memorable Eighty-eighths, in which the Lord appeared wonderfully for his Church in these Lands The first is, that great Appearance of God in the Year 1588. in breaking the *Spanish* Armada, when a Design was formed for ruining the Protestant Interest, both in these Lands and also abroad. Again, a Century of Years after this, when the very same Danger threatned the whole Protestant Interest, especially in these Lands, how wonderfully did the Lord appear in that glorious Revolution in the Year 1688 ? His own Right-Hand did then work Salvation for us And as at that Time the Lord did give us a very remarkable Deliverance, when we were upon the Brink of Ruin so we have been preserved ever since, by a continued Series and Train of remarkable Providences These are some of the special Means by which Christ's Seed have endured in all Ages and Generations.

To proceed now to the *fifth* Thing that I proposed upon this Doctrine, and that is,

To lay before you some Things for confirming you in the Faith of this important Truth, That Christ's Seed shall endure for ever. Let us here take a View of some of the Attempts of Satan, the

the grand Adversary of the Church and People of God, to root out Christ's spiritual Seed , and let us also too consider how, notwithstanding of all these, the Church has been still preserved A few Observations to this Purpose may be of Use to strengthen our Faith in this great Truth.

Before I proceed unto Particulars, you may observe, That in all Ages Satan has still employed all his Malice, Power and Policy, against Christ's Seed, to root them out   There is an Intimation of this in the very first Revelation of the Gospel, Gen iii 15. *I will put Enmity between thee and the Woman, and between thy Seed and her Seed*   This Enmity between the Serpent and the Seed of the Woman, is not only between the Serpent and Christ personal, but between the Serpent and his Seed, that is, Satan and the wicked and ungodly World on the one Hand, and the Seed of the Woman, that is Christ mystical, Head and Members, the Lord Jesus Christ and all true Believers in him, on the other Hand.   The War was first proclaimed in Paradise by the Lord himself, and it continues to this very Day without any Cessation of Arms, and will do so to the End of the World Many Times Satan has thrust sore at Christ's Seed, but he hath never prevailed over them, and never shall Sometimes, indeed, the Church has been brought very low, yea, so low, that, to outward Appearance, she has been as it were consumed, but still she has risen more glorious out of her own Ashes *The Archers have thrust sore at her, but her Bow hath abode in Strength.* Her Motto has always been, *Persecuted, but not forsaken, Cast down, but not overcome.* The Bush burning, and not consumed, which *Moses* saw and wondred at, was a lively Emblem of the Preservation of Christ's spi-

ritual

ritual Seed, in all Ages, from the Fury and Rage of Satan and his Seed. The Attempts of Satan to deſtroy the Church are compared to a Flood, which that old Serpent caſts out of his Mouth after the Woman, that he may cauſe her to be carried away by it, *Rev* xii. 15. I ſhall name a threefold Flood that the old Serpent hath been caſting out of his Mouth againſt Chriſt's ſpiritual Seed, and ſhew you that, notwithſtanding of theſe, they have been ſtill preſerved.

Firſt, A Flood of Profanity, 2*dly,* A Flood of Perſecution, 3*dly* A Flood of Error · By theſe dangerous Floods the Serpent hath ſtill endeavoured to carry away the Woman and her Seed, yet they have lived under them, and ſhall endure for ever.

Firſt, The old Serpent caſts a Flood of Profanity out of his Mouth againſt Chriſt's ſpiritual Seed · Such a Flood did in *Noah's* Days overflow the whole Earth, and ſwelled to ſuch a Height, that God was provōked to ſweep the Inhabitants of the Earth away with a Deluge of Waters, *Gen* vi. 5, 6, 7. And here you may notice, 1*ſt.* That, under this Inundation of Wickedneſs, Chriſt's ſpiritual Seed were brought very low, ſo low that they were confined in one Family, wherein there were no more than eight Perſons, and neither were all theſe eight Perſons of that Number, for there was a curſed *Ham* amongſt them You may obſerve, 2*dly.* That as the Lord preſerved this ſmall Remnant from the wicked Contagion of that ſinful Time, ſo he provided for their Safety againſt the Deluge of Water that came upon the whole Earth, *Heb.* xi. 7. Noah, *being warned of God, prepared an Ark to the ſaving of his Houſe* The Serpent has been caſting out this Flood of Profanity

nity in all Ages againſt the Church ; and we are warned, that, in the laſt Days eſpecially, the Church ſhall be in great Hazard and Danger from it, and therefore thoſe Days of abounding Wickedneſs and Profanity are called *perillous Times*, 2 Tim. iii. 1, 2, 3, 4. And truly he that runs may read it, that there is an univerſal Looſeneſs in Practice, even in the reformed Churches, at this Day ; the common Impreſſions of God are like to wear off the Spirits of Men, it may be ſaid all Fleſh have corrupted their Way , this is for a Lamentation : But yet Chriſt's ſpiritual Seed have been preſerved under this overflowing Flood formerly, and we have Ground to believe they ſhall yet be preſerved.

2dly. Satan caſts out a Flood of Perſecution againſt Chriſt's ſpiritual Seed , he ſtirs up his Inſtruments, the Wicked and Ungodly, to perſecute them. By Perſecution I underſtand all the Violence done by a wicked World unto the People of God, in their Names, Perſons, or Eſtates, by Reproaches, ſpoiling of Goods, Impriſonments, cruel Tortures, and the like , as alſo by killing and ſlaying of them, as not worthy to live in the World, when yet the World is not worthy of them, *Heb* xi. 38. When the Church was in *A-dam's* Family, *Cain* did perſecute his Brother *Abel* to Death · And the Apoſtle teſtifies what Sufferings the Witneſſes for Chriſt did with Patience and Faith undergo, *Heb.* xi 36, 27, 38. I ſhall here mention three remarkable ſuffering Periods of the Church under the Old Teſtament, to which there are three grand ſuffering Periods under the New compared. The firſt remarkable Period of the Church's Sufferings under the Old Teſtament, was that in *Egypt*, when they ſighed by reaſon of

their

their heavy Bondage, and that cruel Edict was published commanding all the male Children to be cast into the River, *Exod.* i. 22. This threatned Ruin and Diftruction to the whole Church and People of God A fecond great Period of the Sufferings of the Church under the Old Teftament, was that from the *Chaldeans* by the *Babylonifh* Captivity, on Occafion of which, it is probable, the 79th *Pfalm* was penned by *Jeremiah*, or fome other Prophet, where the Defolation of *Jerufalem*, and the Sufferings they were brought under, are bewailed after a moft pathetick Manner, particularly in the firft four Verfes. A third memorable fuffering Period of the Old Teftament Church, was that from *Gog* and *Magog*, prophefied by *Ezekiel* in his 38th Chapter It is thought, that by that Prophefy is intended the fore Perfecution which the Church was brought under from *Antiochus Epiphanes* To thefe fuffering Periods of the Church under the Old Teftament, there are three fuffering Periods of the Church under the New Teftament compared.

The firft great fuffering Period of the Chriftian Church, was that Perfecution from *Rome*-heathen, called *fpiritual Egypt*, Rev. xi 8. This began in the Apoftles Days, and did continue, though with various Intermiffions, till the Beginning of the fourth Century It is well known what Cruelties the Chriftians fuffered during this Period, from their heathen Perfecutors, and that many Times, throughout the *Roman* Empire, the Blood of the Chriftians was fhed without Mercy. The fecond grand fuffering Period of the New Teftament Church, is that from *Rome*-antichriftian, called *Babylon the Great*, Rev. xvii 5 It is long fince the Church's Sufferings began from this Adverfary, and the Hiftories of preceeding Ages bear Witnefs how much

she

she h. suffered from this Enemy. There is scarce on ..tion, Province, or City, under the Jurisdiction of *Rome*-antichristian, where the Blood of the Witnesses for Jesus has not been shed Since our Reformation from Popery the old antichristian persecuting Spirit did exert itself even in this Land, in two remarkable Periods, the one before the notable Year 1638. and the other before the memorable Year 1688 and under both these suffering Times the Testimony of the Witnesses for Christ in our Land was stated for the Royal Power and Authority of the Lord Jesus in and over his own House, and that Worship and Government that he himself hath instituted in the same, which all Ranks of Persons in the Land had, by most solemn Covenant Engagements unto the most high God, bound both themselves and Generations to come stedfastly to cleave unto I shall only observe farther on this Head that though the Lord has begun to appear against Antichrist, yet the Storm is not wholly over We in this Land do now enjoy a Calm, but our Brethren abroad are groaning under the Tyranny of this Enemy, and who knows, but, ere the Vial is poured out upon the Seat of the Beast, the Cup may pass over again to us? The third suffering Period of the New Testament Church is that spoke of, *Rev* xx. 8. But this is yet wholly in Prophecy, and therefore we can speak nothing about it. I shall now offer a few Things concerning the Preservation of Christ's spiritual Seed under those Storms of Persecution that have already gone over the Church for confirming you in the Faith of this Truth, that *his Seed shall endure for ever*.

First, Sealing Times have gone before persecuting Times. When *Jacob* is going down with his Family

mily

mily into *Egypt*, the Lord appears to him, and
says, *Fear not to go down into* Egypt, *I will go
down with thee*, Gen. xlvi. 3, 4. This Promise, no
doubt, was supporting to the Faith of the Church
and People of God under the sore Trials that after-
ward they met with in *Egypt*. That great Effusion
of the Spirit at Pentecoste was immediately before
the first Persecution raised against the infant Chri
stian Church at *Jerusalem*, of which you read *Acts*
viii. 1 The Angels of the four Winds are re
strained from hurting *the Earth, the Sea, or the Trees,
till the Servants of God are sealed in their Foreheads,
Rev* vii. 1, 4. There have been solemn sealing Times
in *Scotland* before suffering Times That remarkable Effusion of the Spirit 1596. which we have
already mentioned, went before the first Storm of
Persecution that did blow upon this Church after
the Reformation Also, before the last suffering
Period, the Spirit of the Lord did accompany Go-
spel-Ordinances with discernible Power and Success, to the Conversion and Confirmation of many.
Some of the Christians who were Witnesses to, and
had the Experience of this sealing Work of God,
have lived to our own Times, by this Means a
People were prepared for entring into the Furnace.

2*dly*. We may observe, that Christ's spiritual
Seed have been preserved in suffering Times in
regard Persecution has been the Occasion of the
spreading of the Gospel. The first Persecution
raised against the Church at *Jerusalem* scattered a
broad the Disciples, who *went every where preaching the Word*, Acts viii 4 The Persecution raised
by *Domitian* against the Christian Church brought
the Gospel to the remote Parts of this Island.

3*dly*.

3dly. The Church of Christ has sometimes been brought very low under Persecution ; but yet, in the darkest Times that have gone over her, the Lord never wanted his Witnesses. Under *Achab's* persecuting Reign, *Elijah* complains, 1 *Kings* xix. 14 *I, even I only, am left*, yet *Ver*. 18 *I have left me seven thousand in* Israel, *which have not bowed unto* Baal. Under the cruel Persecutions raised against the Church from *Rome* heathen, the Lord never wanted his Witnesses. Likeways the Lord had still his Witnesses under all the Storms of Persecution from *Rome*-antichristian, in the very darkest Times of Popery there were some found to bear Witness for Truth, and in this Land the Lord hath kept up Witnesses for his Cause and Work, both before and since our Reformation from Popery, notwithstanding all the Severities used by Persecutors.

4thly. We may remark, that the Sufferings of the People of God have been Means blessed for the Conversion of some, and the Confirmation of others. It is an old and true Saying, The Blood of the Martyrs is the Seed of the Church, their Carriage and Behaviour at Stakes, and on Scaffolds, has struck Beholders with a Conviction that the Lord was in them, and with them of a Truth, many particular Instances of this Nature might be given, if it were needful

Finally, All the Church's Persecutions have issued in her farther Enlargement, the more they were oppressed, the more they grew. This hath been verified in all Ages, and particularly in the Church of *Scotland*. It deserves to be remembred, that, notwithstanding of near 28 Years Persecution, by cruel Harrassings, Confiscation of Goods, Imprisonment, Banishment, and Sufferings unto Death, which

which a great Number of all Ranks of Perſons in this
Land were expoſed unto ; yet, at the late glorious
Revolution, there was ſuch a goodly Company in
all Corners of the Land, to appear for and to own
that Cauſe which had been reproached, deſpiſed
and perſecuted, that the Church of *Scotland* might
with Admiration ſay, *Who hath begotten me theſe,
ſeeing I have loſt my Children, and am deſolate, a Captive, and removing to and fro ? And who hath brought
up theſe ? Behold, I was left alone , theſe, where had
they been ?* Iſa xlix. 21.

3*dly.* Satan caſts out of his Mouth a Flood of
Error againſt Chriſt's ſpiritual Seed, and truly
they have been often in very great Danger from
this Flood ; Chriſt warns his Diſciples concerning
it, *Matth.* xxiv 24, 25. *For there ſhall ariſe
falſe Chriſts, and ſhall ſhew great Signs and Wonders,
in ſo much, if it was poſſible, they ſhall deceive the very
Elect. Behold, I have told you before* Alſo his
Apoſtles *Paul* and *Peter* do warn the Churches of
it, 1 *Cor* xi 19 *For there muſt alſo be Hereſies a-
mong you, that they which are approved may be made
manifeſt,* 1 *Tim* iv. 1. *Now the Spirit ſpeaketh
expreſly, that in the latter Times ſome ſhall depart
from the Faith, giving heed to ſeducing Spirits, and
Doctrines of Devils,* 2 *Pet* ii. 1 *There ſhall be
falſe Teachers among you, who privily ſhall bring in
damnable Hereſies, denying the Lord that bought them,*
Alſo the Apoſtle *John,* 1 *Epiſt* iv. 1. *Believe not
every Spirit, but try the Spirits, becauſe many falſe
Prophets are gone out into the World* Satan did begin to caſt out this Flood very early againſt the
Chriſtian Church · There were ſome, even in the
Apoſtles Days, who endeavoured to obſcure or
deny the Doctrine of Juſtification by the free
Grace of God, through the imputed Righteouſneſs
of

of the Lord Jesus, as is evident from the Epistles to the *Romans* and *Galatians* There were others also, who, abusing the Doctrine of Grace, preached up a licentious Liberty. as is evident from the Epistle of *James*. It is remarkable that the Seed of Error has sprung up most in the Day of the Church's outward Calm and Peace, when the Church was delivered from *Pagan* Persecution, and Peace and Liberty were granted her by *Constantine* the Great, she was immediately infested with a Multitude of Errors and Heresies. She enjoyed a short Calm And what is the first Storm that blows upon her? Lo the *Arian* Heresy breaks forth like an impetuous Torrent, and Corruption, both in Doctrine and Practice, did increase from Time to Time, till *Antichrist* that Man of Sin was fully revealed With respect to the Church of Christ in this Land, the State of the Controversy since the Reformation has chiefly been, as we have before observed, about the Government and Worship of Christ's House, until these Days of Degeneracy in which we live, wherein Reason is exalted above divine Revelation, the supreme Deity of the Son of God is impugned, and Man's natural Power and Abilities, with respect to Things spiritual, are extolled, with many other new and dangerous Doctrines, which the old Serpent is this Day casting out of his Mouth as a Flood amongst us.

I shall here offer you a few Remarks concerning this Flood, and the Preservation of Christ's spiritual Seed under the same

First, The Church of Christ has many Times been brought very low by the rising and spreading of Error, this is a Flood that carries away many, and those not of the lowest Size, but such s seem to be tall Cedars in the Church, Men of

the

the greateſt natural Abilities and Endowments, the unſanctified Gifts of learned Men have done moſt Miſchief unto the Church of Chriſt; the Church was once brought ſo low by the Arian Hereſy, that it was ſaid, The whole World is become Arian

2dly In every Period of the Church, the Lord has ſtill kept up his Witneſſes for Truth againſt prevailing Error When the Arian Hereſy did moſt prevail, he raiſed up an Athanaſius to bear Teſtimony againſt it Whatever Error or Hereſies do ariſe, ſome Inſtruments are fitted by the Lord for diſcovering the Dangers of them, and for contending for the Faith once delivered to the Saints

3dly Truth hath always ſhined forth more brightly from under the Vails of Error that Men have drawn over it. Truth is like the Sun, who ſhines moſt brightly when he comes from under the darkeſt Clouds All Attempts that have been made againſt divine Truth, have iſſued in its brighter Manifeſtation, and we have Ground to believe that the Clouds, that ſome are endeavouring at this Day to draw over the Perſon of the glorious Son of God, or any other of the precious Truths of the Goſpel, ſhall be diſſipated and ſcattered by their Luſtre and Glory I proceed to the fifth general Head, to ſhew you why it is that Chriſt's ſpiritual Seed ſhall endure for ever. I anſwer,

Fiſt, This was promiſed to him in the Council of Peace before the Foundations of the Earth were laid In this glorious Tranſaction, all the Elect were given by the Father unto the Son, to be redeemed and ſaved by him, he accepted of the Gift, yea, rejoiced in the Gift and Grant that was made him of a Company of miſerable periſhing Sinners in Adam's Family, to do Service to him up

on

on the Earth. *For his Delights were with the Sons of Men, and his Rejoicing in the habitable Parts of the Earth, before the Mountains were settled, or the Hills brought forth,* Prov. viii 25, 31. &c. The Promise is made to him, that, in every Age and Period of Time, he shall have some of them upon this Earth to be the Objects of this Delight and Joy: *He shall see his Seed,* Isa liii 10. Yea, this Promise is confirmed by the Word of the Oath, *Psalm* lxxxix 35, 36. *Once have I sworn by my Holiness, I will not lie unto* David*, his Seed shall endure for ever.* Also, Verses 3, 4. *I have sworn unto* David *my Servant, thy Seed will I establish for ever.* These are the two immutable Things in which it is impossible for God to lie, therefore his spiritual Seed must endure for ever.

2*dly* This is due unto him as the Reward of his bloody Sufferings In his State of Humiliation he travailed to bring forth a Seed, *Isa* liii. 10. *It pleased the Lord to bruise him, he hath put him to Grief When thou shalt make his Soul an Offering for Sin, he shall see his Seed, and the Pleasure of the Lord shall prosper in his Hand.*

3*dly*. Christ's Seed must endure for ever, that God may have Witnesses for himself in the World. All Christ's spiritual Seed are his Witnesses· The Ministers of Christ are indeed in a peculiar and special Manner his Witnesses, but they are not his only Witnesses. This Honour have all his Saints in some Measure: Therefore, saith he of *Israel,* whom he hath redeemed and called, *Ye are my Witnesses, saith the Lord,* Isa xliii 10. They are Witnesses to his glorious Being and Perfections against the Atheism of the World, *Isa* xliv. 8 *Ye are even my Witnesses Is there a God besides me? Yea, there is no God, I know not any* They are

Witnesses

Witnesses unto the Truth and Reality of the Salvation he hath wrought, against the Unbelief of of the rest of the World, *Isa* xliii. 11, 12, 13. *I, even I am the Lord, and beside me there is no Saviour. I have declared, and have saved. Therefore ye are my Witnesses, saith the Lord.* They are Witnesses unto the Glory and Excellency of this Salvation, against the Contempt the unbelieving World casts upon it To them that believe not, Christ is *a Stone of Stumbling, and a Rock of Offence, but unto such as believe he is precious,* 1 Pet ii 7, 8, 9 They are Witnesses for the Holiness of God, and the Purity and Equity of his Law, against the Unholiness, Wickedness and Profanity of the World Therefore Christ saith to to his Disciples. *Let your Light so shine before Men, that they may see your good Works, and glorify your Father which is in Heaven,* Matth v 6 There was never an Age wherein Christ wanted his Witnesses. When a Deluge of Profanity had overspread the whole World, *Noah,* a Preacher of Righteousness, bears Witness for God against them. Satan never broached an Error under the most subtle Disguise, but the Lord did also raise up some to bear Witness against it · For this End Christ's spiritual Seed must endure for ever, that there may be standing and living Witnesses for the Holiness of God, and for his Truths upon the Earth

4*thly* Christ's spiritual Seed shall endure for ever, because the Spirit is given without Measure unto their Head the Lord Jesus Christ, *the Spirit of the Lord doth rest upon him,* Isa xi 2. He is anointed with the Spirit above his Fellows, and it is for their Sakes that he is anointed, *John* xvii. 19. *For their Sake I sanctify myself. He received Gifts for Men, even for such as did rebel,* Psalm lxviii.

18.

18. The Spirit and all his Grace was given unto him, that he might beget a Seed unto himself, and cherish and nourish them till they should be per-fected in Glory.   The Spirit of the Lord doth rest upon the Head, and is communicated from him unto all his Members, according to that Promise, *Isa.* lix 21. *My Words that are in thy Mouth, and my Spirit which I have put within thee, shall not depart out of thy Mouth, nor out of the Mouth of thy Seed, nor out of the Mouth of thy Seed's Seed, saith the Lord, from henceforth and for ever.*   As the Lord Jesus lives in Heaven, so he must live on Earth by his Spirit in his Members, therefore his Seed shall endure for ever.

5*thly.* Christ's spiritual Seed endure for ever, be-cause he hath obtained Victory over the old Ser-pent ; the Lamb has overcome him already. *Michael,* the Angel of the Covenant, hath prevailed over the Dragon and his Angels.   In the first Pro-clamation of War that was made against the Serpent and his Seed, the Victory was insured to the Seed of the Woman, *Gen.* iii. 15. *He shall bruise thy Head.*   This Declaration of War, and the Promise of Victory made to the Seed of the Woman, was no doubt a surprising Disappointment to the malici-ous Designs and Expectations of the old Serpent : This Promise had its Accomplishment when our Lord Jesus suffered unto Death , then he triumphed over Principalities and Powers, and made a Shew of them openly upon his Cross; Kings of great Armies were foiled, even spiritual Wickedness in high Places ; the Head of *Leviathan* was broke in Pieces by the glorious Head of the Church ; and by reason of his Victory and Conquest over the Powers of Darkness, the Gates of Hell shall never prevail against his Church.   This same Promise is

F   also

alſo accompliſhed every Day, in the Preſervation of the Children of God in the Midſt of their Enemies ; and it will have its final Accompliſhment, when *Satan* is for ever bruiſed under the Feet of Chriſt's myſtical Head and Members, *Rom.* XVI. 20. *The God of Peace ſhall ſhortly bruiſe Satan under your Feet.* The exalted Head of the Church ſhall reign *till all his Enemies are made his Footſtool.*

6thly Chriſt's Seed ſhall endure for ever, that the Lord may be ſeen and glorified in this great Work of their Preſervation. In our Text it is ſaid, *His Seed will I make to endure for ever* I WILL MAKE, whatever Oppoſition may be made to this Work of mine, whatever Adverſaries they may have O ! what of God is to be ſeen in their Preſervation, conſidering the Power and Multitude of their Enemies ? The old Serpent, with all his Power, Malice and Cunning, is againſt them , the World alſo hateth them , they are like *the Lily among Thorns,* Song II. 2. If you inquire what of God is to be ſeen in their Preſervation, I anſwer,

Firſt, The Sovereignty of God, even his abſolute Dominion over the Works of his own Hands, *He doth in the Armies of Heaven, and among the Inhabitants of the Earth,* whatſoever ſeemeth good in his Sight, and *he reproveth Kings for* the Sake of his People, *Pſalm* cv 15 yea, for their Sakes he will take their Crowns from off their Heads, and ſpoil them of all their Glory· He will overturn Empires and Kingdoms for them , The *Babyloniſh* Empire was overturned for their Cruelty againſt the Church and People of God, and the *Perſian* Empire is raiſed up that *Cyrus* might be the Inſtrument of the Church s Deliverance, *Iſa* xlv. 1, 4 *Thus ſaith the Lord to his Anointed, to Cyrus, whoſe*

Right

Right-Hand I have holden, to subdue Nations before him For Jacob *my Servant's Sake, and* Israel *mine Elect, I have even called thee by thy Name · I have named thee, though thou hast not known me.*

2dly The Power of God is manifested in this great Work , he displays the Glory of his Power in setting Limits to the Fury and Rage of Devils and Men against the Church, *Psalm* xlviii 11. His Power is seen in preserving his People in the Furnace, and delivering them out of it , also in reviving them when they are like the dead and dry Bones scattered about the Grave's Mouth.

3dly. The Wisdom of God is also to be seen in the Preservation of Christ's spiritual Seed. Infinite Wisdom has baffled all those Projects that have been set on Foot, by Satan and his Instruments, for the Ruin of the Church, and turned them about for her farther Growth and Enlargement. The Wisdom of God hath brought Light out of the darkest Clouds, and Order out of the greatest Confusion. When the Witnesses for Christ are slain, and the Inhabitants of the Earth are rejoicing, and making merry over their Destruction, lo *the Spirit of Life from God enters into them, and they ascend up into Heaven in a Cloud, and their Enemies behold them,* Rev xi 12,

Finally, His Faithfulness is glorified in their Preservation , his Faithfulness in accomplishing his Word of Promise, made first unto their Head the Lord Jesus *The Lord hath sworn by his Holiness, he will not lie unto David ·* Therefore the lxxxix Psalm is ushered in with a Song of the Faithfulness of God, in the first Verse, *With my Mouth will I make known thy Faithfulness to all Generations.* The Church and People of God have had Reason in all Ages

to

to fay with the Prophet, *Great is thy Faithfulnefs,* Lam. iii. 23.

I proceed now to draw fome Inferences from this Subject.

Infer. 1*ft.* If it be fo, that Chrift's fpiritual Seed fhall endure for ever, hence we may fee, that all Attempts whatfoever to root them out fhall prove ineffectual; *The Gates of Hell fhall never prevail against the Church,* *Matth.* xvi 18. Yea, Jerufalem *fhall prove a burdenfom Stone for all People All that burden themfelves with it fhall be cut in Pieces, though all People of the World be gathered together against it,* Zech. xii 3. All the Attempts of the Enemies of the Church and People of God, againft them, fhall iffue in their own Ruin and Deftruction.

Secondly, If it be fo, then let us turn afide with *Mofes,* and behold with Wonder *this great Sight, a Bufh burning and not confumed* The Church has ever been in the Midft of Danger, yet behold fhe lives. That Day never dawned, wherein it could be faid, that Chrift wanted fome to do Service to him; and that Day fhall never dawn wherein it can be faid that his Seed fails from the Earth. This is a wonderful Work of God, and, if we ferioufly look into it, it cannot but fill us with Wonder and Admiration. I fhall offer a few Things to evidence that this is a wonderful Work of God.

1*ft.* There has been a continued War, without a Ceffation of Arms, thefe five thoufand Years, and more, againft all Chrift's fpiritual Seed, yet they remain. A few Years War frequently depopulates and wears out the moft flourifhing Countries, but here is a War that has been carried on by powerful Adverfaries, by *fpiritual Wickedneffes in high Places, by Principalities and Powers, the Rulers of*
the

the Darkness of this World, even by the Dragon, that old Serpent, who hath managed this War with all his Power, Policy and Skill, yet notwithstanding Christ's spiritual Seed do endure to this very Day, and *shall endure for ever*

2dly. Consider also the Enmity that is in the World against Christ's spiritual Seed, *They are not of the World,* but chosen out of the World, therefore *the World hateth them,* John xv 19 The World are not only Enemies to them, but Enmity against them, they are Enmity against that Doctrine they believe and receive, against him whose Children they are, and against his blessed Image which they bear This Enmity is not for a Time, or for one Age only, but it descends from Father to Son, from one Race to another It is as natural for Men to hate Christ and his Seed, as it is for them to eat and sleep It is the Observe of one, That the human Race moves as naturally to destroy Christ's spiritual Seed, as it doth to preserve its own Kind, yet, notwithstanding of this Enmity, they endure for ever.

3dly. Consider also what dismal Times have gone over the Church, what dreadful Tempests have beat upon her; the Floods of Profanity, Persecution and Error have many Times swelled to such a Height, as they have threatned to swallow her up, yet she remains; this is a wonderful Work of God.

Thirdly, If it be so, that Christ's spiritual Seed shall endure for ever, hence we may see a Bow in the darkest Clouds that may hang over the Church; whatever threatning Dispensations she may be brought under, yet Christ's Seed shall endure for ever With this the Lord's Remnant may and ought to encourage themselves in dark and trying Times.

I shall

I shall upon this Head mention a few dark Providences we are under at this Day, which threaten Danger to the Church of Christ, notwithstanding of which the Lord's People, who are exercised under a Sight and Sense of these Things, may draw Encouragement from this Promise in our Text, *His Seed will I make to endure for ever*

In the *first* Place, Corruption in Principle prevails throughout all the reformed Churches. Ah! what Degeneracy is there from Reformation-Principles? The Doctrine is corrupted, the Wormwood and Gall of Error is mingled with the Waters of the Sanctuary, the Superstition in Worship is made light of by too many, the Hedge of Government that Christ hath set about his House, is broke down by others. We need go no farther than this Church and Land wherein we live, all the Parts of our covenanted Reformation are at this Day assaulted, the Foundations of Doctrine are undermined. Some are not afraid to call in question the supreme Deity and necessary Existence of the blessed God our Saviour. Superstition in Worship abounds through the Land. The Foundations of Government are overturned by others, who, under fair Shews and Pretences, are reviving the old exploded Sectarian Schemes. All these Things are against Christ's spiritual Seed, yet this Promise in our Text is a Bow in the Cloud, *His Seed will I make to endure for ever.*

2*dly* There is an universal Degeneracy at this Time from the Power and Life of Religion. May it not be said of all the reformed Churches, that the Charge given against the Church of *Ephesus* may be too justly applied to them, *Rev.* ii. 5. *Nevertheless I have somewhat against thee, because thou hast left thy first Love.* A Form and Shadow is

come

 come in inſtead of the Life, Power and Subſtance of Religion and Godlineſs , and amongſt us our primitive Love and Zeal are much decayed, *and the Things that remain are ready to die* , yet, Have we not Ground to believe, that becauſe the Head of the Church lives, ſhe ſhall live alſo ? And altho' the Church ſhould be like the dry Bones ſcattered about the Grave's Mouth, yet ſhe ſhall be revived through the Death and Reſurrection of her living and exalted Head, *Iſa.* xxvi. 19 *Thy dead Men ſhall live, together with my dead Body ſhall they ariſe Awake and ſing, ye that dwell in the Duſt*

3 *lly* Corruption in Practice prevails exceedingly in this degenerate Day. Many have no Profeſſion of Religion at all , many that have a Profeſſion of Religion are a Reproach unto their Profeſſion. How unlike unto the Chriſtian Name are many who are called *Chriſtians* ? Sins of all Kinds abound both againſt the firſt and ſecond Table of the Law. A Converſation like the Goſpel is a rare Thing. Many profeſs to look out for Heaven, and hope to be there, yet they are Strangers to a Converſation in Heaven , the moſt Part *ſeek themſelves*, their own Things, and *few the Things of Chriſt* May we not ſay with the Apoſtle that the Walk of many diſcovers that *they are the Enemies of the Croſs of Chriſt, whoſe End is Deſtruction, whoſe God is their Belly, and whoſe Glory is their Shame, who mind earthly Things* This Degeneracy in Practice is very threatning unto the Churches of Chriſt, but yet he who has preſerved a People unto himſelf, under the overflowing Floods of Profanity and Wickedneſs, will ſtill preſerve a Remnant There is one Thing here I would have you to beware of, when you ſee the Walk of Profeſſors unlike their Profeſſion, blame not the holy Religion that

they

they profess; or, when you see the Conduct and Behaviour of any amongst us, unlike that pure Worship, and beautiful Order and Government that Christ has instituted in his House, blame not the Ordinances of Christ; lay the Blame where it should be laid, even upon the Corruptions of Men

4thly The spiritual Glory is very much departed from all the Churches of Christ at this Day, the Purity of the Ordinances, and the special Presence of the Lord in the Ordinances of his own Institution and Appointment, is the Glory of the Church, Zion's God is her Glory, Isa. lx. 19. And when the Lord withdraws his gracious Presence from his own Ordinances, then it may be said that the spiritual Glory is removed. And may we not say, that there is a great Withdrawing of the divine Presence from his own Ordinances amongst his Church and People? Is it not so with a Witness amongst us? Where is that convincing, converting, or confirming Power that sometimes has accompanied the Ordinances of the Gospel? May we not see *Ichabod* written upon our Assemblies, and written upon all our Solemnities? Is not the Hope of *Israel* like a Stranger, like a way-faring Man in all the Churches? But will he altogether leave his People, and cast off his Inheritance? No, he will not, *Psalm* xciv. 14 Look out therefore for his Coming, and live in the Faith and Expectation of his Return to his Churches, *He will arise, and have Mercy upon Zion, the Time to favour her, yea, the set Time will come,* Psalm cii 13.

5thly. Lukewarmness and Indifferency under all these Evils is very epidemick at this Day. *Laodicea's* Disease prevails, and it is both a dreadful Plague and Sin, *Rev.* iii. 16. *Thou art lukewarm, neither*

neither cold nor hot. O! how unconcerned are many though the Doctrine of the Lord's House be corrupted? How indifferent are others though the Government of his House be trampled upon? It is the Sin of not a few, that they are like *Ephraim, a Cake unturned,* cold upwards towards God and the Things of God, and warm towards the Earth and their own Things. But though we should not be concerned for the Truths of Christ, yet he will not want his Witnesses, he will have a Seed to do Service to him, and to bear Testimony unto his controverted and despised Truths.

4thly If it be so, that Christ's Seed shall endure for ever, O then contribute your Endeavours towards the preserving of a spiritual Seed to the Lord Jesus. The Promise doth not exclude the Use of Means on your Part, but ought to quicken and encourage you to use all proper Means incumbent upon you towards this great End. And, in the *first* Place, let me exhort every one of you to be fervent in Prayer, that the Lord Christ may have a Seed to do Service to him. This is a Mean that every Christian ought to use, this is a Mean, as we have told you, that the Church and People of God have used with good Success when they have been brought low. The low State of the reformed Churches at this Time, and all the Providences of God towards them, call aloud for this Exercise, pray then importunately that the Lord may revive his own Work in the Midst of the Year, that he may return to his Churches, that his Work and Power may appear amongst them, and that his Glory may yet be seen in them, pray that he may vindicate his own Truths from the Reproach and Contempt that the Adversaries are throwing upon them, pray that Peace and Truth

G   may

may be within *Jerusalem's* Walls, and then may we hope that Prosperity shall be within her Palaces. 2*dly.* Let me exhort you all, and every one in your several Stations, to exert yourselves for advancing the Kingdom of real Religion and Godliness. Let such as are Magistrates employ their Power and Authority for this End, and let such as are in a more private Station walk so as they may commend Christ and his Truths unto the Consciences of others, this may be a Mean of Establishment unto the Weak, and also of Conviction and Conversion to such as are Strangers unto Christ. *Finally,* Be careful to transmit the Truths of Christ in their Purity to the rising Generation. We in this Church and Land have pure Principles of Doctrine delivered to us in our excellent Confession of Faith, larger and shorter Catechisms, all drawn from that pure Fountain of Truth, the Holy Scriptures. We have pure Ordinances of Worship, and a Government established in Christ's House according the Pattern shewn on the Mount. Let the rising Generation be informed and instructed in these Principles, yea, let it be told to Posterity, that these three Lands, and *Scotland* many Times, have lifted up their Hands and sworn to the Lord, to preserve and maintain the pure Doctrine, Worship, Government and Discipline of Christ's House, and that no Person or Persons on Earth can dissolve the Obligation of the Oath of God. Truth is a sacred Trust committed to us to be kept for the Sake of Generations to come, it is the most valuable Treasure we can leave behind us unto our Children, it is the indispensible Duty of one Generation to deliver this precious Trust safe and uncorrupted to another, yea, to shew unto them the Praises of the Lord, his Strength, and

and his wonderful Works that he hath done, that the Generations to come may know them, and that the Children yet to be born may arise and declare them to their Children, that they may set their Hope in God and not forget the Works of the Lord, but keep his Commandments, *Psalm* lxxviii. 6, 7. Honest and faithful Endeavours of this Kind are an excellent Mean to preserve a spiritual Seed unto the Lord Jesus. Now, may the City of the Lord flourish, and may her Citizens abound in Number like the Grass upon the Earth. Let his Name endure for ever, and his Memorial to all Generations, and let the whole Earth be filled with his Glory. *Amen* and *Amen*.

F I N I S.

The WATCHMAN'S DUTY and DESIRE,

OR,

The PRAYER of faithful Ministers for the Lord's Beauty
on his Church, and Success
in their Work.

A

SERMON

Preached at the Opening of the Synod,
of *Perth* and *Stirling*, at *Perth*, A-
pril 11. 1727.

By the late REVEREND *and* LEARNED *Mr.* WILLIAM
WILSON *Minister of the Gospel at* PERTH.

Printed from his own original Manuscript.

E D I N B U R G H,

Printed for *David Duncan*, and sold at his House,
opposite to the *Weigh-House*, North-Side of the
Street. MDCCXLVII.

Psalm XC. 17.

And let the Beauty of the Lord be upon us; and establish thou the Work of our Hands upon us, yea, the Work of our Hands establish thou it.

THE Title and Inscription of this *Psalm* bears, that *Moses* the Man of God is the Penman thereof. This Epithet, *Man of God*, is frequently given to the Prophets under the Old Testament, and sometimes to the Ministers of the Church under the New Testament, as 2 *Tim.* iii. 16, 17. *All Scripture is given by Inspiration of God, and is profitable for Doctrine, Reproof*, &c. *that the Man of God may be perfect.* 1 *Tim.* vi. 11. *But thou, O Man of God, flee these Things.* *Moses* was called of God to take the Charge and Oversight of the Church in the Wilderness . God set him apart for this great Trust, and furnished him eminently for it · And the Spirit of God gives him this honourable Testimony, *That as a Servant he was faithful in all God's House*, Heb. iii 5 Here we may observe, that it becomes all that sit in *Moses*'s Chair to imitate him in Faithfulness, and in the whole of their Deportment to shew themselves to be Men of God, as we heard, the last Occasion of this Nature, from the forecited 1 *Tim.* vi. 11.

This *Psalm* is a Prayer of *Moses*, wherein he bewails the Calamities that befel the Church and
People

People of God in the Wilderneſs, and withal comforts them under their preſent Miſeries and Troubles, and alſo ſervently prays that the Tokens of divine Diſpleaſure might be removed, that the Lord
may return with Mercy unto his People, 13 & 14 *Verſes*; and that he may build up his Church, and glorify himſelf in their Sight, and in the Sight of their
Poſterity after them, 16 *Verſe*. *Moſes* was a Man
of Prayer ; he many Times ſtood in the Breach,
and turned away Wrath from this People, and
prayed down Bleſſings upon them. Here again we
may obſerve, that all the Church-Miniſters are not
only called to go for God, and from him, to their
People, but it belongs alſo unto them, by their Office,
to go from their People, and for them, unto God,
and to be importunate with him for Bleſſings upon
them : Therefore I hope it will not be unſuitable
to diſcourſe, on this Occaſion, upon a Prayer of
Moſes, the Man of God, for the Church , a Pattern
worthy to be imitated by every one, but eſpecially
by ſuch, who, in regard of their Office, bear the
honourable Character of Men of God : It is the
laſt Verſe of this *Pſalm* I am to diſcourſe upon,
which contains the Concluſion of *Moſes*'s Prayer,
and in it we have two very comprehenſive Petitions
The firſt whereof is, *And let the Beauty of the Lord
our God be upon us*. Where we may notice, *firſt*,
the Bleſſing prayed for, and that is the Beauty of
the Lord. The original Word is by ſome rendred
Pleaſantreſs. Let the Pleaſantneſs of the Lord be
upon us ; let us enjoy that which will make us pleaſant in his Sight, that wherein he delights and takes
Pleaſure. But I ſhall keep by the Phraſe our Tran-
ſlators uſe, being as agreeable to the Original as
any other. The Beauty here prayed for is called
the Beauty of the Lord. The Church is Chriſt's
ſpiritual

spiritual House, his spiritual Kingdom; all her Beauty is spiritual, and it consists in her Conformity unto Jesus her Head and Lord : It is a Beauty derived from him , it is a Beam of his own Glory from the God of Glory shining upon her, *Isa.* lx 1 *The Glory of the Lord shall lighten thee.* On these Accounts the Beauty here prayed for may be called the Beauty of the Lord.

2*dly*. We may observe for whom this Blessing is desired : *Upon us,* thy Church and People in the Wilderness The Church of *Israel* in the Wilderness was a lively Emblem of the Church militant in all succeeding Generations. Though the Church, while here, is still in the Wilderness, still in a militant State and Condition, yet, when the Beauty of the Lord is upon her, there is such a Splendor and Glory about her, as doth distinguish her from all the rest of the World beside.

3*dly* The Church's Relation to God is here asserted . *Our God.* This People in the Wilderness were separate from the rest of the Nations, God had brought them within the Bond of his Covenant, and taken them for his peculiar People A View of the Church's Relation to the Lord Jesus, her Head and Husband, may give Strength and Courage, Life and Vigour, to the Faith of his Servants and People in Prayer.

The second Petition of *Moses,* in my Text, is, *Establish thou the Works of our Hands upon us* Where, *first,* we may notice something implied, namely, their Hands were at Work, they were not idle : *Moses* especially, and others with him, whom God employed in carrying on and advancing his own Work in the Church, they prayed, and joined Diligence with their Prayer , they exerted themselves

as

as became his Servants and Inftruments in building up the Church in the Wildernefs.

2*dly.* We may here likeways obferve what is prayed for, *ramely,* That the Lord may eftablifh the Work of their Hands. The Word rendred *eftablifh,* is fometimes rendred to direct or order, as *Pfalm* XXXVII 23. *A good Man's Steps are order-ed by the Lord.* Direct or order the Works of our Hands, that is, direct us to fuch Meafures as may moft tend to thy Glory, and the Good of thy Church and People. But the Word is ufually rendred to eftablifh or confirm, and two Things may be im-ported in it. *Firft,* When *Mofes* prays that God may eftablifh the Work of their Hands, it is a Prayer for divine Affiftance in the Work, as if he had faid, Lord, put to thy own Hands to thy Work in our Hands, or, Hold thy Hands about our Hands, affift and ftrengthen us in the Work. When the Under-Workers are furnifhed and ftrengthned by the Lord for the Work, then the Work goes on more pleafantly. Again, 2*dly* It is a Prayer that the Lord may append his Seal to his own Work a-mongft their Hands When the Lord crowns the Labours of his Servants with Succefs, then he fhews that he is in them, and with them of a Truth. This is his Seal to the Work of their Hands, and when he thus feals the Work, then the Work of their Hands may be faid to be eftablifhed I fhall take in both thefe, *namely,* Succefs and Affiftance as imported in this Prayer, in the Doctrine I am to offer from it

3*dly* We may here likeways obferve the doubl-ing of the Petition, *Eftablifh then the Work of our Hands, yea, the Work of our Hands eftablifh thou it.* This imports the Senfe they had of the great Neceffity of the Lord's putting his Hand to the Work, by

ftrengthning

strengthning their Hands, and making the Work succefsful, as alfo their ardent and fervent Importunity for it From the Words, thus opened up, I offer the two following Doctrines

DOCT. I *That it is much to be defired by all, but efpecially by the Church's Watchmen and Overfeers, that the Beauty of the Lord may be upon his Church and People.*

DOCT. II *That fuch whom God employs in carrying on his own Work, fhould be importunate with him for Afiftance and Succefs from him.*

DOCT. I *That it is much to be defired by all, but efpecially by the Church's Watchmen and Overfeers, that the Beauty of the Lord may be upon the Church.* This is the Prayer of *Mofes*, the Man of God, for the Church and People of God, and in their Name, *Let the Beauty of the Lord our God be upon us* Here I will endeavour to fpeak a little of this Beauty of the Lord, which is fo much to be defired. 2*dly* I will fhew that it is the Duty, in a fpecial Manner, of the Church's Watchmen, to be concerned that the Beauty of the Lord may be upon the Church. 3*dly*. I fhall offer a Word by Way of practical Ufe.

1. What is this Beauty of the Lord, which is fo much to be defired upon the Church?

I anfwer, There are three Things that contribute to the Church's Beauty, *to wit, Purity, Power* and *Unity* All thefe three are much to be defired, and where they are the Beauty of the Lord may be faid to be upon that Church.

1*ft* There is the *Beauty of Purity.* The Church's Purity doth confift in the Conformity of her Doctrine, Worfhip, Government and Difcipline, unto the Word of God; when every Thing is done in the Church according to the Pattern fhewn in the

the Mount, as the Lord commanded *Moses*, *Exod.* xxv. 40. The Doctrine of the Church is pure, when it is all drawn from that pure Fountain of Truth, the lively Oracles of God : *To the Law and to the Testimony, if they speak not according to this Word, it is because there is no Light in them,* Isa. viii. 20. Her Ordinances of Worship are pure, when they are such as God hath commanded or warranted in his Word, without any Mixture of human Additions or Inventions, which the Lord Jesus condemns as vain Will-Worship, *Matth.* xv. 9. *In vain do they worship me, teaching for Doctrines the Commandments of Men.* The Church's Discipline is pure, when her Censures are such as God hath appointed in his Word ; and truly these are all spiritual, *For the Weapons of our Warfare are not carnal,* 2 Cor. x. 4. The Church's Government is pure, when she is governed by such Officers as Christ hath appointed in his Word, and also by such as he himself hath instituted, every one of them acting in a regular Subordination to one another, and all of them in Subordination to the Lord Jesus, the only Head, King, and Lord of his House, on whose Shoulder the Government is laid, *Isa.* ix. 6.

2*dly.* The *Beauty of Power* is much to be desired likeways. In the Verse preceeding our Text *Moses* prays, *O let thy Work and Power appear before thy Servants and shew thy Glory to their Children.* This *David* desired to see, even the Power and Glory of God in the Sanctuary, *Psalm.* lxiii. 2. The Beauty of divine Power consists in the special Presence of the Lord in the Church with the Ordinances of his own Institution and Appointment. God is said to shine out of the Church, *Psalm.* l. 2. *Out of* Zion *God hath shined* This imports his special Residence in *Zion*, yea, the Church is the Hill
where

where he defires to dwell, *Pfalm* lxviii. 10. The
Church is his Reft, *Pfalm* cxxvii. 14. *This is my
Reft for ever · Here will I dwell, for I have defired it.*
God is faid to be in the Midft of her, *Pfalm* xlviii.
5. In the Midft of her, in her Bowels, fo the original Word fignifies , he is her Life, her Soul. The
Lord in the Midft of her is her Beauty and Excellency : The Church, and all the Ordinances thereof, is like a Body without Life or Soul, when the
divine Prefence is not in her , but when divine
Power is exerted with the preaching of the Word,
and other Ordinances of Worfhip, then the Weapons of our Minifterial Warfare are feen to be
mighty through God, to the pulling down of ftrong
Holds, 2 *Cor* x 4   Then through the Greatnefs
of his Power his Enemies are conftrained to bow,
Pfalm lxvi 3. There may be fome Meafure of Purity where there is little Power , but it will be found
that thefe two go frequently together.   When the
Church lofeth the Beauty of Purity, the Beauty of
Power will quickly depart , and when the Beauty
of Power departs, the Beauty of Purity will not long
fubfift

3*dly*   The *Beauty of Unity* is much to be defired alfo.   The Spirit of God commends it as good
and pleafant for the Members of the Church to
dwell together in Unity, *Pfalm* cxxxii. 1. *Behold
how good and how pleafant is it for Brethren to dwell
together in Unity*   How *pleafant* , it is the fame
Word which in our Text is rendred *Beauty*   The
Church's Unity confifts in Harmony in Doctrine
and Practice amongft her Members , when they all,
and efpecially her Watchmen, *fpeak the fame Things,*
and are knit together in Love and Affection to one
another, then the Beauty of Unity may be faid to
be upon the Church. Purity and Power muft needs
concur to the Beauty of Unity and Harmony, un-

lefs

less Unity have Purity for its Basis and Foundation, the Beauty of the Lord is not in it And if the Beauty of Power depart from a Church, Unity upon the Basis of Truth will not long remain. When the Lord departs from a People, he takes his Peace away with him, and then a perverse Spirit is mingled amongst them.

The *second* Thing I propose, upon this Doctrine, is, To shew that it is the Duty of the Church's Watchmen, in a special Manner, to be concerned that the Beauty of the Lord may be upon the Church. No doubt all the Members of the Church should pray, *Let the Beauty of the Lord our God be upon us :* But it is incumbent, in a special Manner, upon the Church's Overseers, to be concerned that this spiritual Beauty may be upon the Church , to this they are specially obliged by virtue of their Office, and on the Account of the Trust, with respect to the Church's Beauty, committed to them. This will appear, if we consider the following Things.

1*st* With respect to the Purity of the Ordinances of divine Institution there is a special Charge given to the Church's Watchmen, that the Church receive no Spot upon her Doctrine, her Worship, or Government , if she receive any Damage through their Fault. this will be required at their Hands. The Church of *Philadelphia* is commended for her Purity, *Rev* iii 10 *That thou hast kept the Word of my Patience* She had some Measure of the divine Presence with her too, *ver. 8 I have set before thee an open Door, and no Men can shut it , for thou hast a little Strength, and hast kept my Word* She is the Church that amongst all the seven has the fairest Character, and the largest Commendation. Purity, with some Measure of the divine Presence, was her Beauty.
Crown

Crown and Glory. And what is Chrift's Charge to the Angel of that Church, or her Watchmen and Overfeers? We have it in the 11th Verfe, *Behold I come quickly; hold that faft which thou haft, that no Man take thy Crown*

2dly With refpect to the Beauty of Power, though Minifters cannot command the Wind of the Spirit to blow, (the Lord is fovereign, and comes and goes, with refpect to his fpecial and gracious Prefence, as he pleafeth) yet it is incumbent upon them, and that in a more fpecial Manner, to cry. And let the Beauty of divine Power be upon us, if we confider them, *1ft* As the Lord's Remembrancers in behalf of the Church, *2dly* As they are the Church's Watchmen *1ft* If we confider them as they are the Lord's Remembrancers in behalf of the Church, it is incumbent upon them to put him in Remembrance of his Church, and to plead with him on her Behalf, *Ifa lxii 7, 8. I have fet Watchmen upon thy Walls, O Jerufalem, which fhall never hold their Peace Day nor Night. Ye that make Mention of the Lord, keep not Silence, and give him no Reft, till he eftablifh and make Jerufalem a Praife in the Earth Ye that make Mention of the Lord*, in the Margin it is rendred, *Ye that are the Lord's Remembrancers* And who are thefe? No doubt all the People of God may be called his *Remembrancers*, but furely Minifters are fuch in a fpecial Manner They are fuch by virtue of their Office, and it belongs to them, above others, to cry, *Remember thy Congregation which thou haft purchafed of old*, &c. Pfalm lxxiv. 2 *2dly* If we confider Minifters as they are the Church's Watchmen, it belongs to them, in a fpecial Manner, to be concerned that the Beauty of the divine Prefence may be upon the Church. This will appear if we notice two Things that are

incum-

incumbent upon them as they are the Church's Watchmen. 1*st* It belongs to them to watch against those Evils that may provoke the Lord to remove the Beauty of his gracious Presence from his Church. They ought carefully to observe these Corruptions, whether in Principle or Practice, which may sin away the divine Presence It belongs to their Office to shew unto the Lord's People *their Sins, to the House of* Jacob *their Transgressions,* Isa lviii 2 *2dly* As they are Watchmen they should notice the Departure of the spiritual Glory, and to stir up themselves and the Church to use all proper Means for recovering the divine Presence, when it is in any Measure removed. When the Bridegroom departs, it becomes the Children of the Bride Chamber to fast and mourn, *Matth* ix 15. When the Lord removes his gracious Presence in any Measure, it becomes the Ministers of the Sanctuary to stand and weep *between the Porch and the Altar, and to cry, Spare thy People, O Lord, and give not thine Heritage to Reproach,* Joel ii 17

3*dly.* With respect to the Beauty of Unity and Harmony, it is incumbent upon the Church's Watchmen to maintain it where it is, to endeavour to recover it when in any Measure it is lost. The Gospel they preach is the Gospel of Peace, the Embassy upon which they are sent is a Message of Peace. If all the Members of the Church should *keep the Unity of the Spirit in the Bond of Peace,* Eph iv. 3 much more they who by Office are the Ministers of Peace

I now proceed to make some practical Use of this Doctrine, and all the Use I make of it shall be by Way of Exhortation.

If

If it be so, that it is much to be defired by all, but efpecially by the Church's Watchmen, that the Beauty of the Lord may be upon the Church, then this Doctrine ferves to exhort every one of us, efpecially fuch of us as are by Office the Church's Overfeers, to join Iffue with the Man of God, in the Words of my Text, and to pray, *Let the beauty of the Lord our God be upon us* I fhall offer a few Confiderations which fhould move and excite us to this Exercife, and then fubjoin a few Things incumbent upon us, who are the Church's Watchmen, with reference to this.

1*ft* I fhall offer a few Things which fhould move us to be concerned that the Beauty of the Lord may be upon us.

1*ft.* Let us confider the Church has no Beauty at all, if the Beauty of the Lord be not upon her. The Church's Unity and Purity, with the divine Prefence in the Midft of her, are the Things that not only diftinguifh this Society from all others, but exalt the Church above the reft of the World befide The Church is a high Hill, as *the Hill of* Bafhan, *Pfal. lxviii.* 15 and in the 16th *Ver*, *Why hop ye, ye high Hills ? This is the Hill which God defireth to dwell in, yea, the Lord will dwell in it for ever* The leaft Deviation from Truth, when it becomes univerfal, is a black Spot upon a Church, when the Beauty of Power departs, black Formality covers the Church Whatever Flourifh of a Profeffion there may be, yet that Church is like a dead Carcafe in the Lord's Sight, as the Church of *Sardis* was, *Rev. iii.* 1. Again, when Purity and Power are altogether loft, that Church has no Beauty at all, fhe is no more the Spoufe of Chrift, but Satan's Synagogue, as the Church of *Rome* at this Day is.

2*dly.*

2*dly.* Let us confider that the Beauty of the Lord upon the Church makes her beautiful indeed, fhe is then an eternal Excellency, the Joy of many Generations, *Ifa.* lx. 15. Her Beauty is then a real Beauty; fhe is beautiful in her Lord and in Husband's Eyes, he takes Delight and Pleafure in her; fhe is then a Crown of Glory in the Hand of the Lord, a royal Diadem in the Hand of her God, fhe is then his *Hephzibah* and *Beulah*, delighted in and married to the Lord, *Ifa* lxii. 4. Her Beauty is then a moft excellent Beauty; fhe is then beautiful as *Tirza,* comely as *Jerufalem: She looketh forth as the Morning, fair as the Moon, clean as the Sun, Song* vi 4 10. All wordly Beauty and Glory cannot then be compared with the Church's Beauty, yea, the Splendor and Luftre of the great eft and moft glorious Kingdoms of this Earth, are but like a Bubble unto that Splendor and Glory that is upon the Church. When the Glory of the Lord rifeth upon the Church, Zion is then the Perfection of Beauty, *Pfalm* l. 2. *Out of Zion the Perfection of Beauty, God hath fhined.* Again, when the Beauty of the Lord is upon the Church, her Beauty is an aftonifhing Beauty: her Enemies are ftruck with Aftonifhment, yea, fometimes with Terror, at the fpiritual Luftre and Splendor that is feen upon her, *Pfalm* xlviii. 2. *Beautiful for Situation is Mount Zion. Verfes* 4, 5, 6. *The Kings were affembled, they faw it, and fo they marvelled, they were troubled, and hafted away. Fear took hold upon them there.* Yea, *finally,* when the Beauty of of the Lord is upon the Church, then her Beauty is an alluring Beauty; others are engaged to come and join themfelves to this beautiful and lovely Society, *Ifa* lx 1, 3 *Arife, fhine, for thy Light is come, the Glory of the Lord is rifen upon thee.* Ob

serve

ferve what follows in the 3d *Verfe, And the Gentiles fhall come to thy Light, and Kings to the Brightnefs of thy Rifing.*

3dly Confider, when the Beauty of the Lord is upon the Church, the Lord Jefus is therein greatly honoured and glorified; then the gathering of the People is unto *Shilo*, then the Flocks of *Kedar* are gathered unto him, the Rams of *Nebajoth* do minifter unto him, they come up with Acceptance upon his Altar, and glorify the Houfe of his Glory, they fly as a Cloud, and as Doves to their Windows, *Ifa.* lx. 7, 8 Yea, the whole of that Chapter is a Prophecy of the Beauty of the New Teftament Church, and the Glory that fhall redound to her Head the Lord Jefus thereby.

4thly. When the Beauty of Purity, Power and Unity, is upon the Church, then there is a fpecial Luftre and Splendor upon the Members of the Church, both Minifters and People : They have a Luftre of Heaven about them, they appear like the Children of the King. The Church's Seed is then known among the Gentiles, and her Offspring among the People. All that fee them acknowledge that they are the Seed which the Lord has bleffed, *Ifa* lxi 9. When the Beauty of the Lord is upon the Church, her Members appear in the Beauty of Holinefs, *Pfal.* cx 3. *In the Beauty of Holinefs from the Womb of the Morning. Thou haft the Dew of thy Youth* There is then a fweet Savour of Chrift about them, *Hof.* iv 5 *I will be as the Dew to Ifrael* And then, in the 6th Verfe, *His Beauty fhall be as the Olive-Tree his Smell as* Lebanon If the Church has no Beauty at all except the Beauty of the Lord be upon her, if this makes her beautiful indeed, and honours the Lord Jefus, and puts a Luftre and Splendor upon all her Members, thefe

Things

Things should move us to cry, and let the Beauty of the Lord be upon us. I shall add two Things more upon this Head.

5thly The spiritual Beauty is very much departed from the reformed Churches, and there are many Symptoms and Evidences of a Departure of the spiritual Beauty from us. If we look abroad to the reformed Churches, Have not the most Part of them lost much of the Beauty of Purity and Power too, Error in Doctrine, and Corruption in Practice, seem to prevail every where The Ordinances of Worship are corrupted, the spiritual Worship and Government of Christ's House is quite marred in many of them. As for Instance, in our neighbouring Churches of *England* and *Ireland*, though their doctrinal Articles bear some Measure of Conformity to the Word of God, yet, thro' a lordly Prelacy, a carnal Discipline and human Ordinances of Worship, the Beauty of Christ's House is very much defaced amongst them, and gross Ignorance, Immorality and Profanity are the Fruits of this amongst their People Again, with respect to ourselves our Standards of Doctrine are pure, our Ordinances of Worship, our Rules for Discipline and Government, we hope, bear a Conformity to the divine Pattern · Thus far we enjoy as yet some Measure of the Beauty of Purity, yet, alas we may say, our spiritual Beauty is very much departed from us What Heart breaking Divisions, Animosities and Differences have been amongst us ? the Staves of Beauty and Bands have been broke asunder, for the Divisions of our *Reuben* there may be Searchings of Heart. Again, how little of the Power of Religion is to be found amongst us ? Our Exercise bears not a Proportion to our Profession the Life of Religion lies a bleeding, ready to expire in our Streets;

Streets ; that Vigour of Faith and Love, that some-time has appeared, is very much abated. It was a seasonable Warning given us from this Place upon an Occasion of the like Nature not long ago, from *Rev.* ii. 5. *Nevertheless I have somewhat against thee, because thou hast left thy first Love.* Ah ! where is that Lustre and Splendor of Holiness that should be, and sometimes has been the distinguishing Glory of Ministers and People ? Nay, may we not, in the Words of the Spirit of God by the Prophet, bewail, *Lam.* iv. 7, 8. *Her Nazarites were purer than Snow, they were whiter than Milk, they were more ruddy in their Body than Rubies, their polishing was of Sapphire: Their Visage is blacker than a Coal They are not known in the Streets Their Skin cleaveth to their Bones It is withered, it is become like a Stick ?* These and many such Evidences may be offered, that our spiritual Beauty is much departed from us.

Finally, The Departure of the spiritual Beauty is a Forerunner of sad Calamities. When the Beau-ty either of *Purity, Power,* or *Unity,* departs from a Church, it is an Evidence that the Lord is on his Way, if not to unchurch that People, yet to pu-nish them It is remarkable in the 9th of *Ezekiel,* be-fore the Commission is given to the Men with the Slaughter-Weapons in their Hands, to go through the Midst of the City, and to slay utterly Old and Young, in the 3d Verse, the Glory departs from the Cherub to the Threshold of the House. The Departure of the spiritual Glory goes before a Day of Destruction and Desolation Ought not these Things to move us to a Concern that the Beauty of the Lord may be upon us ?

I shall shut up this Doctrine by laying before you a few Things in a special Manner incumbent upon us who are the Church's Watchmen and

C Overseers.

Overseers. We ought not only to pray that the Beauty of the Lord may be upon the Church, but our utmost Endeavours must be used to maintain any Thing of the Beauty of the Lord that is upon us, and to recover any Measure of spiritual Beauty that is wanting, and for this End let us beware of every Thing that may mair the Church's Beauty; more particularly,

First, It is incumbent upon us to beware of every Thing that may marr the *Beauty of Purity*. We ought to keep pure and intire the Ordinances of divine Institution and Appointment, the Doctrine, Worship, Discipline and Government of Christ's House, these, I say, should be kept pure by us, and transmitted pure to our Posterity, that our Children after us may see the Glory of the Lord. We have excellent Catechisms, both Larger and Shorter; an excellent Confession of Faith, for which we desire to bless the Lord, tho' Confessions are now boldly cried down by some in *England,* and others in *Ireland*, (of whom better Things might have been expected) as human and tyrannical Impositions upon the Consciences of Men. But what tho' our Standards of Doctrine be pure? If we do not preach the Word of God purely, the Church's Beauty will be marred by us, it is our unquestionable Duty to hold fast the Form of sound Words, 2 *Tim* i 13 The beaten Path, wherein the wayfaring Men before us have walked, is the safest. Again, it is not enough that we have pure Ordinances of Worship, unless Spirituality in Worship be maintained If Ministers turn flat and dead in the Duties of publick Worship, their People are in Hazard thereby to be hardend, a lifeless and carnal Way of serving the living God opened a Door for all these Popish Ceremonies that have
been

been a Plague upon the Christian Church. When Men once loft the Spirituality of Worship (as the judicious Dr. *Owen* obferves) they behoved to have fomething to fill their natural Eyes, and gratify their carnal Senfes · Hence all thofe gaudy Ceremonies, which Men have defired as Ornaments unto the Worship of God, were introduced into the Church : And what are they all but an Abomination in the Sight of God, and of no other Ufe but to divert Mens Minds from the Spirituality of Worship, and to make them pleafe themfelves with an empty outward Form of Godlinefs ? Yea, farther, it is not enough that we have good Rules for Difcipline, unlefs our Difcipline be managed in a fpiritual Manner, for reaching its fpiritual Ends, *namely* the Conviction and Recovery of fuch as have fallen. Some of us have Occafion to obferve, in Places where grofs Scandals do much abound, that it is very rare to fee any fatisfying Evidences of ferious Repentance amongft them that fall. Surely it becomes us, who are the Church's Overfeers, both Minifters and Elders, ferioufly to inquire how we manage the fpiritual Sword, left their Obduration and Hardnefs be imputable to fome culpable Defect in us *Finally*, With refpect to the Government of the Church, we have fuch Office-Bearers as Chrift hath appointed in his Houfe, *namely*, the Elder who labours in Word and Doctrine, the Elder who rules, the Deacon who takes Care of the poor Members of the Church, we have alfo fuch Courts as Chrift hath eftablifhed in the Church, Seffions, Presbyteries, provincial Synods, and national Affemblies ; it is incumbent upon us to preferve this Government pure and intire Seffions are fubordinate to Presbyteries, and are accountable to them for all their feffional Manage-

ments

ments whatſoever, as Presbyteries are to provincial Synods, and they to the national Aſſembly, and, if the State of the Church did allow of œcumenical Aſſemblies, national Aſſemblies would owe Subjection to them. This is that beautiful Order that Chriſt hath inſtituted in his Houſe. I may here farther obſerve, that, in order to our preſerving the Government pure, it is needful we commit the Government of the Church to faithful Men, yea, the Purity of Doctrine, Worſhip and Diſcipline, as well as that of the Government, are here nearly concerned : Nothing can more endanger the Church's Beauty than corrupt Office-Bearers, and it has been found that a corrupt Miniſtry has ever been the Ruin of the Church, therefore it is incumbent upon us, that we take heed *whom* we receive into the Miniſtry, and alſo *how* we receive Men into the Miniſtry, I ſay, it belongs to us to look well *whom* we receive into the Miniſtry, that they be ſuch, who, ſo far as we can diſcern, have ſome Feeling and Experience of a Work of God upon their own Hearts, and who ſeek into the Miniſtry, not merely to obtain a Livelyhood, or to make a Trade of Preaching, but who have higher and more noble Ends before them, even the Glory of Chriſt, and the Salvation of others. Alſo we ſhould look well *how* we receive them into the Miniſtry, *namely*, that they be taken in in that Way and Manner that Chriſt has appointed his Miniſters to be ſet over his Church, that they be received by that Door at which Chriſt will have all his Miniſters to enter, I mean, at the Door of a regular Election and Call To impoſe and force a Miniſter upon a Chriſtian People, is to exerciſe a Lordſhip and tyrannical Dominion over the Heritage of Chriſt.

2*dly.* Let us take heed that we marr not the Beauty of Power. We should be careful left the divine Presence be removed from us thro' our Sin. For this End, in the *first* Place, a faithful Application of Doctrine is needful on our Part. God has promised his Presence to his Ministers, yet we cannot expect the divine Presence but in a faithful Discharge of our Duty What the Spirit of God speaks by the Prophet *Jeremiah*, concerning the Prophets of that Time, is remarkable, *Jer* xxiii 22. *If they had stood in my Council, and had caused my People to hear my Words, then should they have turned them from their evil Way, and from the Evil of their Doings*, intimating to us, that the Sermons or Preachings of these Prophets had not Success, and that because they were not faithful in their Doctrine. If we would have the Presence of the Lord with us in our Preachings, it becomes us to address ourselves to the Consciences of our Hearers, closely to attack the strong Holds of their natural Corruption, to discover particularly their Sin and Misery by their Apostasy from God in the first *Adam*, and the Help that is for them in the Lord Jesus the second *Adam*, their Ruin by the Breach of their first Covenant, and the only Remedy from this Ruin by the Covenant of Grace We ought to preach the Necessity of a vital Union with Christ Jesus, without which we can have no Communion with him here, and if we have no Communion with him in Grace here, we shall have none with him in Glory hereafter Him we must exhibit as the only beautiful Foundation that is laid in *Zion*, as the precious and chief Corner-Stone, towards him must all our Preachings point, as the Lord our Righteousness and Strength, otherways there will be little Beauty and Glory in them, to him we must lead our Hearers for Righteousness unto

their

their Juſtification, and for the Spirit, in order to the beginning, carrying on, and compleating of a Work of Sanctification • But who is ſufficient for theſe Things ? Yet our Sufficiency is of God. 2*dly*. If we would not mar the Beauty of the divine Preſence, we ſhould endeavour to walk as we preach. Though we ſhould preach faithfully, if our Converſation be not like our Preaching, we may ſin away the Preſence of the Lord from our Miniſtry It is not enough that we commend Chriſt in our Doctrine, we ſhould endeavour to have a Savour of him about us in our Walk. It is not enough that we preach up the Neceſſity and Excellency of Holineſs, (which indeed all Miniſters ſhould do) but we muſt alſo endeavour to have the Beauty of Holineſs upon ourſelves, otherways we will both ſtumble, and harden our People All of us ſhould follow the Example of the Apoſtle, who could ſay to the *Theſſalonians*, 1 *Theſſ.* ii. 10 *Ye know how holily, how juſtly and unblameably we behaved ourſelves amongſt you.*

3*dly*. Let us take heed that we mar not the Beauty of Unity and Harmony. Brotherly Love adorns Church-Members, and eſpecially Miniſters of the Goſpel, Heart Riſings at one another, groundleſs Jealouſies, and ſtriving about Words when there is an Agreement in the Subſtance from whence ſprings Envy, Malice, Railings and evil Surmiſings, 1 *Tim.* iv 6. theſe do all mar the Beauty of Unity. The Command of God, by the Apoſtle, ſhould be regarded by all, but eſpecially by the Church's Overſeers, *Rom* xiv 19 *Let us therefore follow after the Things which make for Peace, and Things wherewith one may edify another* I may here add, that all ſuch as bear Office in the Church, are ſolemnly engaged, when ſet apart to their Office, to

uſe

uſe their utmoſt Endeavours to maintain the Beauty of Purity and Unity, and to obtain the Beauty of Power, yea, this whole Church and Nation are under the moſt ſolemn Engagements to maintain the beautiful Doctrine, Worſhip, Diſcipline and Government of Chriſt's Houſe, Unity in the Lord amongſt ourſelves, and to purſue after the Life and Power of Religion and Godlineſs. This is what is chiefly intended in our national Covenants, which were the Honour of our Land, and a Fruit and Evidence of the Beauty of the Lord upon us, tho' they have been contemned in the ſeveral Periods of this Church, by Men of different Denominations, from different and often contrary Views

I proceed to the *ſecond* Petition of the Man of God in my Text, *The Work of our Hands eſtabliſh thou it;* and a ſecond Doctrine from the Verſe, which is, *That ſuch whom God employs in his Work ſhould be importunate with him for Aſſiſtance and Succeſs in it.* All I intend upon this Doctrine is, in the firſt Place, briefly to ſpeak of the Work the Church's Watchmen are employed in, and then, 2*dly* to ſhew why they ſhould be importunate with him, and, 3*dly.* to offer a Word by Way of practical Uſe.

1ſt What is the Work that the Church's Watchmen are employed in? I anſwer, There is a twofold Work that they are mainly employed in, to wit the Work of Gathering in, and the Work of Building up the Church To gather in Sinners to Chriſt is one Part of the Work that the Lord puts into the Hands of Miniſters, for this End the Miniſtry of Reconciliation is committed unto them, it is for this End they are ſent forth as Ambaſſadors for Chriſt, to intreat Sinners to be reconciled to God, 2 *Cor* v 19, 20 Again, another Part of the Work that they are employed in

is.

is to build up Saints. The whole Church of Believers muft be built up in the Knowledge of Chrift, till they attain unto the Noon Day Vifion of Glory; they muft be built up in Sanctification and Holinefs, thro' Faith, till the Work of Sanctification be compleated in Glorification · For this End Minifters are Shepherds, and it belongs to them to feed Chrift's Sheep and Lambs, Minifters are Stewards of the Mvfteries of God, and it belongs to them to divide the fpiritual Bread, and to give the Children of the Houfe their Food in Seafon · This is their Work, yea, the Church is God's Hufbandry, his fpiritual Building, and Minifters are Labourers together with him, 1 *Cor*. iii. 9. In a Word, a Gofpel-Miniftry, and all Ordinances what foever, are given for gathering in and building up the Church, *Eph* iv 11, 12. *He gave fome Apoftles, and fome Prophets, and fome Evangelifts, and fome Paftors and Teachers*, for the perfecting of the Saints for the Work of the Miniftry, and for edifying the Body of Chrift; this is the Work we are employed in, and all of us fhould be importunate with the Lord, for Affiftance and Succefs from him in the Work. And I offer the following Reafons.

Firft, Upon the Account of the Greatnefs of the the Work. To gather in Sinners to Chrift is a great Work, it is fo great that it requires creating Power, yea, it is a greater Work by far than the firft Creation of Things out of nothing Here the exceeding Greatnefs of *Jehovah*'s Power is put forth, *Eph.* i. 19. The Lord appropriates this Work to himfelf, tho' he employ Minifters as his Inftruments, yet it is his Calling, yea, *the high Calling of God in Chrift Jefus*, Philip. iii. 14.

2dly. Minifters fhould be importunate with him on the Account of their own Weaknefs, they are infufficient for the Work of themfelves, they are

Men,

Men, they are finful Men, they are Men of like Paffions with others ; *This Treafure is in earthen Veffels, that the Excellency of the Power may be of God,* 2 Cor. iv. 7.

3*dly*. The Difficulties that we have to encounter with make this Importunity needful. The ftrong Holds of natural Enmity and Depravation muft be attacked, and thefe ftrong Holds are aided and affifted by all the Power, Malice and Policy of *Satan* ; he is the ftrong Man that keeps the Houfe, and makes all the Refiftance he can unto the Work of the Lord in the Hand of the Church's Overfeers ; he will keep the Poffeffion till a ftronger bind and caft him out. The World alfo bears an inveterate Enmity and Prejudice at the fpiritual Laws, Cenfures and Government of Chrift's Houfe, they will not have this Man to reign over them ; they fay, *Let us break the Lord's Bands afunder, and caft away his Cords from us,* Pfalm ii. 3 In a Word, thofe whom God employs in his Work have Men and Devils againft them, Hell and Earth againft them ; therefore they fhould be importunate that the Lord may give Affiftance and Succefs in the Work. All the Ufe I make of this Doctrine, is in a Word by Way of Exhortation.

If it be fo, that fuch whom God employs in his Work fhould be importunate with him for Affiftance and Succefs in it, this doth exhort us, who are in the Miniftry, in a fpecial Manner, to be importunate with the Lord, that he may put to his Hand to his own Work, that he may be with us in the Work, and give Succefs to our Endeavours. Let us all cry with *Mofes* the Man of God, in the Words of my Text, *The Work of our Hands eftablifh thou it, yea, the Work of our Hands eftablifh thou it.* I fhall offer a few Confiderations to inforce

D   this

this Exhortation, and then conclude with a Word to the Christian People.

First of all, Let us consider the Lord's Work goes slowly on amongst our Hands at this Day, the Work of Gathering in, and the Work of Building up, is very much at a Stand, it is the general and too well-founded Regret of all, who have any Measure of spiritual Discerning, that the Gospel has little Success either for Conversion or Confirmation, that *Israel* is not gathered, that few are brought in to Christ, and that the Work of the Lord goes but slowly on amongst them that are in Christ, that they are not built up in Holiness, that Religion in its Life and Power is very low amongst them These Things have a double Voice unto us in the Ministry.

First, They call upon us to try ourselves, lest there be any Cause on our Part why Matters are so. Have we not Reason to inquire if our Hands are employed with that Activity and Diligence about the Lord's Work that becomes, if we travail as in Birth till Christ be formed in the Hearts of our Hearers, if we have a suitable Concern for Souls upon our Spirits, if we water our Preachings, and other Parts of our Ministerial Work, with Prayer for Success and Increase, if our Walk and Conversation be like our Doctrine, if it be such as becomes the Ministers and Ambassadors of the Lord Jesus? All these Things are necessary Means to make the Work of the Lord go on prosperously in our Hands. But are there any amongst us who will not find Reason, after a serious Communing with your own Hearts, to say, *Lord enter not into Judgment with thy Servant?* 2dly. If the Lord's Work goes slowly on, this calls us to that Importunity that my Text and Doctrine do demand of us. Let us cry,

that

that the Lord may put to his Hand to his own
Work, and make it prosper in our Hands, *The
Work of our Hands establish thou it,* &c

2*dly*. Let us consider, many eminent Instruments,
who were employed in the Work of the Lord,
have been carried off the Stage of late, some of them
in their Prime and Vigour, who, by Course of Nature, might have had their Hands much longer
about the Lord's Work.   This City has smarted
under such Strokes, this Presbytery and this Province, frequently, yea, the whole Church and Land;
and tho' there are not a few that are looking towards
the holy Ministry, yet it is to be feared there are few
to fill up the Rooms of the able Underworkers, who
now rest from their Labours   Our *Judah* may say,
*The Rubbish is great, and the Strength of the Bearers
of Burdens is decayed.*   Should not this move to an
Importunity with the Lord, that he may put to his
Hand to his own Work ? Let us cry, *The Work of
our Hands establish thou it, yea, the Work of our Hands
establish thou it.*

3*dly*. Consider, though all Hands should be at
Work, if the Lord put not his own Hand to the
Work, it will never go on ; the Work is so great,
and we are so weak, that it can never go on without him , the Difficulties are so strong, that we can
never surmount them without him.   *Paul* doth plant,
and *Apollos* doth water, but God doth give the Increase

4*thly*. Importunity has often prevailed with him.
The several Ages of the Church can afford remarkable Instances of this, the infant primitive Church-
Members were all with one Accord in Prayer and
Supplication, when the Holy Ghost came down upon the Apostles, *Acts* ii, 1, 2. They were employed in importunate Prayer, and God came
down

down from Heaven, and did put to his Hand to his own Work. Then, O what glorious Fruit did follow? Thousands were born at once in *Zion*. That great Man of God in our own Land, Mr *Robert Bruce*, was overheard in secret Prayer, before he came to the Publick, saying, I protest I will not go except thou go with me, I will not go except thou go with me. And when he came forth, God was seen to be in and with him, as the Author of the fulfilling of the Scriptures narrates, a Shower of divine Influences did accompany the Word spoken by him.

Finally, God will appear and will put to his Hand to his own Work. If it should be inquired at us, Watchmen, what of the Night? May we not give the Return the Prophet is directed to give, *Isa* xxi. 12. *The Morning cometh, and also the Night?* The Church at this Time is under many threatning Providences that presage a Night, yet these very Providences presage that the Morning is coming. That we are now under threatning Providences is evident, if we consider the universal Degeneracy of the reformed Churches from the Purity, Power, spiritual Life and Vigour that appeared in reforming Days and Times, the great Ones of the Earth do not concern themselves in the Interest of Christ's Kingdom and Glory, farther than they think Religion subservient to their own political Interests, no Care is taken either about Personal, Family or National Reformation, yea, at this Day, the Foundations are boldly struck at, not only by open and avowed Atheists and Deists, that deny all revealed Religion but also by some, who, tho' they profess a Regard for divine Revelation, yet are not afraid to move Debates about the supreme Deity

ty of the Son of God, who is the true God, even
God over all bleſſed for ever. Yea, farther, if we
conſider, that Profanity as a Flood has overflown
the Churches, and that every one of them ſeem to
have fallen into a deep ſpiritual Lethargy, and alſo
the preſent State of the Antichriſtian Kingdom, Antichriſt, for ſome Years bypaſt, ſeems rather to have
gathered Strength, than to be weakned: all theſe
Things preſage that our Night may be yet darker.
Whether the three Days and the Half of Killing
the Witneſſes, mentioned *Rev.* 11 7. be yet paſt or
to come, I cannot determine. I do not think a-
ny can poſſibly determine, tho' various and different
Conjectures have been made, but I may ſay, the
preſent State of the reformed Churches threatens an
overflowing Scourge. Yet, let me alſo add, the
Morning cometh, the Morning of God's appearing
for his own Work, there is a Bow in the Church's
darkeſt Cloud, the Church's greateſt Extremity,
and the Lord's Appearing, have, in all Ages of the
Church, ordinarily tryſted together I ſhall conclude this Head with a judicious Reflection or two
of that great Obſerver of divine Providences, the
Author of the fulfilling of the Scriptures, in his
Appendix to the firſt Part of that excellent Work:
After having obſerved, that the Church has gone
through that long continued and moſt diſmal Trial,
which, under the Time of the Goſpel, until the
Cloſe of Time, was to go over her Head, even
that ſore Bondage from Antichriſt and under his
Reign, ' This Winter being in a great Meaſure now
' paſt, and her Spring begun, (ſays he) there are
' clear and continuing Symptoms, by which ſome
' notable Criſis in her Condition may be diſcerned,
' that after many Conflicts and ſore Wreſtlings,
' ſince her Victory begun over Antichriſt, this
' Time

'Time of the Church seems to fall under that
'more remarkable Assault, which may be looked
'for from this Adversary, before the pouring out
'of the fifth Vial upon his Throne and Seat,
'which, as a Preludium of so great a Victory, may,
'in some Proportion thereto, be more dreadful and
'sharp, for a Time, than any we have seen The
'Scriptures point clearly at this, which shew the
'wrestling Condition of the Church, and a War
'continued betwixt Antichrist and the Lamb,
'even in his falling State, until the last Decision
'put him off the Field, *Rev* xvii. 14. *For the Lamb*
'*shall overcome, and they who are on his Side, who are*
'*called, chosen, and faithful.*' As a Woman when
she is in Travail, her sharpest Showers go before
and hasten the Delivery, so the Church's Victory
over Antichrist may come through one of the so
rest and sharpest Assaults from this Adversary, *Mic.*
iv 13. *Be in Pain, O Daughter of* Zion, *ard go*
forth into Babylon, *for there shalt thou be delivered.*
After all, whatever Steps the Lord may take, this
is sure, the Lord will save *Zion*, and build the Ci
ties of *Judah*, the Time to favour *Zion* is set, and
the set Time is hastning apace Will God appear
for his Work ? Then let us meet an appearing God,
whether in a Way of Judgment or Mercy, with
a fervent Importunity, that he may put to his own
Hand to the Work of Gathering in and Building
up the Church.

I shall conclude all with a Word to the Christi
an People, and there are two or three Things I
would recommend to you

First, Has the Lord employed your Watchmen
and Overseers in his Work, in the Work of Ga
thering in and Building up the Church ? Take heed
that ye weaken not the Workmens Hands; despise

not

not their Persons, but esteem them highly for their
Work's Sake , submit to their faithful Reproofs,
Warnings, Admonitions and Counsels, *Heb.* XIII.
17 *Obey them that have the Rule over you, and
submit your selves, for they watch for your Souls.*

2dly. Be not stumbled at the Lord's Work, on
the Account of the Weaknesses that do attend the
Workmen We whom God has employed in the
Work are earthen Vessels, Men of like Passions
with yourselves, compassed about with Infirmities
as well as you, and you have Reason to bless the
Lord that the Work is committed to such ; you
could not have born the Presence of Angels, had
the Work been in their Hands , and they could
not have dealt with you from a Feeling of your
Infirmities No doubt you may observe the many
Failings that do attend us in our Pulpit-Appearan-
ces, in our Managements in Judicatories, and in the
whole of our Deportment But O remember the
Work we are employed in is the Lord's Work,
therefore stumble not at the Lord's Work in our
Hands.

3dly. Look well how the Work of God thrives
in your Hearts If it doth not thrive in your Hearts,
it doth not prosper in your Hands , if the Work
of Faith with Power be not wrought in you, if you
are not built up in Holiness and Comfort, through
Faith unto Salvation, our Labour is all lost amongst
you

Finally, Join with us in this holy Importunity,
that the Lord may put to his Hand to his own
Work , this God requires from you as well as from
us, and the Gain and Advantage will be yours as
much as ours. If you in this Place were importunate with God for this End, if Ministers and
People in this Province , if Ministers and People
through

through the Land, were exercifed in a holy Importunity for the Return of the divine Prefence a-
mongft us, for more difceinible Succefs unto Go
fpel-Ordinances, this would be a promifing Token for Good, that the Name of this City, the
Name of this Province, and the Name of this Church
and Land, might yet be *Jehovah Shamma*, the Lord
is there.

F I N I S.

STEDFASTNESS in the FAITH recommended,

IN A

SERMON

Preached on *Sabbath*-Evening after the Celebration of the LORD's SUP-PER at *Perth*, *July* 22. 1733.

By Mr. WILLIAM WILSON one of the Ministers of the Gospel there.

To which is prefixed,

A short Account of the Occasion of publishing this, together with some Reasons for his *condemned Conduct* ; directed by the Author to the People of his Pastoral Charge.

E D I N B U R G H,

Printed for *David Duncan*, and sold at his House, opposite to the *Weigh-House*, North-Side of the Street. MCCDXLVII.

Unto the Inhabitants of the Burgh and Parish of PERTH,

GRACE *and* PEACE *be multiplied.*

THE Occasion of publishing the following Discourse, delivered in your Hearing, is a Report made by the reverend Presbytery of *Perth* to the Commission of the late General Assembly, at their Meeting in *August* last, the Tenor whereof follows.

Perth, *July* 25 1733.

THE Presbytery having caused read the Act of the late General Assembly, with respect to Mr. Ebenezer Erskine Minister of the Gospel at Stirling, and the Brethren that adhered to his Protest, whereby they appoint the several Presbyteries, of which the said Brethren are Members, to report to the Commission in August, and subsequent Meetings of it, their Conduct and Behaviour with respect to the Act of Assembly And this Presbytery having made Enquiry as to the Behaviour of two of their Brethren that joined the said Mr. Erskine in his Protest, since said last Assembly, they find, That there is not only a common Fame, but some Members of the Presbytery, who have of late heard the two Brethren preach, did declare, that they continue in their Sermons to reflect upon the

Proceedings

Proceedings of the late and preceeding Assemblies. And the Presbytery appoints the Report hereof to be laid before the Commission of the General Assembly, to meet at Edinburgh *the second* Wednesday *of* August *next to come* — *After the Presbytery had agreed to the above Report, it was moved, that it might be added, as a farther Evidence of the Guilt of these Brethren, That some Members, who had Occasion to hear these Brethren of late, refused to inform the Presbytery, if or not they did in their Sermons reflect on the Judicatories of the Church, which, even in Justice to these Brethren, they were bound to do, had they been innocent. Then the Question being put,* Add this as a Clause to the Report, or not ? *Rolls called, and Votes marked, it carried,* nemine contradicente, Add the said Clause.

This Report the Presbytery was resolved upon at the Close of their Meeting, when some had gone off ; but two reverend Brethren having returned about the Time when they were concluding the above Report, dissented from it, and with them a ruling Elder. My Brother Mr. *Moncrief,* who was also concerned in it, was not present at this Meeting of Presbytery, and I was obliged to leave them before any Thing about the said Report was moved, being to preach our ordinary Week Day's Sermon next Day · But tho' there is little more than the Breadth of one of our Streets betwixt them and me, yet they thought fit to lay this general Charge against me before the reverend Commission, *Of reflecting upon the Proceedings of the late and preceeding Assemblies,* without acquainting me in the least with it If it is agreeable to the Rules of the Gospel, or to common Justice and Equity, to receive a Report of this Nature against a Brother, or to table such a general Accusation, in so publick a

Manner,

Manner, againſt him, without once hearing him upon the Cauſe, I leave i to others to judge.

I am credibly informed, the Sermon I deliver-ed on the *Sabbath*-Evening, after the Celebration of the Sacrament of the Lord's Supper in this Place, was the only Preaching of mine that was mentioned as giving Occaſion to the common Fame that the Presbytery's Report bears, and as the Ground of their general Accuſation. I am not conſcious to myſelf that I delivered any Thing contrary to my Duty, or improper for you to hear upon that ſolemn Occaſion, and therefore I thought it was needful, for the Sake of Truth itſelf, as well as for my Exoneration, to make the following Diſcourſe as publick as the general Charge againſt me has been The *firſt two general Heads*, toge-ther with the *firſt eight Directions* now publiſhed at the Cloſe of the Whole, were only what was de-livered that Evening, and I have, to the beſt of my Knowledge, publiſhed, in the expreſs Words in which I delivered myſelf any Thing I reckon-ed might have given Occaſion to the *common Fame* that the Presbytery's Report bears, and the Reader may judge for himſelf if their was any Ground for the above general Charge and Accuſation. As for the *other doctrinal Heads*, together with the *Ap-plication*, they contain only the Subſtance of what was preached on that ſame Subject the Lord's Day thereafter, and on two Week-Days.

It is now Seventeen Years ſince I had your una-nimous Call to come and labour amongſt you in the Work of the Goſpel The Countenance and Encouragement you have always given me, and your particular Intereſt in me, oblige me to give you ſome Account of my late Conduct, for which I am condemned in ſo publick a Manner.

The

The *Sibboleth* of our divided and diftracted Times is that Act of Affembly 1732. *concerning the Settlement of vacant Churches.* By it the Power of electing and calling Minifters is given to Heritors (a fuch ; yea, the Act is laid in fuch Terms, as, tho' all the Elders and People of a Congregation are reclaiming, yet the Majority of the Heritors, whether they have their Refidence in the Parifh or not, whether they are of the Communion of the Church, of *Scotland* or not, may impofe a Minifter upon them, unlefs the reclaiming People can fix *Error* in Doctrine, or fomething *fcandalous* in Walk and Practice on the Man who is the Heritors Choice. This appears to me to be contrary to the Laws and Inftitutions of the Lord Jefus, the only Lord and Lawgiver unto his Church and People, being contrary to the Apoftolical Practice and Example recorded in the New Teftament, an Encroachment upon the Rights and Charters of the Sheep and Flock of Chrift, and alfo crofs to the End and Defign of the giving of a Gofpel-Miniftry unto the Church

It cannot be pled, That Heritors, as fuch, have any Right or Title from the Word of God to elect or call Minifters Civil Honour ought to be given to every one to whom it is due , and Harmony betwixt Heritors and the People of a Parifh, in an Affair of fuch Importance unto them, as it is moft defirable, fo it ought to be endeavoured by all proper and expedient Means But to give an ecclefiaftical Truft and Privilege, by a Church-Act and Conftitution, to any Set of Men, upon the Account of their Heritage, or other worldly Confiderations, appears to me to be contrary to the Nature of Chrift's Kingdom, which is *fpiritual.* And, as it involves the Judicatories of Chrift's Houfe

in

in Debates and Questions about the civil Rights and Titles of Heritors, which do not belong unto them, so it cannot be vindicated from that *partial Respect of Persons* condemned by the Word of God, which, in Matters of this Kind admits of no Difference betwixt *the Man with the Gold-Ring in goodly Apparel*, and the *poor Man in mean Raiment*, James ii. 2, 3, 4, 5

To impose a Minister upon a *reclaiming* and *dissenting* People, who yet make a *professed Subjection* to the Ordinances of the Gospel, and declare themselves willing and ready to submit to the Ministry of such as are settled amongst them according to the Rules of the Word, appears to me to be contrary to the Apostolical Example and Practice recorded in the New Testament. I shall only touch at two Passages, the one in the first, and the other in the sixth Chapter of the *Acts of the Apostles;* they are both made Use of by our reformed Divines in their Pleadings against the Tyranny and Oppression of the Church of *Rome*

As to the first of them, the Account given by the inspired Historian *Luke*, stands thus Peter *stood up in the Midst of the Disciples*, and it is observed that the *Number of the Names together were about an Hundred and twenty*, Acts i. 15. He acquaints them of a Vacancy in the Apostolical College, by the Treachery and Death of *Judas*, v. 16, 20. He moves that One should be ordained in his Room, and, to direct them in their Nomination, he informs them of the Qualifications requisite in him who should succeed in that important Charge, *Verses* 21, 22. Then it follows, *They appointed Two*, Verse 23 They all joined together in Prayer, and in Prayer made a solemn Reference of the Matter to the Lord, for his immediate Designation of the

par-

particular Perfon, *Verfes* 24, 25. and then the
give forth their Lots in the 26th *Verfe*. The Nomi
nation or Appointment of the Two is made by all
the Hundred and twenty Difciples affembled to
gether, and this muft be admitted, without an e
vident ftretching of the Context, feeing the Num
ber of them is fo particularly condefcended upon,
and the Apoftle *Peter* addreffes them all under the
Appellation of *Men and Brethren* For clearing this
Paffage a little, I make the following Obferves.

1*ft*. This is the *firft* Account we have of any
Officer being given unto the Church after the A
fcenfion of our bleffed Lord, it is the firft Defig
nation and Appointment of a teaching Officer unto
the Church immediately after our Lord's Afcen
fion.

2*dly*. The Apoftle *Peter*, in his Difcourfe unto
the Difciples, makes not the leaft Intimation that
he had any immediate or extraordinary Direction
for the Motion that he now makes unto them,
but only produceth for his Warrant a Paffage from
Pfalm cix. for, fays he, *It is written in the Book of*
Pfalms, ——— *His Bifhoprick let another take*
Therefore, to alledge that *Peter* had Knowledge,
by extraordinary or immediate Revelation, of the
particular Perfon whom God had defigned fhould
fucceed *Judas* in the Apoftlefhip, is fo far from be
ing evident by his Speech, that it appears to be di
rectly contrary unto it

3*dly*. It is moft probable, that the Hundred and
twenty Difciples, affembled together at this Time,
were fuch who, for the moft Part, dwelt in or a
bout *Jerufalem*, where the firft Chriftian Church
was gathered and conftituted, according to the Pro
phecy, *Micah* iv 2. *For the Law fhall go forth of*
Zion, and the Word of the Lord from Jerufalem.
And

And therefore there was no Need for assembling together, upon this Occasion, the Five hundred Brethren by whom Christ was seen at once, and who were scattered throughout *Judea* and *Galilee.* And if it is alledged that the Hundred and twenty here assembled were Church-Officers, this is not only without Warrant from the Word of God, but appears to be contrary to it, in regard the Lord Jesus gave Office, Power and Authority to none after his Resurrection, and before his Ascension, but to his eleven Apostles only, *John* xx. 22, 23 *Matth.* xxviii. 18, 19. As for the seventy Disciples mentioned in *Luke* x as we do not read that their Commission was renewed after the Resurrection of Christ, so their Mission seems to have been only transient and temporary, and designed to prepare Christ's Way into the Places to which he was to come, *Luke* x. 1, 9, 10, 11. And there is no Evidence for it, that any of them were present at this Meeting

4thly. Tho' the Teaching-Officer, designed in this Place, is an extraordinary One, and therefore behoved to have an immediate Commission, yet all the Apostles, beside what was extraordinary in their Office, had every Thing that was proper to all the ordinary Ministers of the Gospel · Therefore we find them sometimes laying aside their extraordinary Character, and acting in the Capacity of other ordinary teaching Elders, so did all the Apostles at the Synodical Meeting · *Jerusalem,* Acts xv. so did the Apostle *Paul* in the Ordination of *Timothy,* 1 *Tim* iv 14. and 2 *Tim.* i. 6 so does the Apostle *Peter,* when he says in his first Epistle, *Chap.* v. 1. *The Elders which are among you I exhort, who am also an Elder.* Hence every Minister of the Gospel is a Successor to the Apostles in every Thing

B

that

that was ordinary and standing in their Work and Office. This will not be disputed by any who own themselves to be of the Presbyterian Denomination.

5thly. There is a great Difference betwixt the Election or Nomination of one to a sacred Office in the Church, and authoritative Mission. This will readily be granted likeways by such as are of Presbyterian Principles. Authoritative Mission to a sacred Work and Office in the Church belongs only to the Office Bearers of the Church, who, according to the Apostolical Pattern and Example, authorize and set apart others for a sacred Function in the Church, with the usual Solemnities of Fasting, Prayer and Imposition of Hands, after Trial of their Gifts and Abilities for the Discharge of the same.

6thly. In the Case of *Matthias*, there is a solemn Reference of the Matter made unto the Lord, for an extraordinary and immediate Decision in this weighty and important Affair, and the Signification of the Mind and Will of God in it is committed unto a Lot. It is needless for us to inquire into the Manner how they gave forth their Lots; only we may observe, what is plain from the Text, that when the Lot falls upon *Matthias*, he is not authorized unto his Work and Office by Prayer and Imposition of Hands, but the Intimation of the Mind of the Lord, by the Lot, is reckoned equivalent to that immediate Mission that the other eleven Apostles had from the Lord Jesus himself, and therefore, without any farther Solemnity, he *is numbred with the eleven Apostles.*

7thly We may observe, That there is nothing extraordinary in the Case of *Matthias*, except what concerned his authoritative Mission, all the pre-

. vious

vious Steps unto it are such as are made according to an ordinary Course of Judgment and Deliberation The Apostle *Peter* lays before them an express Scripture-Warrant for appointing one to succeed in the Room of *Judas*, Verse 20. and points out unto them the Qualifications requisite in him who was to be ordained unto that important Charge, *Verses* 21, 22 and it is said, *They appointed Two*, Verse 23. and there is no doubt but the Two they named were both of them such who they judged had the Qualifications mentioned.   And it is observable that the Leet is restricted to Two, a fewer Number there could not be, unless they had named the particular Person, which could not be done in this Case, because he was to bear an extraordinary Character   Yet the Leet is restricted to Two, even the smallest Number, which is a plain Evidence of the Interest and Concern of all the Disciples here assembled in this Matter, especially when it is considered, that the restricting of the Leet to the smallest Number, was upon the Matter, a restricting of the immediate Determination to One of the Two whom they had named   Farther, The Two who are named are not presented to the Apostles that they may set one of them apart by Prayer and Imposition of Hands, but an Appeal is made by all of them jointly unto the Lord himself, for his immediate Decision in this Matter   Whence it is plain, that the authoritative Mission of *Matthias* is the only Thing that is extraordinary and immediate in this Case, and it is not pled that authoritative Mission does belong in any Case to the whole Community of the Faithful

From these Observes the following Conclusion is plain unto me.

If,-

If, at the first Erection and Constitution of the New Testament Church, the first Teaching Officer, that was given immediately after our Lord's Ascension, was ordained in consequence of the Choice, Nomination or Consent of all the Disciples assembled together, then Ministers of the Gospel ought to be given unto the Church and People of God with their Call and Consent. If it is said, He was an extraordinary Officer, the Argument is yet the stronger, for if, in the giving of an extraordinary Officer, such as bore the Character of Disciples had an Interest in his Nomination, and if their Choice or Consent was thought needful, then it is much more requisite in the giving of ordinary Ministers unto the Church, especially when it is considered that all of them are Successors to the Apostles in every Thing that is ordinary in their Work and Calling

Yea, the Conclusion appears with some more Force and Evidence, when it is considered, that, in the giving of the first Teacher unto the New Testament Church, nothing was taken out of the Hands of the Disciples, but his authoritative Mission, which in no Case belongs unto them. Then, if Apostolical Practice and Example is a Rule or Pattern unto us, it is Violence done unto the Heritage and Flock of God to impose Ministers upon them, when they are both dissenting and reclaiming

The other Passage I name is, the sixth of the *Acts*, and it stands plainly thus. The Apostles represent unto the Multitude of the Disciples the Necessity of chusing some to have the Care and Oversight of the Poor, *Verse* 1, 2. They direct them to chuse some of their own Number for this Effect, and inform them of the Qualifications necessary in the Persons to be chosen, reserving unto
themselves

hemselves what did properly belong unto them as Office Bearers in the Church, namely the authorative Mission of such as should be chosen, therefore say they, *Whom we may appoint over this Business,* Verse 3. The Multitude of the Disciples make the Choice of the seven Deacons in the 5th *Verse*, they present them before the Apostles, and the Apostles, being satisfied with the Choice set them apart unto their Work and Office, with the usual Solemnities of Prayer and Imposition of Hands. And here I make the following Observes.

1st. That the Deacon is the first ordinary standing Officer given unto the New Testament Church after the Ascension of our blessed Lord. The Church of *Jerusalem* was at that Time under the immediate Inspection and Direction of the Twelve Apostles themselves, who did well supply the Place of all the ordinary Ministers of the Gospel, who were given afterwards to this as well as other Churches that were erected and constituted by them.

2dly. There is no material Difference in the Steps previously taken unto the Mission of *Matthias*, and that of the seven Deacons. In the Case of *Matthias*, as was observed, *Peter* addresseth all the Disciples present, and shews them the Necessity of appointing One to succeed in the Room of *Judas*, they name Two, out of which One is to be ordained to this sacred Office. And, in the Case of the Deacons, the Apostles called the Multitude of the Disciples together, and represented unto them the Expediency and Necessity of chusing some to take the Oversight of the Poor, the Disciples make the Nomination of the Seven. All the Difference is in what concerns the Mission of the one and the other. In the Case of *Matthias*, there is a solemn Reference made unto the Lord for an immediate

Designation

Designation of the Person, because he was to bear an extraordinary Character, but, in the Case of the Deacons, there is a particular Designation of the Persons made by the whole Multitude of the Disciples, and they are presented unto the Apostles, who set them apart unto their Office with the usual Solemnity observed in ordinary Cases, because their Office was standing and ordinary. Hence I conclude, That since all the previous Steps unto the Mission of the first Officers given unto the New Testament Church, immediately after the Ascension of Christ, had nothing extraordinary in them, they must be recorded as a plain Pattern and Directory unto the Church in all succeeding Generations, and any Thing that can be reasonably pled, as what should not be a standing Practice in the Church, is that extraordinary Circumstance in the Case of *Matthias*, which was necessary to determine his immediate Mission, and to give him an extraordinary Character

From these two Passages of Scripture we may see, that the first Teaching-Officer, appointed unto the Church immediately after the Ascension of our blessed Lord, was given in consequence of a Choice or Nomination made by the Disciples assembled together, as also, that the first Deacons were given by the Choice or Nomination of the whole Multitude of the Disciples, and all the Circumstances are so particularly condescended upon by the sacred Historian, that we have Ground to conclude, a plain Pattern and Directory is laid down, in these two particular Instances, for the Direction of the Church, in all succeeding Ages, how to proceed in the Designation and Appointment of such as are to bear Office over them · And the inspired Penman having, in the very Front of his excellent and

succinct

succinct History concerning the Erection and Constitution of the New Testament Church, treated so particularly of the Manner of giving the first Teaching Officer unto the Church, and to whom all the Ministers of the Gospel are Successors in all the ordinary Parts of his Calling and Office, as also, having treated of the Manner of the Institution of the first Deacons, he does not afterwards insist upon this Subject, and there was no Need he should do so : Therefore, when he writes of giving of Office Bearers unto the Churches afterwards erected by the Apostles, he wraps up all, according to his usual Manner, in a very sententious Phrase, *Acts* xiv 23 *And when they had ordained them Elders in every Church.* I shall not in this Preface insist upon the native and just Import of the original Word, only it is well known, that in other Translations it is rendred, *When they had appointed them Elders by Suffrages, or Votes, in every Church.* So *Beza*, in his *Latin* Translation of the New Testament.

If Apostolical Practice and Example, in the Erection and Constitution of the New Testament Church, is not reckoned equivalent unto a positive Precept, then we have no Warrant for solemnizing our Christian Sabbath on the first Day of the Week ; yea, the whole Frame of our Presbyterian Church-Government may be overturned, and the Government of the Church modelled according to the Pleasure and Arbitriment of Men. I sincerely wish that nothing of this Spirit may ever appear to be working amongst us.

As the present Practice, of imposing Ministers upon a reclaiming and dissenting Eldership and People, is contrary unto the above Apostolical Pattern and Example, so it appears to me to be

an

an Encroachment upon the Rights and Character of the Flock and Sheep of Christ recorded in his Word. As for Instance, it is the Character of them, that *they know his Voice*, John x 3. They are commanded to *try the Spirits*, 1 John iv 1 And *the spiritual Ear trieth Words, as the Mouth tasteth Meat*, Job xxxiv 3. If a Judgment of Discretion is the Right and Privilege of all the Disciples of Christ, with respect to whatever Doctrines are brought unto them, and if it is a Character of them, that they have a spiritual Knowledge and Discerning of the Voice of Christ in his own Word, it must also be their Right and Privilege to have a Judgment of Discretion about these Gifts, and that Manner of Teaching which is most adapted to their spiritual Edification As there are Diversities of Gifts, so one Gift is more adapted to the Capacity and Edification of one Congregation than another: Therefore, to impose Ministers upon a reclaiming and dissenting Congregation, must be a plain Encroachment upon that Judgment of Discretion, which is the unquestionable Right and Privilege of all that are the Flock of Christ, especially when it is considered, that their Choice may fall upon one who is at least as unexceptionable in the Eye of the Presbytery, as the other who is imposed upon them. And, when this is the Case, every unprejudiced Person may consider, where, according to the Word of God, and common Equity, the Balance should be cast, and if the great and valuable Ends of a Gospel Ministry, *namely*, the Conversion of Sinners, 2 Cor v. 20. the Perfecting of the Saints, and the Edification of the Body of Christ, *Eph* iv. 12. if, I say, these valuable Ends can probably be obtained by imposing Ministers upon a dissenting Congregation, at the Instance of some

Heritors

Heritors, the moft of them perhaps not refiding, or difaffected unto our Presbyterian Conftitution.

This leads me to another Obferve, and it is the laft I make on this Head, *namely*, That if the Power of electing and calling Minifters had been reftricted, by the Act of Affembly, to fuch as are of known and difinterefted Affection to the Government of the Church of *Scotland*, and to the pure Worfhip practifed therein, the Grievance complained of had been more tolerable; we might have reafonably expected that fuch would have had fome Regard in their Calling of Minifters to People of the fame Principles and Sentiments with themfelves, but it is otherways, this Power is given, and that by an ecclefiaftical Act and Conftitution too, to Proteftant Heritors in general, without any other Limitation or Reftriction; whereby the Settlement of many Congregations in *Scotland* is put into the Hands of fuch who will think it no Reflection upon their Character, when I fay, that they are declared Oppofites to the Conftitution of the Church of *Scotland*, and difaffected in Principle to the late glorious Revolution, and to the Proteftant Succeffion in the illuftrious Family of *Hanover*. This is a Compliment I do not know if ever they would have asked of the Church of *Scotland*, and I am fure the Day has been when they would not have expected it. But I do not infift upon this, in regard the keeneft Advocates for the Act have not attempted any Vindication of it.

It is faid, The Point upon which our prefent Teftimony is ftated, is a difputable Point. If, by a difputable Point, they mean a Point that has been and is actually difputed by many, I grant it is fo, and fo is our Presbyterian Church-Government, yea, fo are all the Articles of our Chriftian Religi-

on;

on; they are difputed by too many in this Age: But if, by a difputable Point, is meant a Point that has never been fixed in this Church, or a Point that fuch as are of the Prefbyterian Denomination have difputed amongft themfelves, then I refufe that our Teftimony is ftated upon any fuch difputable Point. The Points upon which our prefent Teftimony ftands are as follows.

That Heritors, as fuch, have no Warrant from the Word of God to call and chufe Minifters, yea, that it is contrary to the Word of God to give this Truft to Heritors as fuch, and particularly to thofe that are not of the Communion of the Church of *Scotland*, and that it is contrary to Apoftolical Practice and Example, to impofe Minifters upon a reclaiming and diffenting Congregation, who are ready and willing to fubmit to the Ordinances of the Gofpel. As thefe are the Points upon which our Teftimony againft the late Act of Affembly is ftated, fo, if it can be made appear that any of the Prefbyterian Denomination (before that Act of Affembly gave Birth to our prefent Difputes) have affirmed, that Minifters may be warrantably fettled over reclaiming and diffenting Congregations, at the Inftance or upon the Call of Heritors, moft of them perhaps not refiding, or not of the Communion of the Church of *Scotland*, or that Minifters may be fettled, according to the Rules of God's Word, in Congregations where the major Part, both of Elders and People are diffenting and reclaiming, tho' the faid diffenting and reclaiming People make a profeffed Subjection unto the Ordinances of the Gofpel, if I fay, they can make it appear that any of the Prefbyterian Denomination have affirmed fuch Things then, they may argue that our Teftimony is ftated upon a difputable Point.

But

But it is not the abovementioned Act of Assembly alone, but some other Proceedings of the Judicatories of this Church, together with some Steps I judged it my Duty to take in Conjunction with my other Brethren, that have been the more immediate Occasion of the condemnatory Sentence that is past against me, of which I offer the following short Account.

Mr. *Erskine* Minister at *Stirling* did, in a Sermon preached in your Hearing at the Opening of our Synod *October* last, with some Freedom and Plainness of Speech, declare the Sinfulness and Unwarrantableness of the Act of Assembly 1732 and of the present Proceedings of our Church-Judicatories in the Settlement of Ministers over reclaiming and dissenting Congregations : The Freedom and Faithfulness he used was so much resented, that three Days were spent in warm Reasonings upon the Sermon, and then, by a small Majority, the Preacher was condemned as censurable for some Expressions emitted by him in his Sermon, and appointed to be brought to the Bar of the Synod to be rebuked and admonished. As he appealed from this Sentence to the general Assembly, so I judged it my Duty, with some others of my Brethren, to protest against and dissent from the same.

When this Cause came before the late General Assembly, they thought fit to affirm the Sentence of our Synod, in the following Terms. *The General Assembly having, at a former Diet, considered an Appeal entred by Mr Ebenezer Erskine Minister at Stirling, from a Sentence of the Synod of Perth and Stirling, wherein the said Synod had found Ground to censure him, and appointed him to be rebuked, on account of several indecent Expressions uttered by him in a Sermon preached before the said Synod in October last,*
tending

*tending to disquiet the Peace of this Church, and im-
pugning several Acts of Assembly, and Proceedings of
the Church-Judicatories, and had appointed him to be
admonished to behave orderly for the future,——the
Assembly found these Expressions vented by Mr Erskine,
and contained in the Minutes of the foresaid Synod's
Proceedings, with the Answers thereto made by him,
to be offensive, and tend to disturb the Peace and good
Order of this Church; therefore they approved the Proceedings of the Synod, and appointed him to be rebuked
and admonished by the Moderator at their own Bar*

Yet none of the Expressions alledged to be emitted
by Mr *Erskine*, nor any Thing given in by him in
his Answers unto the Synod, was found, either by
the Synod or General Assembly, to be contrary to
to the Word of God, or the received and approven
Standards of this Church

Mr. *Erskine* acknowledging *a very great and duti-
ful Regard to the Judicatories of this Church, to whom
he owned Subjection in the Lord, yet, in respect the
Assembly had found him censurable, and had tendered
a Rebuke and Admonition to him for Things he con-
ceived agreeable unto and founded upon the Word of God,
and our approven Standards, therefore he found himself obliged to protest against the foresaid Censure, as*
importing, *That he had in his Doctrine, at the Opening of the Synod October last, departed from the Word
of God, and the foresaid Standards, and that he should
be at Liberty to preach the same Truths of God, and to
testify against the same or like Defections of this Church,
upon all proper Occasions, adhering unto the Testimonies he had formerly emitted against the Act of
Assembly* 1732. *whether in the Protest against it in
open Assembly, or yet in his Synodical Sermon*

If this Cause had been Mr *Erskine's* personal
Cause, I should have judged my Dissent from the
Sentence

Sentence of our Synod sufficient to exoner me in the present Case, but when I considered, that it is a Cause of very publick Concern, and wherein all the Ministers and Members of this Church are so nearly interested, I judged it my Duty to own my Dissent from the Sentence of our Synod at the Bar of the Assembly, who thought fit to refuse the Dissenters a Hearing on that Subject, and when the General Assembly affirmed the said Sentence, I durst not be silent, and therefore, in Conjunction with my Brother Mr *Moncrief*, I signed an Adherence to the above Protestation in the following Terms

We underscribing Ministers, Dissenters from the Sentence of the Synod of Perth *and* Stirling, *do hereby adhere to the above Protestations and Declaration, containing a Testimony against the Act of Assembly* 1732. *and asserting our Privilege and Duty to testify publickly against the same, or like Defections, upon all proper Occasions.*

The General Assembly was so much offended at this our Protestation, that they appointed their Commission, at their Meeting *August* thereafter, to suspend us every One from the Exercise of our Ministry, in case we should not declare our Sorrow for our Conduct, and retract the above Paper we gave in As also to proceed to a higher Censure against us at any subsequent Meeting, if we should be found to act contrary to the foresaid Sentence of Suspension

As the Act of Assembly 1732 appears to me to be sinful, so the above Decision, protested against, appears to me to be such as gave sufficient Foundation and Ground for the Testimony that is given against it, in regard that, by the said Decision of Assembly, not only is our Brother

ther

ther Mr. *Erskine* appointed to be rebuked, but it carries, in its own Nature, a material Declaration that all the Ministers of this Church, who shall upon any proper Occasion, regret from the Pulpit the Sinfulness or Unwarrantablness of that Act of Assembly, or of any other sinful and unwarrantable Proceedings of the Judicatories of this Church, either in the violent Settlement of Ministers, or otherways, must be brought to the Bar of Church-Judicatories, and there be rebuked for the faithful Discharge of their Duty, therefore I have Peace in my own Mind in declaring against this Decision, and that with the Solemnity of a Protestation. Our *Representations* given in to the Commission of the General Assembly, at their Meeting *August* last, and now published to the World, contain our Reasons at large for refusing to *retract* our *Protestation*, to which I refer.

What is now past against me I know, and what I am farther threatned with I may partly know, yet I cannot see every Thing that my above Conduct may expose me unto : But whatever I may be called to endure or suffer, according to my present Views, it is stated upon the three following Points The *first* is, That any ecclesiastical Ordinance or Constitution, contrary to the Laws and Institutions of our Lord Jesus, the only Lord and Lawgiver unto his Church and People, is in it self sinful and therefore can have no binding Force nor Authority over any of the Office-Bearers or Members of the Church of Christ And such the Act of Assembly 1732 appears to me to be, for the Reasons I have already given The *second* Point (and which is yet a more immediate Ground upon which our present Testimony is stated) is this, That the Ministers of the Church of *Scotland*

and ought, upon all proper Occasions, to declare, even from the Pulpit, the Sinfulness that is in any ecclesiastical Act and Constitution, or the Sinfulness and Unwarrantableness of such Proceedings of the Church-Judicatories, whereby the Heritage and Flock of God are opprest, and whereby our Constitution is wounded, by the Opening of a wide Door for the bringing in of a corrupt Ministry into the Church of Christ, especially when the ordinary Means of Representations and Instructions unto our several General Assemblies have been tried, but without Success. This is what the Word of God, our Presbyterian Principles, and our Ordination-Vows and Engagements oblige us unto. This is our Duty, as we are Watchmen set upon *Jerusalem*'s Walls, and appointed to sound the Trumpet, and to give the Alarm of approaching Danger to the City of God The *third* Point is, That this Freedom and Liberty of testifying publickly, upon all proper Occasions, against the publick Sins and Defections of a Church, ought not to be supprest or restrained, and if it is supprest or restrained by an ecclesiastical Act or Decision, then it is the Duty and Privilege of the Ministers and Members of the Church, to testify against any such Sentence and Decision, as what fixeth the Ministers of the Church under sinful and unwarrantable Terms of ministerial Communion. And this is what is our Case with respect to our Protestation against the foresaid Decision of the late General Assembly. We have declared, in our Representations to the last Meeting of the Commission, that we did not intend, by our Protestation, to impugn the Power and Authority of the General Assembly to censure any of the Ministers and Members of this Church upon just and relevant Grounds, or the

Exercise

Exercife of that Power and Authority according
to the Word of God, and the known Principles
of this Church ; and that our forefaid Proteftation
is only a folemn attefted Declaration and Teftimo
ny againft a wrong Decifion of the General Af
fembly, which lays a Reftraint upon minifterial
Freedom and Faithfulnefs · And this Proteftation
we could not retract, becaufe fuch a Retraction
might have been juftly conftructed, not only to be
a Submitting unto a Decifion that lays fuch a finful Embargo upon Minifters, but alfo a giving up
with what is a proper and legal Mean of teftify-
ing, before a Church-Judicatory, againft an unwarrantable Sentence and Decifion   As thefe are
the Points upon which I am fingled out, together
with my other three Brethren, as the Object of the
heavy and fevere Cenfure contained in the Act and
Sentence of the late General Affembly againft us,
fo I hope I have no Ground to be afraid or a
fhamed to own them

The Church of *Scotland* has been honoured to
bear Witnefs in a fpecial Manner to the kingly
Office of Chrift, and that unto him it belongs to
give Laws and Ordinances unto his own Houfe,
and Inftructions unto his Minifters, who are obliged
to *teach all Things whatfoever he hath commended*
them.   And the above Points, upon which our prefent Teftimony is ftated, are the fame, upon the
Matter, with that which a great Cloud of Witneffes in *Scotland* have born Teftimony unto fince
the Dawning of Reformation-Light amongft us.
And tho' I fhould be expofed to fuffer Trouble as
an Evil Doer, even unto Bonds, for the fame, yet
may I hope *the Word of the Lord is not bound,*
2 Tim. ii. 9.

Tho'

Tho' our Mission unto the Work and Office of the Ministry is mediate, yet our Commission and Authority to discharge our Ministry is from the Lord Jesus himself. Every Minister of the Gospel is honoured to be an *Ambassador for Christ*, to act in the Name of Christ, and to *stand in his Stead*, 2 Cor. v. 20. They have both their Commission and also their Instructions from him alone : The Judicatories of his House are only the Channel through which their Commission flows; they are no more than the interveening Means of the Conveyance of that Power and Authority which is derived from the Lord Jesus himself, and none can recal the Commission given unto his Ministers, but according unto the Rules and Directions that he has laid down in his own Word. There is at least some Resemblance in it unto the present Subject : When the Sovereign gives a Commission to any to act in his Name, the Commission comes through the Hands of the Keeper of the King's Seal, and it is sealed by him ; but neither the Keeper of the Seal, nor any of the Ministers of State, can recal the Commission, till the Sovereign declare his Mind and Will in this Matter : Even so, tho' our Commission to preach the Word of the Gospel comes to us through the Hands of them who are intrusted with the Keeping of the Seal of the King of *Zion*, yet no Power nor Authority upon Earth can recal our Commission, but according to the Mind and Will of the Head and King of the Church, declared in his Word unto his Church and People.

I am not convicted of any Thing before the Judicatories of this Church, either in Doctrine or Practice, contrary to the Word of God, our Confession of Faith, or Presbyterian Principles, and

D

there-

therefore it is my Duty to endeavour to fulfil that Ministry among you which I have received from the Lord, and to preach his Word out of Season, as well as in Season, and all that I desire of you is, that you may pray for the Supplies of the Spirit of Jesus unto me, that I may be enabled unto the faithful Discharge of my Duty amongst you, as also that you may receive the Word of Reconciliation which I am honoured to bear, and that, whatever I may be exposed unto in the Discharge of my Duty, you may not be ashamed of my Bonds.

The Burgh of *Perth* was honoured, at the very Dawning of Reformation-light, first of all the Burghs in *Scotland*, to make a noble Stand for our Reformation Rights and Privileges, in Opposition to the Idolatry and ecclesiastical Tyranny of the Church of *Rome*, under which the whole Land groaned at that Time, and ye have distinguished yourselves in a zealous Concern for, and by a steddy Adherence unto our civil and religious Liberties, particularly in the Year 1715. when many of you suffered Banishment from your own Habitations, and endured some other Hardships, after you were overpowered by Force and Violence, and obliged to give Way to the superior Number of those who came against you, and made this Place for some Time the Seat of their displayed Banner against the Revolution Interest, our late Sovereign King *George*, and the Protestant Succession in his Royal Family.

But our good and gracious God did scatter these Clouds, he restored you to your Habitations, he preserved this Place, when some neighbouring Villages were laid in Ashes, and he has followed you since that Time with a Series and Train of remarkable Blessings. All these lay you
under

under so many Obligations to a stedfast Perseverance in the Truths and Way of the Lord.

My present Situation may, I hope, apologize for the Length of this Preface : I intend not in it the Irritation of any, but to discharge myself of what I judge to be a Debt I owe to the People of my pastoral Charge in a particular Manner, whatever the Consequences of this whole Affair towards myself may be As for the Discourse immediately following, my Design, in the several Preachings on that Subject, was, according unto the Measure of the Grace of Christ given unto me, to recommend unto you the Faith of our Lord Jesus, and a stedfast Perseverance in the same.

That you may know the Truth as it is in Christ, and that you may be rooted and built up in him, and may be established in the Faith, is the Prayer of him

Who is one of your Pastors, more willing than able to serve you in the Work of the Gospel,

Perth, Sep. 22d,
1733.

WILLIAM WILSON.

1 COR.

1 Cor. xvi. 13.

Watch ye, stand fast in the Faith, quit you like Men, be strong.

THE Words I have read are amongst the useful and necessary Directions given by the inspired Penman, the Apostle *Paul*, in the Conclusion of this his excellent Epistle to the *Corinthians*, and I hope they are suitable and proper for us to discourse unto you immediately after the solemn Profession of Subjection and Obedience unto the Lord Jesus, that many of you have made this Day in the Sacrament of our Lord's Supper   In this Verse the Spirit of God, by the Apostle recommends three necessary Duties unto the *Corinthians*, and in them unto us all, and every one who professes the Faith of the Lord Jesus, namely, Watchfulness, *Watch ye*, Stedfastness in the Faith, *stand fast in the Faith*, and Christian Courage and Resolution, whatever Dangers and Difficulties may be in our Way, *quit you like Men, be strong*.

The *first* Thing we are here exhorted to, is Watchfulness, *Watch ye*; this is a Duty frequently prest upon the Christian.   After the first Celebration of this Sacrament our blessed Lord exhorts his Disciples unto it, *Matth.* xxvi 41. *Watch and pray, that ye enter not into Temptation*. And this is necessary for the Christian at all Times ; he has always Need to be upon his Watch-Tower, for he lives in the Midst of Snares ; he is surrounded with Enemies, and exposed

poſed to manifold Dangers and Difficulties, and he has the ſtrong Remains of indwelling Sin in his own Heart, therefore, *watch ye*. But I do not inſiſt at this Time upon the Duty of Watchfulneſs, having ſpoken unto it on a former Occaſion of this Nature.

The *ſecond* Thing we are exhorted unto in this Verſe, is Stedfaſtneſs in the Faith, *ſtand faſt in the Faith*. There may be an Alluſion in the Words to the Charge that is given to Soldiers when they are attacked by the Enemy. Every one that is a Chriſtian indeed, is a Soldier under the Banner of Chriſt, he goes a Warfare under the Conduct of the Captain of Salvation, therefore *watch ye, ſtand faſt in the Faith*: As if the Apoſtle had ſaid, You have Enemies, and your Enemies will be upon you, be on your Guard, ſtand firm, give not Way, but keep your Ground, whatever Oppoſition you may meet with, and arm yourſelves with a Courage and Reſolution that becomes the good Cauſe you are engaged in, and the good Captain you fight under, *quit you like Men, be ſtrong*. It is the ſecond Clauſe of the Verſe I am now to diſcourſe upon, and the Doctrine I offer you is this,

> That it is the Duty of the Chriſtian, and it ought to be his Care and Concern, to ſtand faſt in the Faith.

In diſcourſing this Doctrine, I ſhall, in the 1ſt Place, offer you ſome Remarks for clearing our Way upon this Subject. 2*dly*. I will endeavour to ſhew you what you are exhorted unto, when you are called to ſtand faſt in the Faith. 3*dly*. Inquire what it is to ſtand faſt. 4*thly*. I ſhall give you the Reaſons of the Doctrine. And, in the *laft* Place, make some practical Use and Application of the whole.

The *first* Thing propofed, is, To offer some few *Remarks* for paving our Way on this Subject.

In the *1ft* Place, you may obferve that Faith is taken diverfe Ways in Scripture: As for Inftance, fometimes it is taken for the Principles of Faith, or the Truths we are called to believe, so, *Jude* 3. *Content earneftly for the Faith once delivered to the Saints* Again, it is frequently taken for the Grace of Faith, and the Exercife thereof, as, *Gal.* ii 3. *The Life which I now live in the Flefh, I live by the Faith of the Son of God* I fhall exclude none of thefe, but take them both in, in the Sequel of this Difcourfe. Tho' the Principles of Faith, or the Truths we ought to believe, feem to be here principally intended, yet the Exercife of the Grace of Faith is a neceffary and ufeful Mean in order to our Perfeverance and Stedfaftnefs in them.

2dly. The Chriftian's Faith is a valuable and precious Jewel It is called *precious Faith*, 2 Pet. i 1 All the Truths of the Gofpel that he believes are his Glory, and his Stedfaftnefs in them is his Crown, *Rev* iii 11 *Hold that faft which thou haft, that no Man take thy Crown.* True Chriftians have a common Denomination from their Faith They are called *Believers*, every one of them believe in an unfeen Chrift, 1 *Pet* i 8 *Whom having not feen, ye love, in whom, tho' now ye fee him not, yet believing ye rejoice* &c They all live by Faith upon Chrift in his Word of Promife, *Heb* x. 38 *Now the Juft fhall live by Faith*

3dly The Chriftian has many Adverfaries unto his Faith. Hell and Earth, Devils and Men, are

against

against the Christian's Faith. *Satan* endeavours all that he can, either to bereave him of it, or to weaken it, hence is that Warning given to *Peter*, Luke xxii. 31, 32. Simon, Simon *Satan hath desired to have you, that he may sift you as Wheat.* The Men of the World are also Enemies to the Faith of the Christian, the World hateth him, and his Faith too, yea, the World hateth him because of his Faith, *John* xv 19. *Because ye are not of the World, but I have chosen you out of the World, therefore the World hateth you*

4thly. You may observe that the Christian's Faith is many Times sore tried It is tried by manifold Temptations, 1 *Pet* 1 6, 7 *If Need be, ye are in Heaviness through manifold Temptations: That the Trial of your Faith being much more precious than that of Gold that perisheth,* &c All the Graces of the Christian are tried, his Love, his Patience and Submission are all tried But Faith is the leading Grace, and therefore the Trials of the Christian are called the Trial of his Faith, his Faith is in a special Manner tried, and, if it stands out the Trial, all the other Graces of the Spirit will also come forth as Gold when it is tried I shall here give some few particular Instances of the Temptations and Trials that the Christian's Faith meets with

1. The Faith of the Christian is sometimes tried by cross Providences from the immediate Hand of God · So was *Abraham's* tried, when God commanded him to offer up the Son of the Promise, *Isaac*, Gen. xxii 1 and his Faith stood firm under the Trial, for he *accounted that God was able to raise him up even from the Dead: From whence also he received him in a Figure* Heb xi 19 The Christian's Faith is frequently tried by outward

Afflictions

Afflictions from the immediate Hand of God, and also by inward Defertion : This was the Cafe of *Job*, the Hand of God was upon his Body, and upon his Subftance too ; the Lord did likeways hide his Face from him, *Job* xxiii. 8, 9. *Behold, I go forward, but he is not there, and backward, but I cannot perceive him. On the Left-Hand where he doth work, but I cannot behold him : He hideth himself on the Right-Hand, that I cannot fee him.* Yet his Faith ftood firm under this Trial , for, fays he, *Though he flay me, yet will I truft in him,* Job xiii. 15.

2. The Chriftian's Faith is fore tried from the Temptations and fiery Darts of *Satan.* A Meffenger of *Satan* was fent to buffet *Paul,* 2 *Cor.* xii. 7. And there is nothing that *Satan* levels his Temptations fo much againft, as the Faith of the Chriftian , he knows that if he prevails here, all is gained to his Side . Therefore, when *Satan* is permitted to fift *Peter,* Chrift *prayed for him, that his Faith might not fail,* Luke xxii 32.

3. The Chriftian's Faith is fore tried from the World. (1) From the infnaring Pleafures and Profits of this World. So was the Faith of *Mofes* tried , when he was in *Pharaoh*'s Court, all the Pleafures, Honours, and Preferments of the Court of *Egypt* were in his Offer , yea, he had the Profpect of enjoying the Crown and Kingdom of *E-gypt :* But his Faith triumphed over all thefe infnaring Allurements, *Heb.* xi 24 *By Faith* Mofes, *when he was come to Years, refufed to be called the Son of* Pharaoh's *Daughter, chufing rather to fuffer Affliction with the People of God, than to enjoy the Pleafures of Sin for a Seafon.* (2.) From the Frowns and Reproaches of the World. *Mofes's* Faith did likeways meet with this Trial. When he left the

E   Court

Court of *Pharaoh*, and declared himſelf an *Iſrael-ite*, he joined himſelf to the Society of a contemptible and deſpiſed People, the Shepherds of *Goſhen*, who were Servants and Slaves unto the *Egyptians* ; and he behoved to lay his Account with all the Scorn, Contempt and Reproach that *Pharaoh* and his Court could throw upon him · Yet by Faith he overcame all this , for he *eſteemed the Reproach of Chriſt greater Riches than the Treaſures* of Egypt, *Heb.* xi. 26. Yea, not only did he o-vercome the Reproach and Scorn, but even the Fury and Rage of the King , *Ver.* 27. *By Faith he forſook* Egypt, *not fearing the Wrath of the King : For he endured, as ſeeing him who is inviſible.* (3.) The Chriſtian's Faith is frequently tried from the cor-rupt Doctrines that are in the World. Error is often propagated in the Church, in Oppoſition to the Truths of God , and the Tendency of it is to darken and overthrow Truth, and to ſhake the Faith of the Believers, 1 *Cor.* xi. 19. *For there muſt be alſo Hereſies among you, that they which are approved may be made manifeſt.* (4) The Chriſtian's Faith is ſometimes tried by violent Perſecution from the World , the Followers of Chriſt muſt lay their Account with it, to have their Faith tried by the worſt Treatment the World can give them : So it was with the Cloud of Witneſſes mentioned *Heb.* xi. 36, 37. *They had Trial of cruel Mockings and Scourgings , yea, moreover, of Bonds and Impriſon-ments · They were ſtoned, they were ſawn aſunder,* &c. (5.) The Chriſtian's Faith may be tried by ſevere and rough Treatment from thoſe of the ſame Pro-feſſion with them , they may paſs harſh and ſevere Sentences againſt them You have a remarkable Scripture to this Purpoſe, *Iſa.* lxvi 5. *Your Bre-thren that hated you, that caſt you out for my Name's Sake,*

Sake, faid, Let the Lord be glorified. See what the Trial is that thofe here mentioned met with, *they were hated and caft out*, that is, caft out of the Church, caft out of the Society of their Brethren : And by whom were they caft out ? Not by open Enemies, but even by *their Brethren*, by thofe of the fame Profeffion with themfelves And what is the Pretence for cafting them out ? They faid, *Let the Lord be glorified.* Their Brethren, who did caft them out, did pretend a Regard to the Honour and Glory of God in fo doing, yet the Spirit of God fays it was for his *Name's Sake* that they were hated and caft out. I only obferve from this, that there is fomething to be found in the Word of God that meets every Cafe that the Chriftian may be in · If the Faith of any fhall be tried after this Manner, it may be encouraging to them in the Work of the Lord, and in the Way of their Duty, that others that have gone before them have met with the like Trial ; the Cafe is not fingular, for *there is no new Thing under the Sun*

4. The Chriftian's Faith is fore tried, not only from the World, but likewavs from himfelf, from the Remains of indwelling Sin within him, from the Atheifm and Unbelief of his own Heart, *Heb.* iii. 12. *Take heed, Brethren, left there be in any of you an evil Heart of Unbelief, in departing from the living God.* There is a continual War in the Believer, he has the *Company of two Armies* within him, Atheifm and Unbelief fight againft his Faith, and fometimes Unbelief prevails, and carries him down the Stream, *Pfalm* cxvi 11. *I faid in my Hafte, All Men are Liars* The Faith of the two Difciples was very low, and their Unbelief very ftrong, when they faid, *Luke* xxiv. 21 *But we trufted that it had been he which fhould have redeemed* Ifrael . *And befide all*
this,

this, to-day is the third Day since these Things were done. But tho' Unbelief may prevail for a Time, yet Faith shall in the Issue get the Ascendant, *Micah* vii. 8. *Rejoice not against me, O mine Enemy When I fall, I shall arise; when I sit in Darkness, the Lord shall be a Light unto me.*

I proceed now to the *second* Thing proposed, *namely*, To shew you what it is you are called to stand fast in, when you are exhorted to stand fast in the Faith. And here I shall condescend on a few Things wherein you ought to stand fast.

1*st.* Stand fast in the Faith, that is, stand fast in the *Object* of your Faith. Christ himself is the Object of the Christian's Faith, to stand fast in the Faith, is to stand fast in the Lord, *Phil* iv. 1 *Therefore, my Brethren, dearly beloved and longed for, my Joy and Crown, so stand fast in the Lord.* The Christian stands fast in Christ the Object of his Faith, (1) When he keeps his Eye fixed upon him, when he lives habitually within Sight of him . So did *Moses*, he *endured, as seeing him who is invisible*, Heb. xi. 27. And so did *David*, when he says, *I have set the Lord always before me,* Psalm xvi. 8. (2) The Christian stands fast in the Lord, when he maintains high and honourable Thoughts of him at all Times, and in all Cases To stand fast in Christ the Object of Faith, it is to bless him when he *takes*, as well as when he *gives* · So did *Job*, Chap i 21 *The Lord gave, and the Lord hath taken away, blessed be the Name of the Lord* It is to commend him when he frowns, as well as when he smiles . When he frowns, to say, He is holy, just and righteous, *Psalm* xxii 3 *But thou art holy* If any of you are this Day complaining that you have not found him to your
Sense,

Senfe, neither in the Word, nor at the Communion-Table, juftify the Lord and condemn yourfelves · If you are enabled to this, as it is a Sign
that he is prefent unto your Faith, tho' abfent as
to your Senfe, fo it will be fome Evidence of the
Stedfaftnefs of your Faith   (3) To ftand faft in
the Object of Faith, is to lean upon him who is
the Rock and Strength of *Ifrael*   The Chriftian's Life ought to be a Life of conftant Dependence upon the Lord Jefus, *Song viii 5 Who is this
that cometh up from the Wildernefs leaning upon her
Beloved?* Lean upon him for Strength and Furniture for all Duties of Obedience, and for Support
under all your Difficulties . The Glory of your
Strength is in him, it is in his Strength that you
muft go on in your Chriftian Courfe, you muft
walk up and down in his Name, Zech x 12

2*dly.* Stand faft in the *Principles* of Faith   that
is, in all and every one of the *Truths* of God that
you profefs, and which you are called to believe
You ought to hold faft the Principles of Faith, e-
fpecially when the Wind of Error blows *Eph iv 14.
Be no more Children toffed to and fro, and carried about
with every Wind of Doctrine, by the Sleight of Men, and
cunning Craftinefs, whereby they ly in Wait to deceive.*
You ought to ftand faft in the Truths of Chrift, e-
fpecially when they are oppofed or controverted :
As for Inftance, If any of the Truths concerning
the glorious Perfon of Chrift are undermined, if
his *Supreme Deity* and *Neceffary Exiftence* are called in queftion, then we are boldly to own and
avow the fame, if any of the Truths that concern
the Offices of Chrift are oppofed, we ought to
contend for them; if the fupernatural Teaching
of the Spirit is cried down, then we ought to
plead for it , if the Righteoufnefs of Faith is ob-

fcured

fcured or darkned, then we ought to ftand up in the Defence of it, if the kingly Office of Chrift is affaulted, then we ought to bear Teftimony unto it What concerns the kingly Office of Chrift has been juftly reckoned the Word of his Patience given unto the Church of *Scotland* in a particular Manner to contend for, and fhe has been honoured to bear Witnefs unto thefe and the like Truths, *That the Lord Jefus, and he alone, is King over* Zion, *the Hill of his Holinefs, and that the Government is laid upon his Shoulders,* and that *all the Veffels his Father's Houfe hang upon him,* and likeways that he has the ordering of the Affairs of his own Houfe in his own Hand, and the Office-Bearers muft be given unto his own Church and People according to the Rules that he himfelf has laid down in his own Word, and alfo that no lordly Dominion ought to be exercifed over the Heritage and Flock of God · And therefore, if Church-Authority is exercifed beyond the Line of the Word, or in Contrariety unto the Laws and Inftitutions of Chrift, the only Lord and Lawgiver unto his Church, it is not to be regarded Thefe are fome of the Truths that concern the kingly Office of Chrift, and, if any of them is oppofed or denied, then a Teftimony ought to be given unto them. Let Men efteem of it as they they will, it is not only Duty, but an honourable Thing, to give Teftimony to the leaft of them, if I may fpeak fo of any of the Truths of Chrift In a Word, whatever Truth is controverted and born down, to ftand faft in the Faith, is to cleave to that Truth, and to give an open Teftimony unto the fame, when we are called unto it. If you inquire, To whom belongs it to give Teftimony unto controverted and oppofed Truth? I anfwer, in the *firft* Place, It ought to be given in a fpecial Man-

Manner by the *Watchmen* that are set upon *Jerusa-lem's* Walls, they ought to *set their Face as a Flint* in their Master's Cause, they ought to be bold against all Opposition, in his Strength, and under his Conduct, who said, by the Prophet his Type, *Isa* l. 7. *For the Lord God will help me, therefore shall I not be confounded. Therefore have I set my Face like a Flint, and I know that I shall not be ashamed.* Ministers are the Watchmen set upon the Church's Walls, and, if they see Danger coming, they should speak, and not hold their Peace, *Isa* lxii. 6. *I have set Watchmen upon thy Walls, O Jerusalem, which shall never hold their Peace Day nor Night.* Tho' Men should threaten them, tho' Men should endeavour to shut and stop their Mouths, yet the Authority of the Lord Jesus obligeth them to speak, whatever Dangers they may be exposed unto. 2*dly.* As the Watchmen of the City, so all the *Inhabitants* of the City of God ought, in their Stations, and when called unto it, to confess and bear Witness unto opposed Truth, Zion, *thy God confess.* If a Storm of Persecution shall break upon any of us for a Testimony that we have given against the Violence done to the Heritage of God at this Day, a Storm may also fall upon you, if the Watchmen of the City are driven from their Watch-Tower for their Faithfulness in the Discharge of their Duty, it is high Time for the Inhabitants of the City of God to look about them, and to fear least *the Enemy come in like a Flood* upon them. And if, when it comes to your Door, and when you are called unto it, you do not own and confess the Truths which you profess to believe, you betray Conscience and Principle too

3*dly.* Stand fast in the *Profession* of your Faith, *Heb.* x. 23. *Let us hold fast the Profession of our*
Faith

Faith without wavering. We make a Profeſſion of Faith in our daily Attendance upon the Ordinances of the Goſpel : We all make a Profeſſion of Faith in our Baptiſm , when we are baptized it is made by our Parents in our Name . And ſuch of us as have come to a Communion-Table make a Profeſſion of our Faith there · All of you who have been at the Lord's Table this Day have made a publick and ſolemn Profeſſion of your Faith in a crucified Chriſt, you have profeſſed to receive the Teſtimony of God concerning him, and that you are well pleaſed with the Way of Salvation thro' him you have declared, by your ſitting down at that Table, that you have choſen *Jehovah*, even a God in Chriſt, to be your Lord and your God, even him for your Husband and your Portion, and that you are well pleaſed with the Lord Jeſus as a Prophet to teach and inſtruct you, as a Prieſt to juſtify and ſave you by the Obedience of his Life and his Sufferings unto Death, and alſo as a King to reign and rule over you You have profeſſed to devote yourſelves unto his Obedience and Service, and unto a Subjection unto his Laws, Ordinances and Inſtitutions . Stand faſt then in the Profeſſion that you have made And, if you would do ſo, 1ſt. Walk like your Profeſſion; let your Converſation be like unto that holy Chriſtian Profeſſion that you have made, *Phil* 1. 27. *Only let your Converſation be as it becometh the Goſpel of Chriſt* Let your Walk in your Families, and in our Streets, be like the Goſpel of Chriſt, *be not conform to this World, but be you transformed by the Renewing of your Minds* If you conform yourſelves to the ſinful and vain Cuſtoms and Faſhions of this World, you depart in ſo far from the Profeſſion of your Faith. 2dly. Be not aſhamed

ed of your Profession. To stand fast in the Pro=
fession of your Faith, is to own Christ and his
Words, and not to be ashamed of them when they
are reviled, despised and reproached. It has been
observed in the Church, that there is a Multitude
of Professors in a fair Day, and in a cloudy and
stormy Day a Multitude of Apostates from their
Profession. Some make the Religion that is uppermost in the World theirs, the Way that's most
in Vogue, and least obnoxious to Censure, they
chuse that, and fall in with it · But, if you stand
fast in the Profession of your Faith, you will not
be ashamed of Christ and his Words, whatever
your Profession may expose you unto, *Mark* viii.
38 *Whosoever therefore shall be ashamed of me, and of
my Words, in this adulterous and sinful Generation, of
him also shall the Son of Man be ashamed, when he
cometh in the Glory of his Father with the holy Angels.*

4thly Stand fast in the *Ground* of your Faith.
What is the Ground and Bottom upon which the
Christian's Faith leans? It is even the Testimony of
God in his own Word. The Faith of the Christian is built upon the Faithfulness of God, for he
reckons him *faithful that hath promised* · The Veracity and Truth of God in his promising Word
is the only Pillar and Ground of saving Faith :
And if ever you have believed, it is upon the Testimony of God in his Word, evidencing itself by
the powerful Energy of his Spirit unto your Minds,
*your Faith stands not in the Wisdom of Men, but in
the Power of God*, 1 Cor. ii 5 To stand fast in
the Faith, is to cleave to the Testimony of God,
and to credit his Word of Promise, when Sense
fails you, and when Clouds and Darkness surround
you. The Bottom and Ground of the Christian's

F   Faith

Faith ftands always firm and fure, even *when the Floods lift up their Voice, when the Floods lift up their Waves, Thy Teftimories are very fure,* Pfalm xciii. 3, 5   The Chriftian may ftand upon fure Ground, even upon the Teftimony of God, in the Midft of the raging Waves and Billows of Temptations from Satan, and of crofs Difpenfations of Providence from without, *Rom.* iv 20. *He ftagger ed not at the Promife of God through Unbelief*

5*thly* Stand faft in the *Root* of Faith   The Lord Jefus himfelf is the Root of the Chriftian s Faith   Faith fprings from him, for it is the Fruit of the *exceeding Greatnefs of his Power*, Eph 1 19 Alfo Chrift is the Root into which the Believer is ingrafted, and it is by the Means of Faith that he has a Being in him.   Chrift is the Root of all vital Influences unto the Believer . All the Belie ver's fpiritual Nourifhment and Sap, his fpiritual Verdure, Beauty and Fruitfulnefs, are from Chrift his Root   To ftand faft in the Root Chrift, is the fame Thing with abiding in him, *John* xv. 4. *Abide in me*   The Chriftian abides in Chrift, by deriving vital Influences from him daily   As the Bran ches have all their Sap and Nourifhment from the Root, fo your fpiritual Life muft be maintained by a daily Communication of fpiritual Nourifhment from your Root Chrift

6*thly*. Stand faft in the *Fruits* of Faith   Where true Faith is, it brings forth Fruit · *Faith without Works is but a dead* Faith, *James* ii 26   All Du ties of Obedience unto the Law of God, when performed in a right Manner, are the Fruits of Faith, and the Chriftian ought to abound in thefe, *John* xv 8   The Fruits of the Spirit, mentioned *Gal* v. 22. are the Fruits of Faith   The Chrifti an muft not reft fatisfied in any Meafure of Fruit fulnefs

fulnefs he has attained unto, but he ought to increafe and grow in Fruitfulnefs, 2 *Pet.* iii 18.
*Grow in Grace, and in the Knowledge of our Lord
and Saviour Jefus Chrift* 2 Pet. i 5. *Giving all
Diligence, add to your Faith, Virtue, and to Virtue,
Knowledge ; and to Knowledge, Temperance, and to
Temperance, Patience, and to Patience, Godlinefs ;
and to Godlinefs, brotherly Kindnefs, and to brotherly
kindnefs, Charity. For if thefe Things be in you and
abound, they make you that ye fhall neither be barren nor unfruitful in the Knowledge of our Lord Jefus Chrift.*

7thly Stand faft in the *Exercife* of Faith. Faith
muft be exercifed daily If it is not exercifed,
the inward Principle of Grace is weakned, and the
Chriftian withers and decays, *Heb.* x. 38. *Now
the Juft fhall live by Faith, but if any Man draw
back,* &c. He lives by the daily Exercife of Faith ;
and if Faith fails in its Exercife, the Chriftian
draws back, he falls from his Stedfaftnefs

8thly Stand faft in the *Hopes* and *Expectations* of
Faith. The Expectations of Faith are great and large:
Faith expects all the good Things that are contained
in the Word of Promife, *Rom* viii 32 *How fhall he not
with him alfo freely give us all Things?* Faith looks
out for Accefs unto God, and Acceptance in his
Sight, through the Lord Jefus. This is that *Confidence of Faith* which we ought *not* to *caft away,*
Heb x 35 It looks out for Support and Through-
bearing under all Difficulties, *Pfalm* xxiii 4. *Tea,
tho' I walk through the Valley of the Shadow of Death,
I will fear no Evil, for thou art with me* It looks
out for complete Deliverance from all Sin and all
Sorrow, and for a complete Victory over all fpiritual Enemies Faith fays, *In all thefe Things
we are more than Conquerors through him that lov-*
e;

ved us. Faith looks out for a Glory to be revealed hereafter, even for the *Inheritance incorruptible, undefiled, and that fadeth not away, reserved in Heaven for all* the Children of Promise. Quit not then with the Hopes and Expectations of Faith, for these do animate the Christian under the greatest Difficulties, *Rom.* v. 2. *We rejoice in Hope of the Glory of God.*

I proceed now to the *third* Thing proposed, To shew you what it is to stand fast in the Faith, or, to open up a little the Duty of *Stedfastness* that you are here exhorted unto. I shall observe two Things that are implied in it, and then shew you what it is to stand fast in the Faith

First, To *stand fast* implies that the Christian may be *sore thurst at,* that he may depart from his Stedfastness in the Faith He has a Multitude of Enemies against him, and his Enemies want neither Power, nor Malice, nor Subtilty , they have Power to annoy the Christian, and they bear a malicious Disposition against him · The old Serpent and all his Seed have an inveterate Enmity at the Seed of the Woman, and they want not Subtilty and Cunning to ensnare the Christian And here you may observe, 1*st* That the Christian is many Times sore thrust at by his malicious Enemy Satan. Hence saith the Apostle, 1 *Pet* v 8 *Be sober, be vigilant, for your Adversary the Devil, as a roaring Lion, walketh about seeking whom he may devour* He knows well the Christian's weak Side, and he is ready to attack them there. Whatever is a Man's predominant Sin, whatever is the Sin that doth easily beset him, Is it Pride ? Is it Love to the World, or the like ? Satan will adapt his Temptations to it, 2 *Cor.* ii. 11. *We are not ig-*

not ant

rant of his Devices. 2dly The Christian is sore thrust at from the wicked Men of this World, *Pfalm* cxviii. 13. *Thou haft thruft fore at me, that I might fall* He may lay his Account with the worst Names that Men can give him *If they have called the Mafter of the Houfe Beelzebub, how much more fhall they call them of his Houfhold?* Matth. x 25. He may lay his Account with the Fury and Rage of Men against him. The Head and Captain of Salvation cried out, in his Type, *Pfal.* xxii. 13. *They gaped upon me with their Mouths, as a raveuing and roaring Lion.* If the Head met with such Treatment from the World, his Followers need not expect any better Yea, our Lord has forewarned all his Difciples what they are to meet with from the World, *John* xvi 2 *They fhall put you out of their Synagogues, yea, the Time cometh that whofoever killeth you will think that he doth God good Service* 3dly The Chriftian meets with fore Thrusts from indwelling Sin The Apoftle *Paul* had the Experience of the violent Thruſts of this Enemy, *Rom* vii 21, 23 *I find then a Law, that when I would do Good, Evil is prefent with me I fee another Law in my Members, warring againft the Law of my Mind, and bringing me into Captivity to the Law of Sin which is in my Members.*

Se.ndly, The Charge to *ftand faft* implies, that the Chriftian is in Danger of lofing Ground, and falling before the Enemy. One that is in Chrift cannot fall totally nor finally away, yet he is in Danger of lofing his Ground, he is in Hazard of such Falls as may dishonour God, and bring a Reproach upon his holy Profeffion, and break his own Peace. As for Instance, in the *firft* Place He is in Danger of departing from the *Profeffion* of his Faith. *Peter* made a noble Confeffion, *Matth.* xvi 16,

Thou art Chrift, the Son of the living God And a great Teftimony is given by Chrift unto this his Confeffion in the 17th *Verfe* · But how did he fall from it, when at the Vioce of a Maid he denied him with an Oath, and faid, *I know not the Man?* Matth xxvi. 72 2*dly* The Chriftian is in Danger of departing from the *Fruits* of his Faith · The Falls and Sins of eminent Saints are fad Inftances of this, and they are recorded in Scripture, not to encourage us to fin, but as Warnings unto us, they are fet up as fo many Beacons to guard us againft fplitting upon thefe dangerous Rocks Yea, 3*dly.* the Chriftian is in Danger of lofing the *Evidences* and *Expectations* of his Faith, he may lole Sight of his Intereft in Chrift, and may lofe his Hope of eternal Life, *Jonah,* ii. 3, 4 *All thy Billows and thy Waves paffed over me Then I faid, I am caft out of thy Sight.* Thefe and many fuch Things are implied in this folemn Call here given unto us, to ftand faft in the Faith

I proceed now to fhew you what it is to ftand faft in the Faith. I anfwer in general, It is the Chriftian's vigorous and refolute Endeavours, in the Strength of the Lord Jefus, and in the Ufe of all the Means appointed by him, to keep his Ground againft his fpiritual Enemies But, more particularly,

1*ft.* To ftand faft in the Faith, is to ftand in a *watching* Pofture. Thefe two are joined together, *Watch ye, ftand faft in the Faith.* Watchfulnefs is abfolutely needful in order to our Stedfaftnefs, the Chriftian muft ftand upon his Watch Tower, *Hab.* ii 1. *I will ftand upon my Watch* He muft watch all the Motions and Approaches of the Enemy, that he may cry out unto the Head and Captain of

his

his Salvation for Grace to help him in the Day and Time of his Need

2dly. To ſtand faſt, is to ſtand in a *fighting* Poſture ; it is to be ready to fight the Enemy, to reſiſt the Aſſaults, and to repel the Violence of the Enemy, 1 *Pet* v. 9 *Whom reſiſt, ſtedfaſt in the Faith.* The Chriſtian muſt *take the whole Armour of God, that he may be able to withſtand in the evil Day* , and he muſt *in all to ſtand,* Eph vi 13 The Chriſtian's Standing imports his Fighting, and his Fighting imports his uſing Armour The Enemies the Chriſtian has to deal with are ſpiritual, even *Principalities and Powers, the Rulers of the Darkneſs of this World* , and the Weapons of his Warfare are ſpiritual, the Armour, both offenſive and defenſive, is ſpiritual, namely, *the Girdle of Truth, the Breaſt-Plate of Righteouſreſs, the Shield of Faith, the Helmet of Salvation, and the Sword of the Spirit.*

3dly To ſtand faſt, is to ſtand in a *ſuffering* Poſture, that is, to be in a Readineſs to ſuffer for the Truth when we are called unto it , to be ready to ſuffer the Loſs of all Things for Chriſt , the Loſs of our outward Peace and Eaſe, of our Goods and Subſtance, when theſe may come in Competition with any of the Truths of Chriſt , yea, to be willing to part with Life itſelf for Chriſt. The Chriſtian ſtands and keeps his Ground when he ſuffers : yea, in his Sufferings unto Death, he *overcomes by the Blood of the Lamb, and by the Word of his Teſtimony,* Rev. xii 11

4thly. To ſtand faſt, is to *perſevere* in our Chriſtian Work and Warfare, *Matth.* xxiv. 13. *He that ſhall endure to the End, the ſame ſhall be ſaved:* The Chriſtian muſt ſtand, and neither fall back, nor give over , he muſt ſtand, and not ſit down ; he muſt fight, and not faint : *If thou faint in Day*

of

of Adversity, thy Strength is small, Prov. xxiv 10.
The Christian must hold on his Way, *Job* xvii.
9. *The Righteous also shall hold on his Way, and he
that hath clean Hands shall be stronger and stronger.*

5thly. To stand fast, is the Christian's *Endeavour
to keep his Ground* in the Use of all appointed Means,
such as reading and hearing the Word, Meditation,
Self-Examination, and the like. The Duty of
Prayer is likeways a special Mean of Stedfastness in
the Faith, therefore, when the Apostle directs us
to the different Pieces of our Christian Armour, he
recommends Prayer as a notable and useful Weapon for the Christian, *Eph.* vi. 18. *Praying always
with all Prayer and Supplication in the Spirit, and
watching thereunto with all Perseverance and Supplica
tion for all Saints.*

I proceed now to the *fourth* Thing proposed,
namely, To give you the Reasons of the Doctrine:
Why is it that the Christian ought to stand fast in
the Faith ?

1st This is what your glorious Head and Lead
er requires and expects from you. It is his positive
and express Command unto you, *Watch ye, stand
fast in the Faith* This is what may be reasonably
expected from you If you are under the Banner
of Christ, ye are taken as a Prey out of the Hand
of the terrible One, your Head and Captain Ge
neral has delivered your Soul from Death, he has
rescued you unto his own Side out of the Hand of
Satan, he has set you apart for himself, and separated you by his Grace from the rest of the
World; therefore it may be expected that ye should
be stedfast unto him

2dly Unstedfastness dishonours God much, and
therefore provokes him greatly. It brings a Re
proach upon the Holiness and Truth of God : It
dishonours

dishonours him before the World, and brings a Blot upon our holy Profession, therefore it muſt be very provoking unto him, *Pſal.* lxxviii. 57, 59 *They turned back, and dealt unfaithfully like their Fathers; they were turned aſide like a deceitful Bow. When God heard this, he waxed wroth, and greatly abhorred Iſrael*

3*dly.* We ought to ſtand faſt in the Faith, becauſe it is a dangerous Thing to loſe Ground : *If any Man draw back, my Soul ſhall have no Pleaſure in him.* The leaſt Departing from the Profeſſion of our Faith is dangerous, the leaſt Declining from the Way of God is an Inlet to more *Daniel* was very tender in this Matter, when he prayed with his Windows open, *Dan* vi. 10. notwithſtanding of the ſevere Edict and Command of the King.   One might readily have ſaid, It was not prudent for him ſo to do, Might he not have prayed with his Windows ſhut ? If he opened his Windows to direct his Face towards *Jeruſalem*, the Place where the Temple ſtood, Were there not many Mountains betwixt him and *Jeruſalem*, and might he not have directed his Face towards that Place with his Windows ſhut, as well as with his Windows open ? But this was the Caſe · He had made an open Profeſſion of worſhipping *Jehovah*, the God of *Iſrael*, and, if he had ſhut his Windows upon the Commandment of the King, he had departed from that publick Profeſſion   The primitive Chriſtians were alſo very tender of departing from the Profeſſion they had made of their Faith · When their Heathen Perſecutors required them to deliver up their Bibles, they refuſed, when they required them to deliver a Leaf of their Bibles, they refuſed this alſo, and when they offered them their Lives upon delivering any Bit of Paper unto them, neither would

G   they

they yield unto this, becaufe it was required as a
Sign of their giving up with their Chriftian Caufe
and Confeffion.

4*thly*. To ftand faft in the Faith, is the Way to
thrive and profper in the Faith. The ftedfaft Chriftian is always a thriving Chriftian, he has moft of
inward Peace and Serenity in his own Mind, he
has moft of Nearnefs to God, and fpiritual Joy in
in him; and truly the Joy that the People of
God fometimes find in cleaving to the Way of the
Lord, they would not part with it for all the
World's Mirth and Laughter; and the Peace that
they find in the Way of the Lord, they would
not quit with it for all the Pleafures and Profits
of a vain perifhing World; it is a Peace *that paf-
feth all Underftanding*, Philip. iv 7

I proceed now to the *practical Ufe and Improvement* of this Subject.

Inf. 1*ft*. If it be fo, that it is the Duty of the
Chriftian, and ought to be his Care and Concern,
to ftand faft in the Faith, hence we may fee, that
a Chriftian has more to do than to make an outward Profeffion of Faith. Many make an outward
Profeffion of Faith, and this is all they have, this is
all they feek after, but, if you would be Chriftians
indeed, fomething more is needful, you muft be in
the Faith, and you muft ftand faft in the Faith. It is
an eafy Thing to make the outward Profeffion, and
to yield an outward Subjection unto the Ordinances of the Gofpel, to hear the Word, and to communicate, but fomething more is required of you,
you muft ftand in a watching and fighting Pofture,
if the Lord fhall call you unto it

2*dly*. Hence fee the Sin of Unftedfaftnefs in the
Faith. If it is your Duty to ftand faft, it muft be
your Sin to draw back. You that have made

folem

solemn Profession of Faith at the Communion-Table, take heed left you draw back. I shall here give you some Evidences of Unstedfastness in the Faith. 2*dly*. I shall shew you the Sinfulness of it.

In the *first* Place, it is an Evidence of Unstedfastness in the Profession of Faith, when Men turn more remiss and slack in spiritual Duties. It may be you have been frequent in Prayer, and have had something of Fervency in it before the Communion. It is true, solemn Work requires solemn and serious Preparation, but, if you turn formal and negligent in Family and secret Prayer after the Communion, it will be a sad Evidence of your Unstedfastness: The Christian ought to be *praying always with all Prayer and Supplication*, he ought to endeavour to maintain a praying Frame, and to lay hold upon every proper Opportunity for pouring out his Soul before the Lord, *Pfalm* cxix. 164. *Seven Times a Day do I praise thee.*

If you turn unwatchful over yourselves after a Communion, it is an Evidence of your Unstedfastness. It is like that for some Days before the Communion you have kept some Guard over your Words, and over your outward Behaviour, if after the Communion you go from your Watch over yourselves, you turn away from the Profession of your Faith. The Christian must be on his Guard at all Times, he must watch continually over his Heart, over his Words and Actions; he must watch over himself in his Buying and Selling, in his Trading and Traffiquing, in his Eating and Drinking, in every Thing that you do, in the whole of your Walk and Behaviour, you must stand upon your Watch-Tower, *Matth.* xxiv. 42.

3*dly*. If your Affections towards the Lord turn more cool, it is an Evidence of your Unstedfastness.

nefs. I do not fay a Communion-Frame will laft
always, yet the Chriftian ought to have his Affections habitually fet upon the Things that are above,
Col. iii. 2. A Communion-Ordinance is given you
to quicken and increafe your Love to the Lord Jefus, as well as to ftrengthen the other Graces of
the Spirit · You ought to have a growing Efteem
of him, habitual Defires after him, and a conftant
Delight in him, ye ought to exprefs your Love in
to him by fiequent Thinking upon him, *Pfalm* lxiii.
6. *When I remember thee upon my Bed, and meditate
on thee in the Nigh Watches.* And your Love
fhould be exprefled more efpecially in your religious
Duties · If you are carnal in your ordinary Walk,
and formal and coldrife in Piayei and othei Duties, it is an Evidence of your Unftedfaftnefs in the
Profeffion of your Faith.

4*thly.* When Unbelief gets the Afcendant over
the Chriftian, it is a Sign of his Unftedfaftnefs.
It may be you have faid at the Communion-Table,
My Lord, and my God. It may be you have faid,
Let me never call in queftion his loving Kindnefs
again, let me never doubt of the Truth and Ve-
iacity of his Word of Promife · But take heed to
yourfelves, your Faith in a little may be at as low
an Ebb as ever, and your Unbelief as ftrong as ever.
After the firft Communion, all the Difciples faid,
John xvi. 30. *Now we are fure that thou knoweft all
Things, by this we believe that thou can eft foith from
God:* But wheie was their Faith, when that fame
very Night one of them denied him, and all of
them foifook him and fled ?

5*thly.* It is likeways an Evidence of Unftedfaft-
iels in the Faith, when Men waver about the
Truths they profefs to believe, or depart from the
Profeffion

Profeſſion of them, upon Temptations that are caſt in their Way. Some have itching Ears after new Things, others are toſſed to and fro, and carried about with every Wind of Doctrine, they are ſtill halting betwixt two, and are never at any Fixedneſs or Certainty about the Principles they profeſs to believe. Some again are ſoon ſhaken in their Minds, the Frowns of Men, or the Flatteries of Men, will eaſily turn them away from their Profeſſion, and frequently, upon a Pretence that this and the other Truth is not eſſential unto Salvation, they perſuade themſelves that they may let it go. It is true, ſome Truths are of greater Moment and Importance than others, but every Truth of God is worthy to be contended for, *Matth* v. 18. *For verily I ſay unto you, till Heaven and Earth paſs, one Jot or one Title ſhall in nowiſe paſs from the Law, till all be fulfilled.* If you depart from any of the Truths of Chriſt, out of Regard to Man, or for Fear of Man, you diſcover Unſtedfaſtneſs in the Faith.

That you may be guarded againſt Unſtedfaſtneſs in the Profeſſion of Faith that you have made, let me now lay before you a few Conſiderations concerning the exceeding Sinfulneſs of it. 1ſt It is a Giving the Lie unto your Profeſſion. You have made a ſolemn Profeſſion of Faith at a Communion-Table, but, if you fall back, it is an Evidence your Profeſſion was not ſincere. It ſays, that you were *lying unto the God of Truth with your Tongues, and flattering him with your Lips*, Pſalm lxxviii. 36. 2ly It is contrary to the Vows and Engagements that you have come under. You have avouched the Lord at the Communion-Table to be your God: You have ſaid, I will be for him, and not for another. If you now turn unwatchful over yourſelves,

if

if you turn loose or untender in your Walk and Conversation, you walk contrary unto the Vows and Engagements you have professed to come under, and this will be no small Aggravation of your Sin. 3*dly*. Unstedfastness in the Faith exposeth Religion and the Way of God before a wicked World. If you that are Communicants go alongst with them in their sinful Courses and Fashions, Will they not blaspheme in their Hearts, if not with their Mouths, the good Way of the Lord ? Will they not be hardned in their Atheism and Unbelief ? They may be tempted to think and say that there is no Truth nor Reality in Religion, when the Professors of it walk like themselves , and, by reason of your Unstedfastness, the Way of Truth shall be evil spoken of, 2 *Pet.* ii 1 4*thly* It will be wounding to the truly Godly . It cannot but be grieving and affecting unto them, when they see the lax and careless Walk and Conversation of such as have made a solemn Profession of Faith in Christ, and Love towards him. 5*thly*. Your Unstedfastness will bring the Lord's Displeasure upon yourselves, and he may be provoked to manifest his Displeasure against you, by temporal Strokes upon you, 1 *Cor.* xi 30 *For this Cause many are sickly and weak among you, and many sleep* , that is, for unworthy Communicating, and no doubt for the unsuitable Walk and Behaviour of Communicants . If you escape temporal Strokes, you will readily fall under spiritual Judgments ; the Lord may be provoked to cease to be a Reprover unto you, and to leave you unto your own Counsels, to walk in your own Ways.

I proceed to a *second* Use of the Doctrine, and it shall be by Way of Trial and Examination. Is it
the

the Duty of the Chriſtian to ſtand faſt in the Faith?
Then try whether or not you are in the Faith.
You have need to try yourſelves after a Communion, as well as before it ; and it is very needful that
you try yourſelves on this Head : For, if you are
not in the Faith, you can never ſtand faſt in it . If
you have not the Faith of our Lord Jeſus in Truth
and Reality, you can never hold faſt the Profeſſion
of your Faith without wavering.   I ſhall here offer
you ſome particular Characters of ſuch as are in the
Faith, and by theſe you may examine and try yourſelves

1ſt If you are in the Faith, the Word of the
Goſpel has come unto you, *not in Word only, but
alſo in Power*, 1 Theſſ. 1 5   The Preaching of the
Goſpel of Chriſt has been the Power of God,
through the Efficacy of his Spirit, unto your Conviction and Converſion , the Word of the Goſpel
has come with convincing Power unto you , the
Spirit of the Lord has ſet the Lamp of his own
Word within thy Heart and he hath diſcovered
unto thee the great Abominations that are there,
the dreadful Corruption and Depravation of thy
Nature, and thy Tranſgreſſions wherein thou haſt
exceeded · Thou haſt got a Diſcovery of the natural Enmity of thy Heart againſt God, and of the
exceeding Evil that is in the Sin of Unbelief, a
Sin that binds all thy other Sins and Tranſgreſſions upon thee, *John* XVI. 8, 9. *And when he is come,
he will reprove the World of Sin . Of Sin, becauſe
they believe not on me*   The Word has alſo come
with humbling Power unto you , your lofty Looks
have been brought low, your high and ſelf-exalt-
ing Thoughts have been brought down, thou haſt
ſeen thyſelf more vile and loathſom in the Sight
of a holy God than the vileſt Inſect can be in thy

Sight :

Sight· The Difcovery that thou haft 'got of thy
Sinfulnefs and Vilenefs has filled thee with felf-
abafing and felf loathing Thoughts, *Ezek.* xxvi.
31. *Then fhall ye remember your own evil Ways, and*
your Doings that were not good, and fhall lothe your-
felves in your own Sight, for your Iniquities and for
your Abominations. The Word has likeways come
with Light, giving Efficacy unto you, revealing
Chrift the Object of Faith within you· Thou haft
got a Glimpfe of his Glory, and feen him in his
Perfon and Offices, as a full, able and complete
Saviour, as One every Way meet for thy miferable, loft, and perifhing State and Condition, 2 *Cor.*
iv. 6

2*dly* If you are in the Faith, you have given
the Obedience of Faith unto the Doctrine of the
Gofpel, *Rom* vi 17 *Ye have obeyed from the Heart*
that Form of Doctrine which was delivered you If
you are in the Faith, you have given the Obedi-
ence of Faith unto the Word of the Gofpel in the
three following Inftances 1*ft* You have received
the Truths of the Gofpel upon the Teftimony of
the God of Truth Faith is a Receiving of his
Teftimony, *John* iii 33 *He that hath received his*
Teftimon hath fet to his Seal, that God is true
Saving Faith leans to the Truth and Veracity of
God in his own Word Good Education is a good
Mean for beginning and promoting the Work of
Faith But the Faith of all fuch as believe unto
Salvation is bottomed upon the Word of the liv-
ing God, and not upon the Teftimony of Men:
They do not believe becaufe they were educated and
brought up in the Knowledge of the Truths of the
Gofpel, but they receive Gofpel Truth upon the Te-
ftimony of him who is Truth itfelf As this is, a
firm and fure Ground for Faith to bottom upon, fo
the

the Spirit of God fets home his own Teftimony
with abundant Light and Evidence upon the Minds
of all that believe, for the Gofpel comes not unto
them *in Word only, but alfo in Power, and in the Holy Ghoft, and in much Affurance*, 1 Theff. i 5. Moral Arguments for the Truth of Chriftianity are
very ufeful in their own Place, not only to ftop
the Mouths of the Adverfaries of our holy Religion, but alfo as Means to help foreward the Work
of Faith : But faving Faith ftands not in the
Wifdom of Men, it is not built upon the Reafon-
ings of Men, but it ftands upon the Power of
God, that is, in the Teftimony of the God of
Truth, powerfully evidencing itfelf to the Minds
all that believe, 1 *Cor*. 11 5 This is a Myftery
to the Learned of the World that have not learned Chrift, therefore fome of them abufe and reproach it But, tho' they fhould do fo, we preach
the Doctrine *of Chrift crucified, unto the* Jews *a
Stumbling-Block, and unto the* Greeks Foolifhnefs ; *but
unto them that are called, both* Jews *and* Greeks,
Chrift *the Power of God, and the Wifdom of God,*
1 Cor 1 23, 24. 2*dly*. If you have given the O-
bedience of Faith unto the Doctrine of the Gofpel, you have embraced the Promifes, and Chrift
himfelf in the Word of Promife. Faith is an em-
bracing of the Promifes, *Heb* xi 13 The Arms
of Faith, fo to fpeak, are wide and large. Faith
embraces all the Promifes, and him who is *All in
all* the Promifes. Nothing can fill the Arms of
Faith but Chrift himfelf; it is a receiving of him,
John i. 12. *To as many as received him, to them gave
he Power to become the Sons of God.* The Arms of
Faith embrace him for Righteoufnefs unto Juftification, and for Strength unto Sanctification, *Ifa.*
xlv. 24. *Surely fhall one fay, In the Lord have I*

H   *R'gh-*

Righteoufnefs and Strength. Faith receiveth Chrift as the Gofpel-Promife exhibits and offers him, even a wholeChrift, as the only and great Ordinance of infinite Wifdom for Salvation unto the perifhing Sinner, from the Guilt, from the Power, from the Filth and Being of Sin, for Deliverance from everlafting Wrath, and for a Right and Title unto everlafting Glory. 3*dly.* If you are in the Faith, you have given the Obedience of Faith unto the Commands and Precepts of the Word. All the Precepts of the Law are the Commandments of a God in Chrift unto the Believer · He receives the Law out of the Hands of him who is *Zion's* King and Lord : All the Commands of it are his Commandments unto his Subjects, and they are inforced upon them with the powerful and ftrong Arguments of his dying and redeeming Love ; and Obedience to them is required as an Evidence of their Love unto him, *John* xiv 15. *If you love me, keep my Commandments.* The Believer gives the Obedience of Faith unto the Commandments of Chrift, by devoting himfelf unto the Fear and Obedience of the Lord Jefus, he loves the whole Law of God, becaufe it is a Tranfcript of the Purity and Holinefs of God, *Pfalm* cxix 140. *Thy Word is very pure therefore thy Servant loveth it.* The Law is holy, the Commandment holy, juft and good, therefore the Believer breathes after Conformity unto it, *Pfalm* cxix 5. *O that my Ways were directed to keep thy Statutes.*

3*dly.* If you are in the Faith, you are formed and framed according unto the Doctrine of Faith : *Ye are God's Workmanfhip, created in Chrift Jefus,* Eph. ii. 10 The framing of the Heart according to the Truth of the Gofpel, is expreffed by the Lord's *putting* his *Law in the inward Parts,*

and

and writing it in the Heart, Jer. xxxj. 33. **And**
this is that Truth in the inward Parts in which
the Lord delights, *Pfalm* li. 6. When the Heart
is formed according to the Truth of the Gofpel,
there is a fupernatural Principle and Difpofition
implanted in the Man, whereby he is difpofed and
inclined to love the Lord, and to yield Obedience to his commanding and providential Will,
to honour and to glorify God, to value and efteem
all the Truths of Chrift Every one of them bulk
more in the Man's Eye than the whole Creation
befide. If any of the Truths of God were laid
in the Balance, they would, in his Efteem, weigh
down every other Thing . A Heart fafhioned according unto the Faith, is the Heart that is right
with God Some fpeak of a good Heart towards
God, of a fincere Heart, and the like, but they
know not what they are faying . The Heart that
is right with the Lord, is the Heart that is fanctified by the Word of Faith , it is a Heart that is
purified by the Faith of the Operation of God;
it is the Heart that is humbled and meekned by
the Word of Truth If you have not this Heart
within you, you are Strangers to faving Faith.

4*thly.* Every one that is in the Faith, is a Mar-
tyr for it in Refolution. The Chriftian dares promife nothing in his own Strength, but he can promife much on the Head of his Surety, *Phil.* iv. 13.
*I can do all Things through Chrift which ftrengthneth
me* When the Chriftian comes under the Banner
of Chrift, he refolves to follow him through good
Report and bad Report, through Honour and Difhonour; to appear in his Station for the Truths
of Chrift, if they fhould be oppofed and born
down , and to follow Chrift in a ftormy Day, as
well as in a fair Day ; when the World frowns,

as

as well as when it fmiles, upon his Christian Pro
feffion.

I come now to the *laft* Ufe of the Doctrine, and
this fhall be in a Word to three Sorts of Perfons
1*ft* To fuch as have a Profeffion of Faith, and no
more. 2*dly*. To fuch as are young Beginners in
the Faith 3*dly*. To all and every one of you
that have made a folemn Profeffion of Faith, e-
fpecially to fuch as have the Faith of our Lord
Jefus in Truth and in Reality.

1*ft*. I fhall fpeak to fuch as have a Profeffion of
Faith, and no more. We have Ground to fear
that many have made a folemn Profeffion of Faith
in a crucified Chrift at a Communion-Table, who
are Strangers to him, and who know him not, and
who have none of the Characters that we have juft
now given of thofe that are in the Faith I fhall
offer two or three Things for your Conviction, and
then addrefs you in a Word by Way of *Exhortation*. In order unto your Conviction, confider, in
the *firft* Place, that your Profeffion is little worth,
and it will do you but little Service, if you have
not the Faith of our Lord Jefus in Truth and in
Reality. Your Profeffion will not carry you
through in the Day of your Strait, it will never
bring you to Heaven Yea, if you are looking
and hoping for Heaven, you will meet with a fad
Difappointment in the End. Your State and Con
dition will be the fame with that of the foolifh
Virgins in the Parable, who had Lamps, but no
Oil in their Lamps : And when they fay, *Lord,
Lord, open to us*, he anfwers them, *Verily, I fay unto you, I know you not*. And tho' you may fay in
that Day, *We have eaten and drunk in thy Prefence*,
yet he fhall fay unto you, *I tell you, I know you not
whence*

whence you are. *Depart from me, all ye Workers of Iniquity*, Matth xxv. 11, 12. Luke xiii 26, 27. 2dly. It is a dangerous Thing to have a Profession of Religion, and no more · You run the greatest Risque, for Publicans and Harlots will enter into the Kingdom of God before proud, self righteous Professors, *Matth* xxi. 31 A dreadful Hell and a horrible Eternity abide you, you will meet with a sad Surprize in the End, *Isa* xxxiii 14 *The Sinners in Zion are afraid, Fearfulness hath surprised the Hypocrites Who among us shall dwell with the devouring Fire ? Who among us shall dwell with everlasting Burnings ?*

Let me now address you in a Word by Way of *Exhortation* ; and our Exhortation unto you is, O be concerned to have the Faith of our Lord Jesus in Truth and in Reality. As you are Christians by Profession, study to be Christians indeed And you that have been at a Communion-Table, study to know a saving Faith in him in whom ye have professed Faith after such a solemn Manner In order to this I offer you the following Advices ; 1st. Be convinced of your Unbelief, all that believe in the Lord Jesus have been convinced of their Unbelief, *John* xvi 9 A Sight of the Unbelief of the Heart may be a Mean, through the Blessing of the Lord, to obtain the Spirit of Faith 2dly. Consider, that tho' you are destitute of Faith, yet you may obtain it All that have Faith once wanted it none of them were born Believers It is by their new Birth that all of them become Believers. Those that have Faith were once under the Power of Unbelief as you are, they were once as dark and blind as you are, they were as much alienated from the Life of God as you are . *But God, who is rich in Mercy, quickned them when dead in Trespasses and Sins*, Eph. ii. 4, 5 . 3dly. Consider from

whom·

whom it is that you may obtain the Grace of Faith. It is given by the Lord Jesus, he is the Author and Finisher of Faith: He begins the Work of Faith, and he carries it on. Faith is the Gift, even the free *Gift of God*, Eph. ii 8 4thly Attend upon the Means by which Faith is wrought. The Word preached is one special Mean of Faith, *Rom* x. 17. *Faith cometh by Hearing, and Hearing by the Word of God* Look unto him who is the Author of Faith, that he may work Faith in you. Come with your atheistical and unbelieving Heart unto him, he promiseth freely the Spirit and Grace of Faith. The Spirit of Faith is in that Promise, *I will pour Water upon him that is thirsty, and Floods upon the dry Ground I will pour my Spirit upon thy Seed, and my Blessing upon thine Offspring One shall say, I am the Lord's*, Isa xliv 3, 5 The Grace of Faith is in that Promise, *A new Heart also will I give unto you, and a new Spirit will I put within you: And I will take away the stony Heart out of your Flesh, and I will give you an Heart of Flesh*, Ezek. xxxvi. 26. Look unto the Lord for the Grace that is in the Promise, Prayer is an appointed and instituted Mean for the obtaining of it. *Thus faith the Lord God, I will yet for this be inquired of by the House of Israel, to do it for them*, Verse 37. If you were crying under a Sense of Unbelief for the Spirit and Grace of Faith, it would be a Token for Good, that the Seed of Faith is already sown by the Holy Ghost in your Hearts

I come, in the *second* Place, to speak a Word to young Beginners in the Faith Several have been at the Communion-Table in this Place, who were never Communicants formerly, and some of you have begun in young Years to make a fair Profession of Faith in the Lord Jesus. Faith, in its first

Begin-

Beginnings, is often like a Grain of Muſtard-Seed, both tender and weak, and ſcarce diſcernible. We have it in our Commiſſion to ſtrengthen the weak Hands, and confirm the feeble Knees, to encourage you that are beginning to ſet out in the Way of the Lord · And our Heart's Deſire for you is, that you may ſtand faſt in the Faith of Chriſt, being rooted and grounded in him. Let me then addreſs you that are of the younger Sort, eſpecially ſuch of you as have been at a Communion-Table: If there are any young Motions of Heart among you towards the Lord Jeſus Chriſt, if there is any young Senſe of the Need of Chriſt, or any young Deſires after him, if there are any Outgoings of Faith upon him, I would ſuggeſt the following Things unto you.

1ſt. Look well to it, that any Work that is begun in you be real and ſaving: And for this End examine and try yourſelves, try if Chriſt is formed within you A wrong Caſt at your firſt Out-ſetting in the Way of the Lord is dangerous, and may ſtick to you all your Days · If you ſit down upon a wrong Foundation, all your Building will fail to the Ground, it will not ſtand when the Winds blows and the Rains deſcend, *Matth.* vii. 7. If ye have been under Convictions, take heed leſt ye *ſtay long in the Place of the breaking forth of Children*, Hoſ. xiii 13 Many have Convictions who were never converted. If your Convictions have been genuine and kindly, you have found no reſting Place for you, but on the Foundation-Stone that is laid in *Zion* If your Convictions have had a gracious Iſſue, you have found no Peace, no Quiet, but in the Blood of Jeſus, applied and brought home by the Spirit of God through Faith in his Name. The Blood of Chriſt

E 3

is the only effectual Balm for that Wound that the
Law makes in the Conscience.

2dly. Bless God for any young Beginnings that
are with you. If the Lord has been dealing with
you by his Spirit in a Work of Conviction and
gracious Illumination, O give Thanks unto him
for it They are highly favoured and privileged
who are reached by the Grace of Christ at any Time,
but more especially such who are prevented by his
Grace in their younger Years : He stops the Course
and Current of their Rebellion against him early,
and enables them to glorify him, by giving the Beginning of their Days, and the Prime and Flower
of their Love unto him, who is altogether lovely,
and who alone is worthy to be loved · The Kindness of thy Youth and the Love of thy Espousals
shall be remembred, and shall not be forgotten,
Jer. i. 2

3dly. You have Reason to be on your Guard,
and to take heed to yourselves . For *Satan* will endeavour to crush any begun Appearances of the
Work of the Lord within you, he will do all
that he can to snib any young spiritual Growth that
is within you, lay your Account with it, that he
will lay Snares for you, and beset you with his
Temptations. No sooner do any set their Faces towards Christ than *Satan* raiseth a Storm against
them, and he may raise a Storm against you, from
some Airth that you are least expecting.

4thly Cherish any Beginnings of the Work of
God within you, encourage Convictions, and do
not stifle them : *Quench not the Spirit,* 1 Thess. v.
19 It is a dangerous Thing to quench any of the
Motions and Workings of the Spirit of God. Im-
prove any Dawnings of Light upon your Minds;
the Dawning of the Day is a Forerunner of the
Rising

Rising of the Sun. If the Lord has made the least Beam of spiritual Light to shine into thy Heart, look out for a clearer and fuller Discovery of the Lord Jesus unto my Soul, sit not down upon any Thing that you think you have attained, but press after Growth in Grace and in the Knowledge of the Lord Jesus Christ: *Count not that you have apprehended ; but, forgetting those Things which are behind, reach forth unto those Things which are before · And press toward the Mark, for the Prize of the high Calling of God in Christ Jesus,* Philip. iii 13, 14.

5thly. O be concerned to be well rooted in Christ! Col. ii. 6, 7 *Walk in him, rooted and built up in him, and established in the Faith, as ye have been taught.* If you would be rooted in the Faith of Christ, pray for the *Spirit of Wisdom and Revelation in the Knowledge of Christ,* Eph. i 17. Every saving Discovery of Christ unto the Soul, is rooting and establishing unto the Christian ; it confirms and strengthens his Faith, *John* ii 11. *Jesus manifested forth his Glory, and his Disciples believed on him.* If you would be rooted in the Faith of Christ, let Faith be daily exercised upon him, 1 *John* v. 13. *These Things have I written unto you that believe on the Name of the Son of God, that ye may know that ye have eternal Life, and that ye may believe on the Name of the Son of God.* If you enquire what is the Meaning of it, when he says, *These Things have I written unto you that believe on the Name of the Son of God, that ye may believe,* &c. I answer, it is as much as if he had said, Believe over and over again, believe better than ever you have done, you must ay be exercising Faith upon the Lord Jesus : By the repeted Acts of Faith the Habit of Faith is strengthned, the Eye of Faith grows still clearer the oftner its looks to its glorious Object, *Psalm* xxxiv. 5. *They looked unto him*

I   *and*

and were lightned. The Hand of Faith is ſtill ſtronger the oftner it lays hold upon the Lord Jeſus.

6thly. Scar not at the Croſs of Chriſt. *If any Man will come after me, let him deny himſelf, and take up his Croſs and follow me.* I warn you of it, that if you would be the Diſciples of Chriſt indeed, you muſt take up the Croſs; the Croſs is the beaten Path unto our Father's Kingdom. If you think this a hard Saying, yet I dare ſay the Croſs of Chriſt looks worſe at a Diſtance than when it is brought near : The nearer the Croſs of Chriſt comes, it is ſomething the lighter and the eaſier, therefore ſcar not at the Croſs of Chriſt · Chriſt himſelf bears the heavieſt End of his own Croſs, and he gives all his Diſciples a Back for every Burden he lays upon them, Chriſt and his Croſs are above all the ſinful Pleaſures, Joys and Comforts of the World. The Reproach of Chriſt is a rich Treaſure. *If ye be reproached for the Name of Chriſt, happy are ye, for the Spirit of Glory and of God reſteth upon you.* The Croſs of Chriſt is the Way to the Crown, and it is but a ſhort Way you have to bear the Croſs: *For our light Affliction, which is but for a Moment, worketh for us a far more exceeding and eternal Weight of Glory,* 2 Cor. iv. 17.

I proceed now, in the *third* Place, to ſpeak a Word unto you all and every one that have a ſolemn Profeſſion of Faith in Chriſt, and eſpecially to ſuch of you as have the Faith of our Lord Jeſus in Truth and in Reality. Let me exhort you in the Words of the Spirit of God, by the Apoſtle, in our Text, *Stand faſt in the Faith* I ſhall offer you ſome Arguments to inforce the Exhortation, and conclude with ſome Words by Way of *Direction* and *Advice.* To inforce the Exhortation then, conſider, in the

1ſt

1*ft* Place, The Stedfaftnefs of the Chriftian in his Faith glorifies God, it honours and glorifies him before the World · All the People of God are Witneffes for God upon Earth, *Ifa.* xliv 8. *Ye are even my Witneffes.* They ought to bear Teftimony before the World, unto the Holinefs of God, by ftudying Holinefs in all Manner of Converfation : They ought to bear Teftimony unto the Truths of God, by cleaving unto them, efpecially when any of them are controverted and born down. *To ftand faft in the Faith,* and that in the Face of Oppofition, glorifies God in an eminent Manner : It is a glorifying of God in a Way that does not and cannot take Place in Heaven : The Saints in Heaven have no Oppofition made unto them, for Heaven is the Place of the Saints Reft , there is none to hurt nor deftroy in all his holy Mountain. But this Honour have all his Saints upon Earth, that they are called to glorify him in the Face of Oppofition, and of ftrong Oppofition made by Satan and the World unto them. *Rom.* iv. 20. it is faid of *Abraham, He ftaggered not at the Promife of God, but was ftrong in Faith, giving Glory to God*

2*dly.* Confider that Faith is a precious Thing. Whatever Way you take Faith, it is precious . If it is taken for the Object of Faith, the Lord Jefus, he is infinitely glorious and excellent in his Perfon, and precious in the Eyes of all them that believe, 1 *Pet.* ii 7. If by Faith you mean the Principles of Faith, or the Truths that we ought to believe, they are all precious. Truth is a precious *Depofitum,* or a precious Truft, given unto the Church and People of God, a Truft given unto them to keep and preferve fafe; and if any of the Truths of God are controverted, one Generation

tion fhould deliver them off their Hands, with a Teftimony, to another, this is a Debt one Generation owes to another. We are unfaithful to Pofterity, if we fuffer any Vail to be drawn over any divine Truth, without a Teftimony unto it *For he eftablifhed a Teftimony in Jacob, and appointed a Law in Ifrael, which he commanded our Fathers that they fhould make them known to their Children,* Pfalm lxxviii 5.

3*dly* Ye are under manifold Obligations to ftand faft in the Faith If you have the Faith of our Lord Jefus in Truth and Reality, the redeeming Love of Chrift is a ftrong Bond upon you to continue ftedfaft in the Faith : *The Love of Chrift fhould conftrain you,* 2 Cor. v. 14. The Grace of God, manifefted in your effectual Calling, obligeth you to this, *Heb* iii. 6. *Wherefore, holy Brethren, Partakers of the heavenly Calling, confider the Apoftle and High-Prieft of our Profeffion, Chrift Jefus.* The Vows of God are upon you, your Baptifmal Vows bind you to this, as alfo the folemn Engagements you have profeffed to come under at the Lord's Table

4*thly.* Confider, whatever you may be expofed unto on the Account of your Stedfaftnefs in the Faith, nothing fingular befals you. *For through much Tribulation we muft enter into the Kingdom* Have you Difficulties in the Way ? Thefe are the common Fate of all that have gone to Heaven before you : Have you Satan and his Temptations to conflict with ? So had they all : Have you an evil Heart of Unbelief to wreftle againft ? So had they Have you Violence from the World to encounter with ? So had they, *Rev* vii. 14 *Thefe are they which came out of great Tribulation, and have wafhed their Robes, and made them white in the Blood of the Lamb.*

Yea,

Yea, not only the Followers of the Lamb, but their Head, Lord and Captain himfelf had the greateft Difficulties in his Way. *It is enough for the Difciple that he be as his Mafter, and the Servant as his Lord.*

5*thly* Ye have good Furniture provided for you, to enable you to ftand faft in the Faith : All the Grace that is in the Lord Jefus your Head, it is laid up in him for your Behoof and Advantage. Are you foolifh? In him are hid all the Treafures of Wifdom and Knowledge, and the Spirit of Wif-dom and Council is given by the Head unto his Members · Are you weak and without Strength? With him there is everlafting Strength, and he is the Glory of your Strength, *Pfalm* lxxxix. 17. Do you want Armour wherewith to fight the Ene-my? He has it to give you, *even the whole Armour of God*, Eph. vi 13. The Chriftian's Armour is the *Armour of God*, it is Armour of his framing and making, it is Armour of his giving, it is proven and tried Armour Do you want a Head? The Captain of Salvation is in the Field before you : Your *King fhall pafs before* you, *and the Lord on* your *Head*, Mic. ii. 13.

6*thly*. Confider the many Promifes that are gi-ven you, to encourage you to Stedfaftnefs in the Faith Upholding and ftrengthning Grace is pro-mifed you, and the Promife is given you as an An-tidote againft all flavifh and difquieting Fears, *Ifa-th 10 Fear thou not, for I am with thee, be not difmayed, for I am thy God · I will ftrengthen thee, yea, I will help thee, yea, I will uphold thee with the Right-Hand of my Righteoufnefs*. It is not enough that you make a fair Beginning in the Way of the Lord, but you muft alfo perfevere and hold on · *For he that fhall endure unto the End, the fame fhall be faved,*

Matth.

Matth. xxiv. 13. *The Righteous shall hold on his Way, and he that hath clean Hands shall be stronger and stronger,* Job xvii. 9. The stedfast Christian is the overcoming Christian, and many Promises are made to the Overcomer · *He that overcometh shall eat of the Tree of Life, which is the Midst of the Paradise of God,* Rev. ii. 7. He shall *eat of the hidden Manna; and the white Stone, and in the Stone a new Name written,* shall be given unto him, *Rev.* ii. 17. Yea, he shall be set down with Christ in his Throne, *Rev.* iii 21. *He that overcometh shall inherit all Things,* Rev. xxi 2.

I shall now shut up all with some Words by Way of *Direction* and *Advice* unto you If you would be stedfast in the Faith, then, 1*st.* Let not the World get too much Room in your Hearts. The Man that loves the World more than Christ, and the Truths of Christ, can never stand in the Faith When the Pleasures and Profits of this World, when his outward Peace and Ease, or the like, come in Competition with the Things of Christ, he grips to the World, and to the Things of it, and lets the Things of Christ go · So it was with *Demas,* 2 Tim iv 10 *For* Demas *hath forsaken me, having loved this present World.* You may no doubt have a moderate Concern and Care about the Things of this Life , you ought to *provide Things honest in the Sight of all Men,* Rom. xii. 17. But many give up themselves to an immoderate Love to the World, under Pretence of a moderate Care about it, and this is both sinful and dangerous; for, *if any Man love the World, the Love of the Father is not in him,* 1 John ii 15

2*dly.* Beware of Self-Confidence. If you trust unto yourselves, you cannot stand. *Peter* had too

much

much Self-Confidence, when he said, *Though all Men should be offended becaufe of thee, yet will I never be offended. Although I fhould die with thee, yet will I not deny thee.* And that fame very Night he got a fad Proof of his own Weaknefs, when he denied his Mafter thrice, *Matth.* xxvi 35, 74.

If you truft unto Grace received, you will readily fall from your Stedfaftnefs, *Pfalm* xxx. 6, 7. *In my Profperity I faid, I fhall never be moved. Lord, by thy Favour thou haft made my Mountain to ftand ftrong. Thou didft hide thy Face, and I was troubled.*

3*dly.* Think not any Sin a little Thing. You ought to hate all Sin whatfoever, *Pfalm* cxix. 104. *I hate every falfe Way.* If a Man begin to think any known Sin a fmall Thing, he cannot ftand, he will foon fall from his Stedfaftnefs.

4*thly.* Efteem highly all the Truths of Chrift. As you ought to think no Sin a little Thing, fo neither fhould you think meanly of any of the Truths of God No Sin is fo little that it ought not to be witneffed againft, and no Truth is fo fmall, that it ought not to be contended for. If any of the Truths of Chrift are controverted and born down, let the Oppofition made unto Truth endear it the more unto you, *Pfalm* cxix. 23. *Princes alfo did fit and fpeak againft me ; but thy Servant did meditate in thy Statutes.*

5*thly* Beware of lofing Sight of your Head and Captain the Lord Jefus Chrift ; keep him in your Eye Every new Look of Faith unto him brings in frefh Life and Vigour unto the Soul. Live within Sight of him that is invifible. When an invifible God is feen by a Man, all Things elfe difappear, *Heb.* xi. 27.

6*thly.* Beware of the Fear of Man · *The Fear of Man bringeth a Snare,* Prov. xxix 25. The Frowns

or

or Smiles of Men are little to be regarded *Ceafe ye from Man, whofe Breath is in his Noftrils : For wherein is he to be accounted of?* Ifa. ii 22.

7thly. Lay your Account with Tribulations for the Teftimony of Chrift : *In the World ye fhall have Tribulation*, John xvi. 33. If you have been honeft Communicants, you are refolved through Grace to follow Chrift, whatever difficult and rough Steps may be in your Way : And none of thefe ought to difcourage you, for there is that to be found in Chrift that can counterbalance all Hardfhips and Difficulties, all Loffes and Croffes that you may be expofed unto, *Rom.* v. 3, 4, 5. *We glory in Tribulations alfo, knowing that Tribulation worketh Patience, Patience, Experience, and Experience, Hope; Hope maketh not afhamed, becaufe the Love of God is fhed abroad in our Hearts by the Holy Ghoft which is given unto us.*

8thly Live upon Chrift your living Head and Life-giving Root. You need the Supplies of his Grace daily. Any Meafure of Grace that you have received, any fenfible Tafte that you have got of his Love in the Word, or in the Sacrament, this Day, will not bear you up, nor carry you through under new Straits and Difficulties that you may meet with the next Day; you muft have new Supplies of the Grace and Spirit of Jefus for every new Duty, and for every new Difficulty. He is a Head of Counfel and Conduct unto his Church and People : Live then upon him for Counfel and Direction under all the Difficulties of your Wildernefs-Journey. He is alfo a Head of Strength unto you : Go on therefore in his Strength, making Mention of his Righteoufnefs, even of his only. It is by a conftant Communication of vital Influences from Chrift your Root, that you muft ftand

faft

ist in the Faith ; therefore make Use of him, derive Furniture and Strength daily from him. *Live
continually by the Faith of the Son of God,* Gal. ii.
10.

9thly. Beware of the least Declinings from the
Way of God, 1 *Thess* v. 22 *Abstain from all Appearance of Evil.* If you turn aside in the least
from the Way of the Lord unto By-Paths, you
may have Difficulty to find the right Path again.

10thly. Put on the whole Armour of God. You
can never stand unless you have on your Armour ;
a naked Man falls before the Enemy : You must
put on your Armour, and likeways handle your
spiritual Armour. Let Truth in the inward Parts
be your Guide , let the Righteousness of your Head
and Surety be your Breast-Plate ; let Humility and
Meekness adorn your Steps ; make Use of the
noble Shield of Faith : Let that Hope that anchors
within the Vail be your Helmet : Learn to handle
the sharp two-edged Sword of the Spirit, even the
Word of God . It is by this that you must make
your Way through a Host that may encamp against
you, *Eph.* vi. 13,——18.

11thly. Be in the Use of those Means by which
you may be preserved stedfast in the Faith. Read
the Word of God much, study to be well acquainted with the Scriptures, let your Minds be
well stored with the rich Treasures of divine Truth
that are laid up in the Word, *Psalm* cxix. 11. *Thy
Word have I hid in mine Heart, that I may not sin a-
gainst thee.* Meditate upon his Word daily, and
look to your Remembrancer the Spirit of Promise,
that he may bring the Words of Christ to your
Remembrance in the Day and Time of your Need,
John xiv. 26. Watch likeways and pray, lest ye
enter into Temptation : Pray that he may *deliver*

K *your*

your Feet from falling, that you may walk before God in the Light of the Living, Pfalm lvi. 13.

12*thly.* If you would ftand faft in the Faith, there are fome fpecial Acts of Faith I would recommend unto you. 1*ft.* The rolling and committing Acts of Faith, *Pfalm* xxxvii 5. *Commit thy Way unto the Lord;* in the Margine it is rendred, *Roll thy Way upon the Lord:* And this is the very fame Thing with cafting our Burdens upon him, *Pfalm* lv. 22. *Caft thy Burden upon the Lord.* You ought to commit all your Concerns for Time and Eternity unto him, 1 *Pet.* iv. 19. *Commit the Keeping of your Souls to him in Well-doing, as unto a faithful Creator.* And you may be perfuaded of it, *that he is able to keep that which ye have committed unto him against that Day,* 2 Tim. i. 12. 2*dly.* I recommend unto you the Exercife of the refting and leaning Acts of Faith, *Pfalm* xxxvii. 7. *Reft in the Lord,* reft upon his Word as good Security for your fpiritual and eternal Concerns, reft upon his Word as good Security likeways for all Things that you need in Time; he will withhold nothing that is good from you. Reft upon himfelf in the Word as your Staff and Stay, even when you walk in Darknefs, *truft in the Name of the Lord, and ftay your felves upon your God,* Ifa. l. 10. Lean to him, and depend upon him, in every Step of your Wildernefs-Journey, *Song* viii. 5.

Finally, Let the Grace of Patience be exercifed. This is needful for the Chriftian in order unto his Stedfaftnefs, efpecially under fhaking and trying Difpenfations of Providence. Study a patient Submiffion unto the providential Will of God, and a quiet and patient Waiting for a gracious Iffue unto all your Trials and Difficulties, *Heb.* x. 36. *For you have Need of Patience, that after ye have*

have done the Will of God, you might receive the Pro-mise. Now, may *the God of all Grace, who hath call-ed us unto his eternal Glory by Christ Jesus, after that ye have suffered a While, make you perfect, stablish, strengthen and settle you.* To him be Glory and Do-minion for ever and ever, *Amen.* 1 Pet. v. 10.

F. I N I S.

THE
BLESSEDNESS
LOST IN
The First *Adam*,

To be found in

CHRIST the Second *Adam.*

Being the Subſtance of ſome

SERMONS
ON

PSALM lxxii. 17.——— *And Men ſhall be
bleſſed in him*———

By the late REVEREND *and* LEARNED *Mr.* WILLIAM
WILSON *Miniſter of the Goſpel at* PERTH.

With a PREFACE prefixed,

To the Gentlemen of the *Deiſtical Principles* in or
about the Burgh of *Perth.*

E D I N B U R G H,
Printed for *David Duncan,* and ſold at his Houſe,
oppoſite to the *Weigh-Houſe,* North-Side of the
Street. MDCCXLVII.

Advertisement to the Reader.

*T*HE *following Sheets contain the Substance of some Sermons lately delivered, in my ordinary Course of Preaching, in one of our Churches on the Lord's Day I had not the remotest Intention of making them publick when I preached them; but the following Preface accounts for the Occasion of it.*

When the Contagion of Infidelity *in Principle, which cannot miss to be attended with* Looseness *and* Profaneness *in Practice, is spreading; when the Name of* Christ *is nauseous to many; when* Preaching *of* Christ *is become a Term of Reproach and Contempt, and is cried down as an Engine to drive all* rational Preaching, *(as they speak) yea,* Mortality *itself, out of the World; tho' it cannot but be affecting to me, as it is to the most judicious in this Place, that I have any such under my pastoral Charge to deal with; yet I do not grudge to take hold of the Occasion they have given me, to cast in my Mite, in speaking from the Press for him whom* Men despise, *and whom the* Nations abhor, *even for our exalted and glorious* Redeemer, *whose Name shall be remembred with Honour unto all Generations.*

TO THE

Gentlemen of the DEISTICAL PRINCIPLES in or about the Burgh of *Perth*.

YOUR *unfubfcribed Miffive*, fent to my Houfe by an unknown Hand, *Tuefday's* Night before our late National Faft, ye have thought fit to make publick, not only by difperfing your Copies of it both in this Place and in the neighbouring Country, but by fpreading them to more diftant Places. Your Defign is evident and plain ; and therefore I thought myfelf obliged to take this publick Notice both of you and your Conduct.

As for the malicious Infinuations contained in your invidious *Queries*, wherewith your Paper is fwelled, and whereby you flyly attack my Character, I am not afraid that they fhall do the leaft Hurt or Prejudice unto it : And, if you have any Confcience at all, I am perfuaded I have a Teftimony in your own Breafts, that there is no Truth in any of your wicked and railing Infinuations. Therefore I fhall not take any farther Notice of them, than to tell you I am not furprifed with the Treatment you give me, I am warned of it : I have the Honour to be his Servant by Office, who has told me, That *the Difciple is not above his Mafter, nor the Servant above his Lord;* and, *if they have called the Mafter of the Houfe* Beelzebub, *much more*

shall

shall they call them of his Houshold, Matth. x. 24, 25.

But it is not at me only, it is at revealed Religion, it is at the Gospel through me, that your envenomed Arrows are directed : And tho' you have not the Assurance to come from behind the Curtain, to own your Wickedness, yet you have pulled off the Mask in your Paper, when you declare, that you reckon the Doctrines of the Gospel, which I am honoured and called to preach, are *airy Speculations concerning Faith, mere Phantoms in Religion, which are nowhere to be found but in School-Divinity, or in the Brains of a hot Enthusiast,* &c. It is for this Reason that I have addressed you under the Character I have given you, and I do not think that I should have done you any Injury, tho' I had designed you Ἄθεοι, that is, *without God* Your Wickedness has more aggravating Circumstances in it, than theirs to whom this Character is given by the Spirit of God, *Eph.* ii. 12

After the manifest Contempt you have discovered of the plain Preaching of the Truths of the Gospel amongst you, I do not think any Thing that is dropt from my Pen will be much regarded by you Yet I must tell you, that I judge it very applicable to you, what an eminent Divine in the last Age writes concerning Men of the same Complexion with yourselves, *I know not* (says he) *whether it were not more for the Honour of Christ, that such Persons would publickly renounce the Profession of his Name, rather than practically manifest their inward Disregard unto him.*

Tho' you have no Regard for me, yet, if you have any for yourselves, the following Sheets contain the Substance of some Sermons delivered on a Subject that deserves your serious Consideration. Your Missive led me to some Enlargements in tran-

scribing

scribing the Copy for the Press; particularly to the Reasonings, in the first three Inferences, with such as despise revealed Religion, and to whom the Preaching of the Gospel of Christ is Foolishness. I was induced, from the two following Reasons, to make them publick, the one is, They contain, as full as was delivered, what I spoke on the Occasion of an *Itinerant*, (from whence he came I know not) who brought to this Place a pretended Picture of our blessed Redeemer in some Part of his Sufferings: And tho' I spoke nothing but what my Duty and Office obliged me unto, yet you have represented me, first in the publick Prints, as preaching Principles that had a Tendency to *Blood* and *Confusion*, and now, in your Missive, as the Author of a *Riot* and *Insolence* committed by the Mob, &c. I am well pleased that you have done me the Honour to make me share in the Reproach that your Predecessors in Opposition to the Gospel did throw upon the first and best Ministers of the New-Testament Church, whom they stiled *Deceivers of Mankind*, and such as *turned the World upside down*.

The other Reason that moved me to make them publick is, They contain the Subject I was preaching upon when I received your Missive; and I judged it my Duty to lay before the World a short Summary of the Truths of the Gospel, which I am neither afraid nor ashamed to preach and own, and which you, after a very bold Manner, have represented, in Town and Country, as *airy Speculations* and *mere Phantoms in Religion*. As it was my Design, in preaching on this Subject, to lead you to Christ for eternal Blessedness, for I endeavoured to declare something concerning the Fulness and Glory of his Person and Mediation, and the Necessity of Faith in him for eternal Salvation; as also, of

a vital

a vital Union with him, that Men may bring forth the Fruits of Holiness, and may yield acceptable Obedience unto God : If these Things are *any Speculations* and *mere Phantoms* in your Eyes, you despise, and that unto your own Destruction, the Wisdom, Grace and Love of God shining forth in Gospel-Revelation. I am satisfied, that when the several Members of your *Club* were preparing their Revilings and Cursings against me, I was employed in bringing forth the Blessing unto you : But, if you continue to despise the Blessing that was offered you, the Word of the Gospel, which I have preached amongst you, will be Witness thro' Eternity against you.

It will unriddle a great Part of your Missive, when I tell you what is the Spring of all your malicious Resentment against me . It is because I concurred with the *Session* of *Perth* in their Endeavours to suppress the profane Diversions of the Stage in the School, a Practice that has an evident Tendency to corrupt the Minds of our Youth, and to debauch them in their Morals , yet the Master of the School did, with a particular Insolence, despise the friendly Advice and Admonition of the Session by their Committee, under a Pretence that he was accountable only to the Presbytery for his Managements in the School : It is because I endeavour to declare from the Pulpit against the overspreading Wickedness and Profaneness of the Age, and those Seminaries of it, or peculiar Incentives to it, which go under the Name of *Assemblies* and *Balls* : It is because I warned the People of my Charge against that Indignity done to the Son of God, by an unknown Stranger his carrying about a pretended Picture of him in his Sufferings for a common Shew . It is because I joined

ed with the *Seffion* of *Perth* in the regular Steps
they took for bringing to a fair and impartial Trial
a very flagrant Report of Scandal in the Mafter of
the Grammar-School, and for this the *Seffion* of
Perth, the moft confiderable Body of this Kind in
the Bounds of the *Presbytery*, and who are daily
wreftling againft a Torrent of Profanenefs, muft
be lafhed with your virulent Tongues and Pens.
It is for the above, and the like Reafons, that you
hifs like *Serpents* or *Adders* in the Path againft me;
and yet you have the Affurance to pretend, in your
Miffive, a Refpect to the Doctrines of Morality:
But you have confirmed me, that it is my Duty to
hold on in what, by Way of Ridicule, you term
the beaten Path, even tho' the Reproofs of the
World fhould gall and torment you.

It is like fome may think I have paid you too
great a Compliment, when I have taken any Notice of you at all, but I affure you, if you continue in your *profane Banter*, I fhall never judge it
worth my While to make any Return unto you. In
the mean time, I fincerely wifh you well, and it
is my daily Prayer for you, That you may be re-
claimed from the Error and Wickednefs of your
Way.

Perth, Sept. 16
1735.

WILLIAM WILSON.

Psalm lxxii. 17.

*His Name shall endure for ever; his
Name shall be continued as long the
Sun; and Men shall be blessed in him,*
&c.

THE Penman of this excellent *Psalm* is
David, the Royal Psalmist, it is the
last *Psalm* that he penned, as you may
see from the last Verse: It bears the Title
of *a Psalm for Solomon*, and it is probable it was
penned when *David* resigned the Government into
the Hands of *Solomon* his Son, the History of which
you have, 1 *Kings* 1 33. Though the *Psalm* contains a Prayer for a prosperous and happy Reign
to King *Solomon*, *yet a greater than* Solomon *is here*.
Solomon was a very eminent Type of the Lord Jesus;
he was a Type of him in the Names that were given him, he was called *Jedidiah* when he was
born, *that is*, Beloved of the Lord, 2 *Sam*. xii. 25.
So Christ is the Son of his Father's Love, his *beloved Son in whom he is well pleased*. Again, the
Name *Solomon* signifies *Peaceable*; this Name was
given him, because *Israel* enjoyed great Peace and
Tranquillity under his Government, 1 *Chron*. xxii.
9. Christ is the *Prince of Peace*, his Kingdom is
a Kingdom of Peace, all his Subjects enjoy a glorious Peace, they have Peace with God; and that
inward *Peace of God, which passeth Understanding*, is
one of Christ's Legacies unto them; it is the Royal

B   Gift

Gift and Grant of their King, *John* xiv, 22. *Solomon* built that stately and magnificent Fabrick, the Old Testament Temple, Christ *builds the Temple of the Lord, and bears all the Glory,* Zech. vi. 13. He is both the Foundation and Builder of his Church, and he bears away all the Glory from his Type. *Solomon* was famous for his Wisdom, but all the Wisdom of *Solomon* was only a faint Shadow of him who is the *Wisdom of God,* and *in whom are hid all the Treasures of Wisdom and Knowledge.* *Solomon* had immense Riches, but *all Fulness* dwells in the Person of Christ, *unsearchable Riches* are with him, all the immense Treasures of Glory and Grace are in his Hand It is Christ, the promised *Messiah,* the glorious Antitype of King *Solomon,* who is principally intended in this *Psalm,* the general Strain of it is so high and lofty, the Expressions are so great and strong, that they cannot be applied to any other : It is only of him that it can be said, *They shall fear thee as long as the Sun and Moon endure, throughout all Generations,* Verse 5 It is he alone who *comes down* by the Doctrine of his Word, and by the Grace of his Spirit, *like Rain upon the mown Grass, as Showers that water the Earth,* Verse 6. His Kingdom alone is a *Kingdom of Righteousness,* and of *abundant* and perpetual *Peace,* Verse 7. It is to him that the Promise is made, *That he shall have Dominion from Sea to Sea, and from the River to the Ends of the Earth,* Verse 8 And this Promise gives us Ground to expect a more glorious Enlargement of the Kingdom of Christ Though his Person and Government are much despised at this Time in the World, and even amongst those who bear the Christian Name, yet *they that dwell in the Wilderness shall bow before him, and his Enemies shall lick the Dust,* Verse 9. But, not to insist upon the preceed

ing

ing Part of the *Pfalm*, the Words I have read are a plain Prophecy and Promife concerning the *Meffiah*, the Lord Jefus Chrift, he was the Object of the Faith, Hope and Expectation of the Old Teftament Church ; *for to him gave all the Prophets Witnefs*, they fpoke of him as a-coming, they bare Witnefs unto his Perfon, unto his Sufferings, and the Glory that fhould follow And, amongft others, *David* was an eminent Witnefs unto the Perfon of Chrift, unto his Sufferings and Death, and the Glory that was to follow thereupon. *His Name* fays he, *fhall endure for ever, and Men fhall be bleffed in him.* The Expreffions are too great to be applied to any mere Creature In the Words then you have a Prophecy, 1. Concerning the perpetuating of Chrift's Name unto all Generations ; *His Name fhall endure for ever* 2. Of the great Benefit and Advantage Men fhall reap by him ; *They fhall be bleffed in him* And, 3 of the univerfal Subjection of *Jews* and *Gentiles* to his Kingdom , *All Nation fhall call him bleffed.*

The firft Thing remarkable in the Verfe is a Promife concerning the perpetuating of the Name of Chrift, *His Name fhall endure for ever.* What is his Name ? *Prov* xxx 4. His Name is *fecret*, he has a Name that none knows but he himfelf. His Name is *wonderful*, his Name is a *great* Name, he hath *a Name above every Name.* By his Name we are to underftand Chrift himfelf, and every Thing whereby he makes himfelf known unto us, all the glorious Perfections and Excellencies of his divine Nature are his Name ; all his Titles and Office-Characters that he bears are his Name , his Word and his Ordinances are his Name · *His Name fhall endure for ever*, that is, his moft renowned Fame fhall be publifhed and declared in all Ages and Generations.

Generations. He shall never want Heraulds of his
Glory, and Trumpeters of his Praise, *One Genera-*
tion shall praise him to another . The Glorious Honour of his Majesty shall be proclaimed, they shall
declare his mighty Acts, *Men shall speak of the*
Might of his terrible Acts, and declare his Greatness,
Psalm cxlv. 4 5. 6. Our Lord Jesus got to himself
a great Name in the Victory that he obtained over
the Power of Darkness, *namely*, over Sin and Satan,
over Death, Hell, and the Grave, he has *triumph*
ed gloriously over them, and therefore he hath a
Name above every Name   The glorious Fame of
what he has done, of the Satisfaction that he has
given to the Justice of God, of the Atonement
that he has made for Sin, of his bruising the Head
of the old Serpent, and of the everlasting Righte
ousness that he has brought in, the Report and
Fame of all this shall endure for ever   He shall
be known in all Ages and Generations as *Immanu-*
el, God with us, as *Jehovah* our Righteousness,
our Peace, our Strength, our Healer, our Redeemer, and our Sanctifier, as our great Prophet,
Priest and King, as the great God our Saviour. It
is remarkable, is is said, His Name *shall* endure,
whatever Opposition may be made to this glorious
Name, yet it *shall* endure. It has been the great
Plot of Hell in all Ages to banish this Name out
of the World, or to darken this illustrious and glorious Name ▓▓▓▓the same Design is pursued with all
the Rage and Cunning of the old Serpent in the Age
wherein we live. The Person of Christ is blasphem
ed, his Word is reproached and traduced, his
Grace is rejected, and his Ordinances are despised·
But his Name shall endure for ever, the divine
Glory of his Person shall shine forth brightly from
under all the Clouds and Vails that Men endeavour

draw over it, his Word shall stand its Ground against all the Batteries of Hell, his Ordinances and Institutions shall be maintained and preserved in his Church, if Men pervert or corrupt them, he will not want some Witnesses for the honour of his Name against any Injuries that are done to them, for *a Seed shall do Service unto him, and it shall be accounted to the Lord in a Generation, they shall come and shall declare his Righteousness*, Psalm XXII 30, 31.

The next Clause in the Verse is, *His Name shall be continued as long as the Sun* These Words are very important and emphatick, our Translators in the Text have followed the Seventy. The original Word, which is here rendred *continued*, is not oft used in Scripture, I shall not offer any critical Commentary upon it, but confine my self to the Translation given us in the Margine, where it is rendred, *He shall be as a Son to continue his Father's Name for ever* The Father's great Name is continued in the Son, he is the essential Image of the Father, *the express Image of his Person*, Heb. 1 2. All the essential Attributes and Perfections of the divine Nature are in the Person of the Son, the Father's great Name is in him, *Exod.* XXIII. 21. Is the Father the supreme, the independent and self-existent God? So is the Son, therefore it is said, *He that hath seen the Son, hath seen the Father also; for he is in the Father, and the Father in him*, John XIV 10. Again, he shall be as a Son to continue his Father's Name for ever, that is, the Father's great Name is made known to Men in the Person of his Son, as he is *Immanuel*, God with us: It is *in the Face*, or in the Person of Christ, that the *Light of the Knowledge of the Glory of God* is given unto Men, 2 *Cor.* IV. 6. That great Name of God,

The

The Lord, the Lord God, merciful and gracious, is no where to be seen, it is nowhere to be read, it is nowhere to be known, but in the Person of the Lord Jesus : The Love, the Mercy, and the Grace of God, are vented upon Sinners only in and through him, for it is in him that Men are blessed. This is a short Hint at what has been delivered on the first Part of this Verse

I proceed now to the *second* Part of the Verse, which contains the great and unspeakable Benefit that comes to Men by Christ, *Men shall be blessed in he:* This is the same Promise, upon the Matter, with that which was given to *Adam* immediately after the Fall, *Gen* iii. 15. and which was renewed to *Ibiaham, Gen* xiii 3 and xxii 18 *In thy Seed shall all the Nations of the earth be blessed* The Apostle *Paul* declares, that this was the Gospel which was preached to *Abraham,* Gal iii. 8. *Abraham* saw the Day of Christ in this Promise, and was glad. This Promise That *Men shall be blessed in him,* is a short Sum of the Gospel. And in it you may notice, 1*st.* What it is that is promised, it is Blessedness : The Blessedness here promised is spiritual and eternal Blessedness; it is that Blessedness that was lost by the Entrance of Sin, it includes all these *spiritual Blessings in heavenly Places* that are bestowed upon all that believe. 2*dly.* You may notice where it is that this Blessedness is to be found, *in him;* that is, in the Lord Jesus, who is God manifested in the Flesh, and who bears the Character of the second or last *Adam,* 1 *Cor.* xv. 45. and *the last* Adam *is a quickning Spirit.* He bears this Name, because he is the Head of a new Family, who are redeemed from among Men by his Blood, and whom he quickens by his Spirit But I am afterwards to open up more fully what is

imported

imported in thefe Words, *in him.* 3dly. You may here likeways notice who they are that are blef-fed in him, they are *Men*, Men fhall be bleffed: Not the Angels that finned, but Men, for he took not on him the Nature of Angels, or, he *taketh not hold of Angels, but of the Seed of* Abraham *he taketh hold,* Heb ii 16. He took hold on our Nature, and preferves a Remnant of Mankind from Ruin and Deftruction, when all the apoftate Angels are fhut up under Chains of Darknefs. Again, *Men fhall be bleffed in him,* not innocent Men, or Men that have not finned, but finful and rebellious Men *Adam,* in a State of Innocence, ftood in no Need of Chrift the Redeemer and Mediator He is the Saviour of finful Men, a Help found out for perifhing and loft Men; *He received Gifts for the Rebellious, that God the Lord might dwell amongft us.* Again, *Men fhall be bleffed,* that is, Men indefinite-ly, *Gentiles* as well as *Jews* The Words of our Text point at New Teftament Times, when *the Bleffing of* Abraham *comes upon us Gentiles* Under the Old Teftament Difpenfation, the Revelation and Promife of the Bleffing was confined for a confider-able Time to one Nation, but now the middle Wall of Partition is broken down, and we *Gentiles are madeFellow Heirs* and *Partakers of his Promife in Chrift by the Gofpel,* Eph iii. 6 4thly You may notice in the Words the Manner how it is promifed Men *fhall* be bleffed, that is It is the unchangeable and irreverfible Purpofe of his Will to blefs Men in his own Son the Lord Jefus Chrift When *Satan* feduced our firft Parents into Sin, he no doubt thought he had brought all Mankind into utter and inevitable Ruin and that he had made them as cur-fed and miferable as himfelf This was the geeat **Plot and Defign of Hell :** But in the Promife God

intimates

intimates his Purpose of Love, whereby the Deſign of Hell is counterplotted and diſappointed, for *Men ſhall be bleſſed in him*, as if it had been ſaid, The whole Race of Mankind ſhall not periſh, *the Captives of the mighty* Power of Darkneſs *ſhall be taken away*, and *the Prey of the Terrible ſhall be delivered*. Satan has done his utmoſt to ruine them, but I will make my great Power and Grace to be known in the Redemption and Salvation of a Remnant of Mankind, in and by my own Son the Lord Jeſus. The Doctrinal Propoſition that I offer you from the Words is this,

That it is in the Lord Jeſus Chriſt alone, that ſinful and miſerable Men may find ſpiritual and eternal Bleſſedneſs · Or, That the Bleſſedneſs that Men have loſt in the firſt Adam, it is to be found in the Lord Jeſus the ſecond Adam.

The Doctrine is evident from the Words of the Text; and, for Explication of it, I ſhall, in the 1ſt Place, premiſe a few Things for paving our Way on this Subject. 2dly I ſhall ſhew you what is imported in the Expreſſion, *In him Men ſhall be bleſſed.* 3dly. Give you ſome Account of that Bleſſedneſs which is to be found in Chriſt. 4thly. Shew you how it comes to be ſo, or, why it is that the loſt Bleſſedneſs is to be found in him. And then, in the *laſt* Place make ſome practical Uſe and Improvement of this Subject.

I return to the firſt general Head, *namely*, To premiſe a few Things.

1ſt. When God made Man at the Beginning, he made him happy and bleſſed. When Man came out of his Creator's Hands, he was bleſſed with the Image of God, *Gen.* 1. 26, 27. *And God ſaid, Let us make*

make Man in our own Image, after our Likeness.—So God created Man in his own Image, in the Image of God created he him. This Image of God, in which Man was created, was some Resemblance and Likeness which he bore unto his glorious Creator, in Knowledge, Righteousness and Holiness, and this was Man's peculiar Glory and Excellency, to bear the Image of God, he was crowned with this Honour and Glory above all the other Works of God's Hands in this lower World. But this was not all the Blessedness that was bestowed upon him, for God condescended to become a promising God to him, he promised him Life upon Condition of perfect Obedience to his Law, this Condition Man was able to perform without any Difficulty The Promise of Life upon this Condition is implied in the Threatning of Death in case of Disobedience, *Gen* ii. 17. and plainly declared elsewhere in Scripture, *Rom.* x. 5. When God made a Promise of Life unto Man upon the Condition of his Obedience, he condescended to make him his Friend and Confederate, and here he dealt with him in the Way of a Covenant, this was a higher Degree of Blessedness bestowed upon Man. And indeed the Distance between God and the Creature is so great, that tho' reasonable Creatures do owe Obedience to him as their Creator, yet they cannot expect the Fruition of him as their Blessedness and Reward, but by some voluntary Condescension on God's Part, which he was pleased to express to our first Parents by the Way of a Covenant, and this Covenant is that which is ordinarily called the *Covenant of Works,* wherein the whole Race of Mankind were included and comprehended, the first *Adam* being their common Head and Representative, *Rom.* v 12,———— 20.

C   2*dly.*

2dly. Tho' God made Man bleſſed, yet he did not abide in this bleſſed and honourable State : Our firſt Parents, being ſeduced by *Satan*, did voluntarily and wickedly depart from God their Bleſſedneſs ; they tranſgreſſed his Covenant by the Breach of the poſitive Command that was given them for the Trial of their Obedience, *Gen.* iii, 6. This Sin and Diſobedience of the firſt *Adam* was the Defection of the whole Race of Mankind from God their Bleſſedneſs and their Reward , they all *ſinned in him*, and by his Diſobedience every one of them are *made Sinners*, Rom. v. 12, ————18, 19. Hence,

3dly The whole Race of Mankind, by their Sin and Rebellion againſt God, are under his Curſe, and obnoxious to his Sin-revenging Juſtice. When Sin entred into the World, the Curſe of the broken Law took hold on *Adam* and all his Family ; for, *Curſed is every one that continueth not in all Things which are written in the Book of the Law to do them,* Gal, iii 10 Therefore, tho' God made Man bleſſed, Man by his own Sin has loſt the Bleſſedneſs that God gave him, and brought himſelf under the Curſe and Wrath of a righteous and holy God This is that miſerable Eſtate into which our Apoſtaſy and Defection from God has brought us; we have forfeited every Thing that is good, and have made ourſelves liable unto every Thing that is evil; we have loſt that beautiful and glorious Image of God after which we were created , we have loſt the Favour and Friendſhip of God , we have forfeited that Life that was promiſed unto us in the firſt Covenant, and we are every one born under the Curſe of the broken Law ; we are Children of Wrath by Nature, and, while we are in our natural State, the *Wrath of God abideth on us.*

4thly.

4*thly.* Though all Mankind are under the Curfe, yet the whole Race are not left to perifh in this deplorable and miferable Condition, for God has, out of his mere good Pleafure, from all Eternity, elected fome to everlafting Life, even fome of that apoftate and finful Family *For whom he did foreknow, them he did predeftinate,* Rom viii. 29. They are *predeftinate to the Adoption of Children,* Eph. i. 5. And it is for this End, that an eternal Revenue of Glory may be given unto God, Father, Son and Spirit, in their Redemption from Sin and Wrath, *Eph*. i. 5, 6.

5*thly.* The Blefednefs that Men have forfeited by Sin is to be found in the Lord Jefus, and nowhere elfe, there is *no Salvation in any other,* and *there is none other Name given under Heaven among Men, whereby we muft be faved,* Acts iv. 12. The Incarnation, Obedience and Death of the eternal Son of God, is the great Mean provided, in his adorable Wifdom and Love, for our Redemption from that Wrath and Curfe we are under, and for bringing back unto us the Blefednefs that we have loft. But this leads me to

The *fecond* Thing propofed in the Method, which is, To open up the Import of the Expreffion, *Men fhall be bleffed in him.* It is the Import of thefe two Words, *In him,* that I am to confider, and there is very much wrapt up in them.

They import, in the *firft* Place, that Chrift is the *Treafure-Houfe* of all fpiritual and eternal Blefednefs unto Men : *In him are hid all the Treafures of Wifdom and Knowledge,* Col ii 3. They are *hid in him ;* that is, they are laid up, or treafured up in him : He is made the firft Recipient of all that Blefednefs that is defigned for Men in Time

or

or Eternity : All the Bleſſings that are prepared in the Purpoſe of God for the Veſſels of Mercy, are lodged in the Perſon of his Son, to be diſpenſed and communicated by him , for *it pleaſed the Father that in him all Fulneſs ſhould dwell*, Col. 1 19. He becomes the Treaſure-Houſe of all ſpiritual Bleſſings to Men, three Ways 1. By his Father's eternal Deſignation and Appointment 2. By the Covenant-Tranſaction with him. 3. By his actual Manifeſtation in the Fleſh.

1ſt. He is the Treaſure-Houſe of all ſpiritual Bleſſings by the Deſignation and Appointment of his Father . He is deſigned in the eternal Purpoſe of God to be the ſecond *Adam*, the Head-Repreſentative of a new Family, even of a Remnant of the ſinful and miſerable Poſterity of *Adam*, who were given him to be redeemed and ſaved by him; therefore he ſays himſelf, *Prov.* viii. 23. *I was ſet up from everlaſting* He was ſet up to be the Mediator, betwixt God and Man , he was ſet up to be the Centre of Union and Communion betwixt Heaven and Earth , he was ſet up to be our Redeemer, both by Price and Power, to be a juſtifying and ſanctifying Head unto us, to bring in an everlaſting Righteouſneſs for Juſtification, and to communicate the Spirit of Holineſs unto us for our Sanctification : In a Word, he was ſet up to be *the Captain of our Salvation, to bring many Sons unto Glory,* through his Obedience and Death. And, by this eternal Conſtitution and Appointment, he is become the Treaſure-Houſe of all ſpiritual Bleſſings to Men ; therefore all the Fulneſs that dwells in his Perſon is aſcribed to the Sovereign Good Will and Pleaſure of the Father, *Col.* i 19 and for the ſame Reaſon the Elect are ſaid to be *choſen in him,* Eph. i. 4. The ſovereign Good-Will and Pleaſure

sure of God (which admits of no Cause or Motive without himself) is the only Source and Spring of our Salvation.   When we are said to be *chosen in him*, the Meaning is, that he is the great Mean found out and provided in the infinite Wisdom of God for our Recovery from Sin and Ruin, and for our obtaining everlasting Blessedness, hence the giving of the Son to be the Redeemer and Saviour is mentioned in Scripture as the Fruit and Effect of the sovereign Purpose of Love to Sinners, *John* iii. 16. and herein the *manifold Wisdom of God* is eminently displayed   If the Wisdom and Love of God, in the Constitution and Appointment of his own eternal Son to be the Redeemer and Saviour, is not believed and humbly adored it is rejected and despised, and if it is rejected and despised, then you reckon the only Mean that infinite Wisdom hath pitched upon for bringing back Blessedness to Men to be Foolishness; and, if this is Foolishness in your Eyes, your Condemnation must be as inexcusable, as it is certain and inevitable

2dly Christ is the Treasure-House of all spiritual and eternal Blessings, by virtue of the Covenant-Transaction betwixt Jehovah and the eternal Son considered as the second *Adam*, is plainly declared in Scripture, *Psal* lxxxix 3. *Zech.* vi 13. In the Covenant of Works the first *Adam* was considered as a publick Person representing all his natural Seed, God dealt with him as their Head and Representative, he was Trustee for them, their Stock was lodged in his Hands, perfect Obedience was required as the Condition of Life, Death was threatned upon the least Failure : But *Adam* broke this Covenant, he lost the Right and Title to Life, and involved himself and his Posterity into Sin and Misery. In the Covenant-Transaction with the

second

second *Adam*, there is a sovereign Grant of the Father, giving and delivering to his eternal Son, to be redeemed and saved by him, a certain definite Number out of *Adam*'s Family, who were beheld lying in the Ruins of Sin by the Breach of the first Covenant Hence Christ, speaking of them, calls them, The Men given him by the Father out of the World, *Thine* (says he) *they were, and thou gavest them me*, John xvii. 6,——9. In this Transaction the Son is considered as a publick Person, standing in their Law-Place, Room and Stead, undertaking to do and suffer every Thing that was necessary to save them from Sin and Wrath, and to possess them of eternal Life More particularly, he undertook to assume their Nature into a personal Union with his divine Nature, and in that Nature to fulfil the Condition of Life ; that is, to yield the perfect Obedience that the Law or Covenant of Works demanded as a Condition of Life , also, to bear the Punishment incurred by the Breach of that Covenant, and to endure that Curse and that Wrath that was the Desert of Sin, to die that very Death which by the Law is the Wages of Sin. In a Word, he undertook to redeem, or buy back, at the Price of his own Blood, the forfeited Blessing, and to deliver by the Power of his Spirit the lawful Captives, and to rescue them, not only from the Guilt, but also from the Power, Filth, and Being of Sin, and from the Dominion and Tyranny of Satan. All this you have in the following Scriptures, *Psalm* xl. 6, 7, 8 *Isa.* xliii. 21. Chapter liii throughout *Dan.* ix. 24. *Isa.* xlix. 24, 25. As the Lord Jesus, in the Covenant-Transaction with him, was an undertaking Head, so he was also a receiving Head · All the Blessings designed for the elect Sinners were delivered into his Hand.

Hand : He received on their Behalf all the Promifes of the Spirit, of Grace and Glory, yea, of every good Thing which they were to receive on the Account of his undertaking for them   Hence it is faid, that *Grace was given us in Chrift Jefus before the World began*, 2 Tim. 1. 9 that is, in him as our Head and Reprefentative Alfo *eternal Life*, which includes all the Bleffings wherewith Men are bleffed in Chrift, is faid to be *promifed before the World began*, Tit i. 2.   To whom was the Promife then made ? To the great New Covenant Head, the Lord Jefus Chrift . On account of this Transaction with him, he is defigned the Father's *Servant*, Ifa. xlii. 1.   And, on account of his fulfilling his Engagement, as alfo becaufe of that Fulnefs of Grace that is in his Perfon, and the Fulnefs of Merit and Virtue that is in his Obedience, in his Death, and daily Mediation, he is declared in the Word of the Gofpel to be *given for a Covenant of the People*, Ifa. xlii. 6.   This Covenant-Transaction is that Bottom and Foundation on which the whole Building of Mercy and Grace ftands , and it is laid open in the Word and Promifes of the Gofpel, as a Foundation of our Faith and Hope for all Bleffednefs fpiritual and eternal

  3*dly*. Chrift is the Treafure Houfe of all fpiritual Bleffings, by his affuming our Nature into a perfonal Union with his divine   This he did in the Fulnefs of Time, in confequence of his eternal Undertaking, *Gal.* iv. 4   *John* 1. 14 *The Word was made Flefh, and dwelt among us* Who is it that was made Flefh ? *The Word*, that is, the fecond Perfon of the adorable Trinity, who is defcribed in the Beginning of this Chapter from his Eternity and Omnipotence manifefted in the creating of all Things. His Manifeftation in the Flefh is the

great

great Mystery of Godliness, 1 Tim. iii. 16. If we behold him in the glorious Constitution of his Person, as he is *Immanuel, God with us*, his Name may justly be called *Wonderful*. He is the mighty God, the Father of Eternity, yet *a Child born unto us* : He is God, and he is Man too, he is God and Man, in two distinct Natures and one Person for ever. The Union of these two distinct Natures in one Person is the Effect of the manifold Wisdom of God, and what we should rather adore and admire than curiously search into, it is a Mystery that the Angels desire to look with Reverence and Admiration into. By assuming our Nature into a personal Union with his divine, he is become the rich Treasure House of all spiritual Blessings unto us, for *in him dwells all the Fulness of the Godhead bodily*, Col ii 9. He *received Gifts for Men*, or in the Man, *in Adam*, so it is in the Original, *Psalm* xlviii. 18. *Grace is poured into the Lips* of the second *Adam*, Psalm xlv 2. The Spirit in all his Gifts and Graces doth rest upon him, for *God gave not the Spirit by Measure unto him*. His Disciples, in the Days of his Flesh, *saw the Glory* of God in him, and *beheld him as full of Grace and Truth*, John i. 14. and they acknowledge, that all the spiritual Blessings that they enjoyed, they found them in him, and received them from him, and every one that believes will make the same Acknowledgment with them, *Of his Fulness have all we received, and Grace for Grace*, John i 16

Secondly, Men shall be blessed *in him* ; it imports, that he is the Conduit of all spiritual Blessings unto Men. The Grace, the Love, and the Mercy of God, have a Vent upon Men through Christ, and only through him. God out of Christ is a consuming Fire to Sinners ; his Justice, his Holiness, his

his Faithfulnefs, are all againft the Sinner. And here you may obferve, that fpiritual Bleffings are conveyed unto Men through the Perfon, Death and Mediation of the Lord Jefus, by the Means of the Word, and by the fpecial Energy of his holy Spirit.

1ft. He is the Conduit of fpiritual Bleffings unto Men in his *Perfon* It is in his Perfon, as he is *Immanuel*, God with us, that we have any comfortable and gracious Difcoveries of God ; it is only in him that we may look with Hope and Expectation toward God : God comes to us in the Perfon of his Son in a Way of Grace and Mercy, and in him we may draw near with Hope and a holy Confidence unto God, *John* xiv 6 *I am the Way* : He is the Way in which God comes unto us, and the Way in which we may come to God, and there is not another Way Whatever Difcoveries of the Being and Perfections of God are given us by the Light of Nature, yet Nature's Light cannot afford us the leaft Ground of Confidence or Truft in God for Redemption from the Curfe that Sin brings us under, or Deliverance from the Wrath that it deferves · Why, the Light of Nature fpeaks nothing of the Perfon of Chrift the Redeemer, the only Days Man betwixt God and us , it cannot inform us of an Atonement for Sin, or any Reparation made of the Difhonour that is done unto the great God, the fupreme Ruler and Governor of the World, by the univerfal Defection and Apoftafy of Mankind from him, whereby every individual Perfon is become a Rebel, yea, is continually rebelling againft his fovereign Authority and Government. Likeways the righteous and holy Law difcovers unto us the Holinefs and Purity of God the great Lawgiver ; it informs us that we are Sinners,

and

and obnoxious to his Wrath ; it both finds us and leaves us under the Curfe, but fpeaks nothing of a Way of Reconciliation unto God : It is only in the Perfon of Chrift, as he is revealed in the Word of the Gofpel, that any comfortable Difcoveries of the Glory of God are given. In him *Mercy and Truth are met together ;* in him *Righteoufnefs and Peace kifs each other* mutually ; in him all the glorious Excellencies and Perfections of the divine Nature dart forth the comforting and refrefhing Beams of Mercy and Grace, in him the Faithfulnefs, Juftice, and Holinefs of God fpeak *Peace on Earth, and Good-Will towards Men ; for God is in Chrift reconciling the World to himfelf.*

2dly He is the Conduit of fpiritual Bleffings to Men in his *Obedience* and *Death.* The Lord Jefus, according to his eternal Undertaking, did actually in Time fubftitute himfelf in the Room of Sinners, he was made under the Law, he fuffered and died in their Room and Stead. In the perfect Obedience of his Life he fulfilled all the Demands of the Law as a Covenant of Works ; and, by his Obedience unto it, the broken *Law* was *magnified and made honourable :* Greater Honour was done to the Law in the Obedience of the Son of God, than *Adam* by his Obedience could have given, if he had continued in a State of Innocence. Likeways, in his Sufferings unto Death, he bore that Punifhment that was incurred by the Breach of the Law, and thereby gave Glory to the rectoral Juftice of God, and to his Faithfulnefs in the Threatning. The Satisfaction that Chrift gave unto the Law and Juftice of God for Sin and Sinners, was finifhed and completed in his Death, and therefore our Redemption and Reconciliation are frequently afcribed unto the Death of Chrift in
Scripture.

Scripture. By this full and compleat Satisfaction that he gave unto the Justice of God, an offended God is atoned, and an everlasting Righteousness is brought in : The great Surety, having paid all the Debt, obtained the Discharge in his Resurrection from the Dead : He is now ascended into Heaven, and is *set down on the Right-Hand of the Majesty on high*, and conveys all spiritual Blessings thro' this glorious and costly Channel of his Obedience and Death. Redemption from Sin, Reconciliation unto God, and all other spiritual Blessings, flow unto Men thro' the Blood of the Lord Jesus Christ, *Eph.* i. 7. *Col.* i. 20,

2*dly*, He is the Conduit of all spiritual Blessings to Men, by the Means of his *Word*. The rich Treasure-House of all spiritual Blessings is opened up in the Word of the Gospel : The Gospel reveals Christ ; it is a Preaching of him in his Person and Offices, as the great Ordinance of God for our Justification and Sanctification, and for our compleat Redemption and Salvation. Christ, the Treasure-House of all spiritual Blessings, was first opened up in the first Promise, *Gen.* iii. 15 and afterwards to *Abraham, Gen.* xii. 3, 18. After the first Revelation of Christ, the Discoveries of him were like the *Morning-Light, that shineth more and more unto the perfect Day ;* they grew fuller and clearer from Time to Time, till he himself appeared in Person on Earth, and by his Death rent the Old Testament Vail asunder. Under the New Testament Dispensation he is clearly revealed in his Person and Offices : The Glory of his Person and the Blessings that are purchased by him, are unvailed · Every Word, every Offer and Promise of the Gospel, every Command to believe, every Call and Invitation that is given you to come to

the

the Lord Jefus, is an Opening up of the rich Treafures of fpiritual Bleffings that are in him.   In this
Word that is preached unto you, *Men fha'll be bleffed in him*, all the Bleffings that are in Chrift are
brought nigh unto you, his Righteoufnefs and Salvation are brought unto your Door.

  4*thly*. He is the Conduit of all fpiritual Bleffings
unto Men by his *holy Spirit*.   In the bleffed Oe
conomy of our Redemption and Salvation by the
Lord Jefus Chrift, the effectual Application of all
purchafed and promifed Bleffings is committed unto the Holy Ghoft, for this End he is promifed,
and for this End he is given by Chrift ·   Hence he
is called *the Spirit of Wifdom and Revelation in the
Knowledge of Chrift;* becaufe he gives the faving
Knowledge of him, *Eph* 1 17   Chrift is not only revealed by the Word, but he is revealed by
the Holy Ghoft within the Hearts of all that be
lieve, as the Apoftle *Paul* doth exprefs it, *Gal* 1.
15, 16.   And, left any fhould think that this
was extraordinary, and peculiar to the Apoftle *Paul*,
(though there is no Doubt that *Paul* had an extraordinary Revelation of Chrift to fit him for the extraordinary Office and Character that he was to
bear) he fpeaks of a faving Revelation of Chrift by
the Holy Ghoft, as what is common to all that are
effectually called, and peculiar to them alone, he
expreffeth it by the Lord's *fhining into their Hearts*,
2 Cor iv. 6   This Work of the Spirit, whereby
he applies the Redemption purchafed by Chrift, is
his powerful Teftimony concerning Chrift unto
the Souls of all that believe, according to the Promife, *John* xv. 26 *He fhall teftify of me*   The
Word is no doubt the Teftimony of the Spirit concerning the Lord Jefus in his Perfon and Mediation,
but the Teftimony of God in the Word is alfo
                                                    brought

brought home unto the Minds of them that believe, by the fupernatural Power and Energy of the Holy Ghoft. Hence it is faid concerning the *Theffalonians,* That the Gofpel *came not unto them in Word only, but alfo in Power, and in the Holy Ghoft,* 1 Theff. 1 5. When the Spirit of God brings home the Teftimony of God in his Word unto the Heart of a Sinner, the Word carries along ft with it its own Evidence, and all that believe reft upon God's own Teftimony in his Word concerning his Son, evidencing itfelf in its own Light and Power unto their Minds : Hence their *Faith is faid to ftand, not in the Wifdom of Men, but in the Power of God.* 1 Cor. ii 5. The Holy Spirit is alfo promifed to fhew the Things of Chrift, *John* xvi 14 *He fhall glorify me, for he fhall receive of mine and, fhew it unto you.* And what is it that he fhews ? He fhews the Glory and Excellency of the Perfon of Chrift, the Glory that is in his Undertaking and in his Obedience and Death, the Fulnefs of Merit and Virtue that is in the Satisfaction he gave the Suitablenefs that is in all his Offices for the Mifery we are under. Thefe and the like are the Things that the Holy Ghoft fhews And he fhews them not by the bare outward Revelation of them, but by giving a fpiritual Ability to difcern and know the Things of God; *He gives us Underftanding to know him that is true,* 1 John v 20 He creates in the Heart that Faith whereby we are enabled to receive and apprehend the Lord Jefus Chrift for our Redemption and Salvation from Sin and Wrath. It is a certain Truth, that none can partake in any of the Bleffings that are in Chrift, unlefs they are applied by the fupernatural Energy of the Holy Ghoft, and if Men deride and defpife his Work, they fhall meet with a fatal Difappointment in the End.

End. The Contempt that is caſt by many upon the Spirit of Chriſt, in his ſpecial and ſupernatural Operations, it is a plain Evidence of the Truth of his own Word, 1 *Cor.* ii 14 *The natural Man receiveth not the Things of the Spirit of God, for they are Fooliſhneſs unto him, neither can he know them, becauſe they are ſpiritually diſcerned*

I ſhall conclude this Head with obſerving, that there is a beautiful and glorious Order in the Communication of divine Bleſſings : All the Bleſſings deſigned in the Purpoſe of God for ſinful and miſerable Men are delivered into the Hands of the Son, they are treaſured up in him as the Head of the new Covenant, they are purchaſed by his Blood, they are revealed and offered in the Word and Promiſes of the Goſpel, and effectually conveyed by the Holy Ghoſt unto all Chriſt's ſpiritual Seed

Thirdly, Men ſhall be bleſſed *in him*, imports the Neceſſity of an Inbeing in Chriſt, in order to an actual Participation of the Bleſſings that are in him. We are every one by Nature in the firſt *Adam;* and as we are in him, we are under the Guilt and Power of Sin, and conſequently under the Curſe and Wrath of God · We muſt needs be cut off from that corrupt Root from whence we ſpring, and ingrafted in the Lord Jeſus Chriſt, otherways we cannot partake of the Bleſſedneſs that is in him. A Branch has no Benefit from a Root, unleſs it is ingrafted in it. All Communion betwixt the Head and Members reſults from Union betwixt them. If we have not a vital Union with Chriſt the living Head, we can have no Communion with him in his Bleſſings, if we are not in him, we have no Intereſt in his juſtifying Righteouſneſs, nor in his ſanctifying Spirit ; if we are not in him, we have not any Right or Title to Glory : Union is the Foundation of Communion, and Communion reſults fults from Union.   The Union that we are speaking of, is that which is ordinarily called the *mystical Union*, it is a most close and real Union; it is resembled to the Union that is betwixt a Foundation and a Building, and to the Union betwixt the Head and the Members, and to that which is betwixt the Root and the Branches, yea, to that which is betwixt the Husband and the Wife But all these Comparisons are only Shadows of that Union which is betwixt Christ and his People, for *he that is joined to the Lord is one Spirit,* 1 Cor. vi. 17.   The two special Ligaments and Bonds of this Union are the *Spirit* and *Faith* .   The holy Spirit is the primary and first Ligament of this Union, he descends from the living Head into the Heart of a Sinner, in his convincing, enlightning and quickning Virtue and Power, and he lays unto the dead Sinner, *Live*, and that very Moment in which the Breath of spiritual Life is breathed into the Heart of a Sinner, Faith, the other Ligament and Bond, springs up and takes hold on Christ.

Having touched, on the former Head, at the Necessity of a supernatural Work of the Spirit of Christ, in order unto our partaking of the Blessedness that is in him, let us take a View of Faith, the other Ligament of the mystical Union It is the appointed and the instituted Mean for uniting us to Christ, and interesting us in his Salvation; it is the only uniting Grace, though, where it is, it is never alone but has Repentance, Love and all the other Graces attending it . Hence *Christ* is said to *dwell in our Hearts by Faith* Eph iii 17. On this Account our Justification is ascribed to Faith, *Rom* v. 1. Likeways our Sanctification, for the *Heart* is *purified by Faith*, Acts xv. 9. Also we

are

are said to be *saved through Faith*, Eph. ii. 8. through Faith, as it is the Mean of God's Appointment for interesting us in Christ himself, and in all his spiritual Blessings. The Grace of Faith has a special Aptitude and Fitness in it for this End, for it is a self-denying, a self emptying, and a self abasing Grace. It renounceth all Confidence in the Flesh, and leans unto the Lord Jesus Christ alone, it renounceth Confidence in every Thing else beside Christ himself for Deliverance from Sin and Wrath, for Acceptance in the Sight of God, and for a Right and Title unto eternal Life   The Language of Faith is, *In the Lord have I Righteousness and Strength.* Faith credits the Record of God in the Word, concerning his Son, as true, it approves of the whole Plan and Device of Salvation through Jesus Christ, as suited unto the divine Perfections, to the Case of perishing and lost Sinners, and to the Persons own Case in particular, and, upon the Warrant of God's own Word, trusts unto, or rests upon Christ himself for the whole of his Salvation, for Salvation from Sin as well as from Wrath, for Salvation from the Power as well as from the Guilt of Sin, for Sanctification as well as Justification. And this Faith is *not of ourselves, it is the Gift of God,* it is a Blessing promised and given by the Lord Jesus, it is one of the Fruits of his Spirit, hence the Holy Ghost is called the *Spirit of Faith,* 2 Cor. iv 13 By the Means of the Grace of Faith the mystical Union betwixt Christ and the Believer is completed, and from this Union results that actual Propriety and Interest which all that believe have in Christ himself, and in all the Blessings that are purchased by his Death and treasured up in his Person and revealed and offered in his Word For of him are ye *in Christ Jesus,* who of God is

made

made unto us Wisdom, Righteousness, and Sanctification, and Redemption, 1 *Cor* 1. 30.

I proceed now to the *third* Thing proposed for
Explication of the Doctrine, which is, To speak
of those *Blessings* wherewith Men are blessed in
Christ. They are great and many, even *all spiritual
Blessings in heavenly Places*, Eph 1 3. And what all
these are, what Tongue can declare, or what Heart
can conceive ? The Riches of Christ are truly unsearchable Riches I can only give a few Instances
of those Blessings that are to be found in him ; every
one of them have an unspeakable Worth and Excellency in them.

1*st*. *Justification* in the Sight of God is a Blessing wherewith Men are blessed in Christ ; *In him
shall all the Seed of Israel be justified, and shall glory*.
We are every one concluded under Sin , we are
guilty before God, and under the Sentence of
Death , we have no Merit to purchase, no Moyen
to procure Pardon and Remission of Sin , we are
destitute of a Righteousness wherewith to appear before a righteous and holy God , our best Duties,
and what Men may reckon their most virtuous Actions, when presented before a holy God, they are
all as an unclean Thing, they are all but *filthy Rags*.
In Justification Sin is pardoned and the Person of the
Sinner is accepted as righteous in the Sight of God :
When one is justified, he is acquitted and absolved
from the Sentence of Condemnation , the Hand-
writing of the Curse, that was standing against
him, is cancelled and blotted out, and he is declared righteous (so to speak) at the Bar : But the
Judgment of God is always according to Truth ;
none can be declared righteous without a Righteousness . But where is this Righteousness to be

E   found

found ? With us there is nothing but Guilt and Sin, we must plead guilty at the Bar: The Righteousness, on the Account of which we must be justified, is only to be found in the Lord Jesus, he has brought in a perfect and an everlasting Righteousness, a Righteousness that honours both Law and Lawgiver Every convinced and self-condemned Sinner who stands trembling at the Bar, may plead this Righteousness for Justification, and all who take Hold of it by Faith are justified in the Sight of God: *Their Righteousness is of me, saith the Lord*, Isa liv. 17. *This is the Name wherewith he is called*, THE LORD OUR RIGHTEOUSNESS, Jer xxiii. 6. He bears this Name, that every justified and pardoned Sinner may remain an eternal Debtor to his free Love and rich Grace, therefore *let him that glorieth, glory in the Lord*.

2dly. *Peace* and Reconciliation with God. *God is in Christ reconciling the World unto himself*, 2 Cor. v. 19. We lost the Favour and Friendship of God in the first *Adam*. When Sin entred into the World, it set God and Man at Variance, it made a great Rupture, a wide Breach betwixt Heaven and Earth, the whole Creation could never have made up the Breach. But the eternal Son of God stooped to stand in the Gap, and to make up the wide Breach, he alone was able for this Undertaking, being both God and Man, he was a meet Mediator of Peace and Reconciliation He is the only Days-Man, who lays his Hand upon the offended and offending Parties, and he is the only proper Umpire of the Variance between Jehovah and us, *He is our Peace*, Eph ii 14 *He hath made Peace through the Blood of his Cross*, Col i. 20 And God is to be found in him a God of Grace, and of Peace and Goodwill towards Men.

3dly. *Sanctification* is only to be found in him, 1 Cor. i. 30. *Christ is made of God to us —— Sanctifica-*

tion.

tion. In the firſt *Adam* we have loſt the Image of God, our whole Nature is corrupted and depraved, our Works are abominable. *Their is none that doth Good, no not one.* Where is the Image of God to be found? Or where is Holineſs to be had? Only in the ſecond *Adam,* the Lord Jeſus. As his Righteouſneſs is imputed to all that believe for Juſtification, ſo he is the Fountain-Head and Spring of Sanctification unto them, the Spirit of Holineſs deſcends from the holy Head unto all his Members, when they are united to him: In their Union with him, a Principle of Purity and Holineſs is implanted in them, hence they are called *his Workmanſhip, created in Chriſt Jeſus unto good Works,* Eph. ii. 10. And this Principle of Purity and Holineſs infuſed in them, it is the Image of God reſtored unto them. It is called the *Waſhing of Regeneration,* and the *Renewing of the Holy Ghoſt,* becauſe the Spirit of the living and holy Head begins the Work of Sanctification, in Regeneration, and, as he begins it, ſo he carries it on by Ordinances and Providences, by the Word and by the Rod, by every Mean of his own Inſtitution and Appointment, till it is complete in Glorification. To conclude this Head, unleſs Men are Partakers of the Spirit of Holineſs from the holy Head, there is no Holineſs in any of their Works, there is no Holineſs in their Duties, nor in any of their Actions. And do not deceive yourſelves, *Without Holineſs no Man ſhall ſee God.* If you are not holy, you cannot have Communion with him, neither in Grace here, nor in Glory hereafter.

4*thly* The *Adoption* of Children is another Bleſſing wherewith Men are bleſſed in Chriſt. By our Apoſtaſy from God in the firſt *Adam,* we are caſt out of God's Family, we have loſt the Right of Sonſhip,

Sonſhip, and all the Privileges of the Sons of God; we are Strangers and Foreigners to the Family of God. And it is in the Lord Jeſus the Head of the new Family, that the Right is recovered and the Privileges of Sons reſtored, hence the Elect are ſaid to be *predeſtinated unto the Adoption of Children by Jeſus Chriſt*, Eph. 1 5 that is, by him as the Head of the whole Family of God, therefore, *to as many as receive him, to them gives he Power to become the Son, of God*, John 1. 12 The Lord Jeſus Chriſt, the ſecond *Adam*, he is the firſt and great Heir of all Things, *Heb.* 1 2. The Right unto the whole of the forfeited Inheritance is in his Perſon, according to the Covenant Tranſaction with him, and *as many as receive him* by Faith, are taken in to the Family of God. *he gives them Power to become the Sons of God*, that is, he gives them the Right and Privilege of Sonſhip For in him, who is the great Head of the Family, they are made Sons and Heirs, even *Heirs of God, and joint Heirs with Chriſt*, Rom viii. 17 In him they are Heirs unto all the good and great Things that are contained in the Promiſe. While you are in the firſt *Adam*, you are Children of Wrath, you are Heirs unto the Curſe of the broken Law, and the Sin revenging Wrath of God · It is in the Lord Jeſus the ſecond *Adam*, that you muſt be the Heirs of Promiſe, he has the *Keys of the Houſe of* David in his Hand, *he opens and none can ſhut he ſhutteth and none can open* He admits into the Family, and keepeth out of the Family, according to his good Pleaſure.

5thly. *Acceſs to the Preſence of God* is another Bleſſing wherewith Men are bleſſed in Chriſt, *Heb.* x 19 *Having therefore, Brethren, Boldneſs to enter into the Holieſt by the Blood of Jeſus by a new and living Way which he hath conſecrated for us through*

tre

the Vail, that is to say, his Flesh When Sin entred into the World, all friendly Intercourse betwixt God and Man was broke up. Sin shut us out from the Presence of God it stands as a great Mountain, and as a Partition-Wall betwixt God and us. But in Christ this Partition-Wall is broken down, there is a Way prepared for us into the Holiest of all, the Stumbling Blocks are taken out of the Way, according to the Prophecy, *Isa.* lvii. 14, 15 *Cast ye up, cast ye up, prepare ye the Way, take up the Stumbling Block out of the Way of my People* For thus saith the high and lofty One that inhabiteth Eternity, *whose Name is Holy, I dwell in the high and holy Place, with him also that is of a contrite and humble Spirit* God condescends to come down and dwell with Men Why? the Way is prepared, the Stumbling-Blocks are removed, Justice is satisfied, the Faithfulness of God to the Threatning is glorified, his *Law is magnified and made honourable.* Now God comes to us thro' the Blood of his own Son, and we have Access to him that same Way, even *through the Vail of Christ's Flesh*, that is, through a crucified and slain Christ, we have Access to God with Hope and Confidence of Acceptance in all Duties of Worship, through him we have Communion with God both in Grace and Glory · This is indeed a wonderful Way of Access to God May we not say of it, *It is the Doing of the Lord, and let it be wonderful in our Eyes?*

6thly The *Life of Glory* hereafter is a Blessing wherewith Men are blessed in Christ. This Blessing was lost by Sin, and it is only to be found in the Lord Jesus Christ By the Life of Glory I understand all that Blessedness and Felicity that is reserved for the Heirs of Promise, even the *Inheritance incorruptible, undefiled, that fadeth not away,*

reserved

reſerved in Heaven for them · This Glory, it is Glory to be revealed, it is vailed from us in our preſent State; for *Eye hath not ſeen, nor Ear heard,
neither have entred into the Heart of Man, the Things
which God hath prepared for them that love him* It
is expreſſed in Scripture by *being ever with the Lord,*
1 Theſſ iv. 17. By *ſeeing his Face in Righteouſneſs,
and being ſatisfied with his Likeneſs,* Pſalm xvi. 15.
Seeing him as he is, 1 John iii. 2. *Seeing Face to
Face,* 1 Cor. xiii. 12.

7thly. To ſhut up this Head, God gives *himſelf*
in Chriſt unto Men. This is indeed a comprehenſive Bleſſing, it is the Sum and Subſtance of all
other Bleſſings. When Man fell, he loſt Bleſſedneſs, that is, he loſt God himſelf, in Chriſt God
himſelf is to be found as our chief Joy, as our eternal Bleſſedneſs and Reward: This is the great
new Covenant Gift and Grant unto us, *I will be
your God, and ye ſhall be my People,* Jer xxxi 33
Behold, then, *the Tabernacle of God is with Men, and he
will dwell with them, and they ſhall be his People, and God
himſelf ſhall be with them, and be their God,* Rev xxi 3.
Jehovah, Father Son and Spirit, gives himſelf unto
Men in the Perſon of our great *Immanuel,* and,
through his Death and Mediation, to be their Portion and Inheritance, their Husband and Father,
their Bleſſedneſs and Glory. O what amazing and
condeſcending Grace and Love is here! Well
may it be ſaid, *Men ſhall be bleſſed in Chriſt.*

I proceed to the *fourth* general Head, and that
is, To enquire how it comes to be ſo, or why it is
that Men are bleſſed in Chriſt

I anſwer, 1ſt. This is intirely owing to the
Goodwill and Pleaſure of God, this is the original Spring and Source of the whole of our Salvation

There

There was no Cause, no Motive without himself, that moved him to be a God of Blessings to Men ; we are blessed in Christ, because so it seemed good in his Sight   The whole Work of our Redemption and Salvation by Jesus Christ is ascribed to *the good Pleasure of his Will*, Eph 1 5   It is *according to his good Pleasure, which he hath purposed in himself*, Verse 9.

2*dly* It is for the Manifestation of the Glory of God   This is the great End of all the Works of God , for *the Lord hath made all Things for himself,* that is, for his own Glory, *Prov* xvi. 4. For *of him, and through him, and to him are all Things, to whom be Glory for ever and ever,* Rom. xi. 36. The Work of our Redemption and Salvation, by Christ Jesus, is the chief of the Works and Ways of God, and the Manifestation of his Glory is the Design of this great Work of God , and the divine Glory shines forth more brightly here than in all the other Works of God. The adorable Sovereignty of God is manifested in blessing fallen Men, and in shutting up the Angels who sinned under Chains of Darkness . Yea, glorious Sovereignty shines forth in bestowing the Blessing upon some of Mankind, while others are passed by.   Here there is an unsearchable Depth ; *How unsearchable are his Judgments, and his Ways past finding out ? Who may say unto him, What dost thou ?* If any will contend with their Maker, how will they manage the Plea against him ? For all are guilty, all are sinful before him , and he might have justly dealt with the whole Race of Mankind, as he has done with the fallen Angels.   Here the awful Justice of God, the spotless Purity and Holiness of his Nature, and his untainted Veracity and Truth to the penal Sanction of his righteous Law, do all shine forth, for *God spared not his own Son.* What greater Evidence can there be of the Evil of

Sin,

Sin, of God's infinite Hatred and Deteſtation at it, and of the Excellency and Importance of his Law, than his giving his own Son to be the Propitiation for Sin? As nothing leſs could vindicate the Honour and Authority of his Law than this amazing Inſtance of Love, ſo it was a publick Declaration to the whole World, unto Angels and Men, of the Holineſs and Purity of his Nature, and of his inexorable Juſtice and Equity, as the ſupreme Rector and Governor of the World It is one of the Letters of his great and glorious Name, that *he will by no Means clear the Guilty* His Juſtice and Holineſs cannot admit of Forgiveneſs without a Satisfaction. Again, the Glory of Grace and Mercy is wonderfully diſplayed here: An Atonement is made for Sin, and a Satisfaction is given unto the Juſtice of God, that Mercy and Grace may have an Egreſs upon Men, to the Honour of the Holineſs and Faithfulneſs of God. Juſtice and Judgment are the Habitation of his Throne, and Mercy and Truth go before his Face, therefore we are bleſſed with all ſpiritual Bleſſings in Chriſt, *to the Praiſe of the Glory of his Grace*, Eph 1. 6. and *that in the Ages to come he may ſhew the exceeding Riches of his Grace in his Kindneſs toward us through Chriſt Jeſus*, Eph. ii. 7. Alſo, what a glorious Diſcovery is there of the manifold Wiſdom of God, in finding out ſuch a proper Mean for our Recovery from Sin and Miſery, whereby the Honour of God, his Law and Government are ſecured, and the higheſt Glory is brought unto him out of the greateſt Evil, even the Sin and Fall of Man, and whereby Man is raiſed to a State far more glorious and excellent than that in which he was placed at his firſt Creation? Likeways the perſonal Glory of God is manifeſted here; the electing Love of the Father, the

redeeming

redeeming Love of the Son, and the applying Love of the Spirit, shine forth in the Contrivance, Purchase, and Accomplishment of our Salvation: These glorious Discoveries, both of the personal Glory of God, and of the adorable Perfections and Excellencies of his Nature, in the Business of our Redemption and Salvation, will be the subject Matter of the Contemplation, Admiration, and Praise of Angels and Men through Eternity.

I proceed now to make some practical Improvement of this Subject. And the first Use may be by Way of *Information* and *Instruction*.

1*st* If it is so, that sinful and miserable Men may find Blessedness in the Lord Jesus, and only in him, hence we may see the miserable Estate and Condition of those who are without Gospel-Revelation, they know not, neither can they know where Blessedness is to be found, they are *in Darkness, in the Regions of the Shadow of Death, without God, and without Hope in the World.* The Apostle testifies, that *the invisible Things of God from the Creation of the World are clearly seen, being understood by the Things that are made, even his eternal Power and Godhead, so that they are without Excuse,* Rom. i. 20 Yet the wisest and most learned among the Heathen never made that Improvement they might have done of those Discoveries which the Light of Nature gave them of the Being of God, and of some of his glorious Excellencies and Perfections, they never walked up to that small Light they had And, in all their pretended Searches after Wisdom, any Knowledge that they had of the supreme Being discovered their gross Ignorance about him, for *the World by Wisdom knew not God.* How inconsistently with themselves, and with

F

what

what Uncertainty, do they speak about the chief
Good? They knew not what it was, and generally
they placed it in indulging themselves in their carnal and sinful Pleasures. Every one of them were
in the utmost Darkness about the Way of Reconciliation to God, and of acceptable Worship, Service and Obedience unto him. Such of them as
have commended Virtue, have lived in the grossest
Wickedness themselves. Every Thing was reckoned indifferent among them, that did not break
Society, or disturb the publick Tranquillity: And
none of them knew any higher Origin, from which
virtuous Actions spring, than Self-Interest, Self-Ap-
plause, or one's own Honour and Esteem. A Regard unto the Authority, the Honour and Glory of
God, never entred into their Thoughts: In all
their virtuous Actions, *they sacrificed unto their own
Net, and burnt Incense unto their own corrupt Drag.*
Therefore, however useful some of their Rules they
laid down concerning Morality might be for human Society, yet all their virtuous Actions were
nothing but *splendid Sins* in the Sight of God, as
an eminent Light in the primitive Church did express himself. This was the miserable State and
Condition in which the Gospel did find the *Gentile*
World, when it was first published among them,
under gross Darkness and Ignorance of God, *vain
in their Imaginations, having their foolish Hearts
darkned. Professing themselves wise, they became Fools;
changing the Glory of the incorruptible God into an
Image made like to corruptible Man, and to Birds,
four-footed Beasts, and creeping Things, and giving up
themselves to all Manner of Uncleanness, and to vile
Affections.* In a Word, the Gospel found them
altogether under the Power of *Satan, the God of
this*

this World, the Spirit that worketh in the Children of Disobedience, Rom. i. 21, 22, 23, &c. Eph. ii. 2.

When I have mentioned the Morality of the Heathens, and the Grounds upon which their Philosophers pled for it, I must here observe, that it is a strong Evidence of the natural Darkness that is upon the Minds of Men, that under the Light of the Gospel, when God speaks plainly and clearly unto us, Morality should be taught upon no better Foundations and Principles than those upon which the Heathen Philosophers built their Schemes A Scheme of Morality, which has Self-Interest for its principal and leading Motive, that has no Respect to Christ as its Author and Ground of Acceptance, or to the Glory of God as its End, is plain *Heathenism.* It is too open and evident, that there is a deep Plot of Hell, in the Age wherein we live, to pluck up by the Roots the true Origin, Spring and Ground of all acceptable Obedience unto God, and to bring Men back to Paganism Hence it is that the Renovation of our Natures by supernatural Grace, a vital Union with the Lord Jesus in order to the bringing forth the Fruits of Holiness in Heart, Life and Conversation, Faith in him for the Acceptance of our Persons and all Duties of Obedience, are Doctrines that are nauseous to the Men of this Age, that pretend to be of a more refined Taste; and hereby they discover that *their Understandings are darkned,* that they are *alienated from the Life of God through the Ignorance that is in them,* and that they have no Taste, no Discerning of the Things of God : Whatever their Pretences to Morality or Wisdom are, yet their Principles have a native Tendency to banish Holiness out of the World, and to introduce Profanity and Looseness in Practice The Run of Profanity and Lasciviousness

through

through the Land, is one of the Fruits of the loose
and corrupt Principles that are vented in the Age
The Men of the Principles that I have named,
whatever their Opinion of themselves may be, are
no better than their Heathen Predecessors, *without*
Christ, Strangers to the Covenant of Promise, and
without God in the World, Eph ii. 12. Yea, their
Sin is more highly aggravated in regard they have
the Light the Heathen World had not, and their
Judgment and Condemnation will bear a Proportion
on to their aggravated Guilt and Sin.

2*dly*. If it is so, that Blessedness is only to be
found in Christ, hence see the Insufficiency of natural Religion to lead Men to Happiness and Blessedness. A Set of Men in the present Age, who
who have rejected the Bible, or that Revelation
that God makes of himself in his Word, and to
whom the Doctrine of Christ, and every Thing that
concerns his Person and Mediation, is Foolishness,
affirm, That there is a Sufficiency in what they call
natural Religion, for obtaining eternal Felicity and
Blessedness, or, " That the Laws of Nature do ly
" obvious to the Observation of every Man that
" inquires with Attention into the Nature of
" Things, and in themselves are a certain and
" sufficient Rule to direct rational Minds to Hap'
' piness, and our observing of these Laws is the
' Mean or Instrument of our real and lasting Feli-
" city " From these and the like Principles that
are vented in the present Age, it follows, that there
is no Necessity of divine Revelation, if we ob
serve the Laws of Nature, which ly obvious to e
very Man, we may be blessed and happy without
it : And consequently there is no Need of Christ,
his Death and Mediation, his Spirit and Grace
we observe the Laws of Nature, we may be blessed

and

and happy without him. Yea, many in this degenera-
ted Age are not aſhamed openly to own, that the
whole of divine Revelation is an Impoſture, that the
Goſpel is a *cunningly deviſed Fable*, and that the common Notices that we have from the Light of Nature,
of the divine Being and Goodneſs, are ſufficient to
conduct Men to Bleſſedneſs. Theſe and the like are
the Principles upon which the ancient Heathen Phi-
loſophers rejected the Goſpel of Chriſt, and, being
vainly puffed up with an Opinion of their own
Wiſdom, looked down upon this bleſſed Device
of Salvation through Chriſt as *Fooliſhneſs*.

Beſide what was obſerved on the former Head,
concerning the Ignorance and Darkneſs that prevailed in the World before Goſpel Light did ſhine
amongſt the Nations, is it not plain that all Mankind are Sinners before God? The Heathens themſelves have acknowledged it, the Deſpiſers of revealed Religion cannot refuſe it. Is not Sin a Tranſ-
greſſion of the Law of God? Is it not Rebellion a-
gainſt his ſovereign Authority? Is it not contrary
to his Purity and Holineſs? If it is acknowledged
that there is any ſuch Thing as Sin in the World,
all this muſt be acknowledged likeways. Again, if
Sin is an inſolent Affront offered to the Majeſty of
God, if there is an irreconcilable Contrariety in it
to his holy Nature, the Wiſdom, Juſtice, and Holineſs of God make a penal Sanction to his Law neceſſary, and his Faithfulneſs pleads for the Execu-
tion of the threatned Puniſhment. Hence it is an
important and weighty Queſtion, *Wherewith ſhall a*
guilty Sinner come before the Lord, or bow himſelf be-
fore the moſt high God? Or, How ſhall a guilty Sinner ſtand before him? The Juſtice, Faithfulneſs,
and Holineſs of God demand that the penal Sanction of the Law ſhall be executed, the Honour of
the

the Law and Lawgiver muſt be maintained : What
can give Relief to the Conſcience perplexed and
diſtreſſed under a Senſe of Guilt ? What can be a
ſufficient Plea for the Sinner againſt the Juſtice and
Faithfulneſs of God ? Can the Religion of Nature
looſe the Difficulty ? Can the Laws of Nature inform us of any proper Mean whereby Sin may be
pardoned, and at the ſame Time the Diſhonour done
to the great God repaired, his Faithfulneſs maintained, and the Honour and Authority of his Law
vindicated ? Nay, if the Conſcience is awakned,
the Terror and Dread of the righteous and holy
Law of God immediately ſtrikes the Sinner, the
Religion of Nature cannot tell him where his Relief is to be found, it cannot direct him to any proper and ſuitable Mean of Relief : In the preſent
Caſe, the Sinner, if he could, he would, with *Adam*,
flee from the Preſence of God, and hide himſelf
from his Juſtice, but there is no Poſſibility of his
covering himſelf from the Eye of God, or of ſhel-
tering himſelf from the Stroke of his Hand · Therefore the laſt Shift and Reſort of the miſerable and
ſelf-deceiving *Deiſt*, for quieting his guilty Conſcience, is his Notion of the general Goodneſs of
God. God, ſays he, is infinitely good, and therefore,
if we repent of our Sins, that is, if we are ſorry
for them, and return to our Duty, he will ſurely
pardon and forgive. Not to inſiſt upon the Contrariety that is in Man's corrupted and depraved
Nature unto that Sorrow for Sin, and that Return
to Duty, that is pretended, and conſequently the
Impoſſibility thereof, which may be obſerved afterwards, the Queſtion at preſent is about a ſuitable
Reparation of the Diſhonour done to God, and what
is a ſufficient and ſure Foundation for Peace unto
a Conſcience awakned under a Senſe of Sin. Is

not

not God infinitely juft, as well as infinitely good? Does not his Juftice and Holinefs require that the Honour and Authority of his Government fhould be maintained, and that the Sanction of the Law fhould be executed? What Security has the miferable *Deift* for it, that has alledged that Repentance can be acceped for the Ends and Purpofes named? Who told him this? If he fays, It is evident from the Goodnefs of God, it is as evident that the Juftice of God pleads for the Punifhment Is he a Debtor for the Egrefs of his Goodnefs unto any of his Creatures, far lefs for his pardoning Grace and Mercy to finful Creatures? It would not be reckoned a fufficient Security for any Government among Men, if Rebels and Criminals in every Cafe fhould have a Title to Pardon upon their Repentance, fuch a Principle as this would unhinge Government, and open a Door for the greateft Diforders amongft Men, the Authority of human Laws could not at this Rate be maintained. Can Men think that their Repentance is a fufficient Atonement for their heinous Rebellion againft the Sovereign of Heaven and Earth, or that it is fufficient to maintain the Honour of his Government, and Authority of his Laws?

If Men own their Dependence upon God, and his Authority over them, muft they not likeways own that perfect Obedience without Sin is due unto the great Creator? And is it not as true that none can anfwer this Debt and Obligation that they are under? Therefore, how can we expect to be accepted in that Sorrow for Sin, or in that Return to Duty which is alledged? Can a Repentance which anfwers not the Demand of the Law and our Obligation to Duty, be accepted for itfelf? And, if it cannot be accepted for itfelf can it make an Atonement for any other Tranfgreffions? To conclude

clude this Head, When that Revelation of the only Mean and Way to obtain Blessedness in and by the Lord Jesus Christ, which God gives us in his own Word, is rejected, what Security can miserable Men have for obtaining Peace and Reconciliation with God? Or what can they pretend unto as a sufficient Bottom and Foundation for Peace, Quiet, and Rest to their own Consciences under a Sense of Sin? Yet vain Man, like the wild Ass's Colt, will run himself into the greatest Labyrinths and Difficulties, rather than submit his carnal Reason and Wisdom, which is but Blindness and Folly, to that Revelation which God makes of himself in his Word. The Root of all the Opposition that is made both now and formerly to the Word of God, the Person of Christ, and the Way of Salvation through him, is that natural Enmity that is in the Hearts of Men against God. *The carnal Mind is Enmity against God, for it is not subject unto the Law of God, neither indeed can be* Rom. viii 7

3ly If it is so, that Blessedness is to be found in Christ, hence see the Excellency and Glory of divine Revelation Life and Immortality are brought unto Light by the Word of God The Word informs us where Blessedness is to be found, *Men shall be blessed in him* The whole Subject of divine Revelation is great, excellent, and glorious, it is such as becomes its Author it proclaims and declares to Men that God himself is its Author, if they will not wilfully shut their own Eyes against the glorious Light that breaks forth from the Word The great Design of divine Revelation is to inform us how Sin entred into the World, of the exceeding Evil that is in it, and the Ruin and Misery it brings upon Mankind, and also to declare unto us a Way of Reconciliation unto God, and of Redemption and Deliverance from Sin, and all the difmal Fruits and Effects of it, to the Honour and Glory of all the divine Excellencies and Perfections. The Origin of Evil was a Myftery to the Heathen Philofophers of old : They had fome Conviction that Mankind was corrupted and depraved, their own Confciences told them fo much, their daily Experience bore Witnefs unto it, the Miferies and Calamities wherewith they faw Mankind affected were fo many Evidences of it . But how Sin entred into the World, they knew not. Both in this, and in every Thing that concerns Deliverance from it, they *groped for the Wall like the Blind, they groped as if they had no Eyes, they ftumbled in their Noon-Day as in the Night, they were in defolate Places as dead Men.* But the Word of divine Revelation plainly declares unto us how Sin entred into the World, what Way the whole Race of Mankind are corrupted and depraved, together with all the difmal Effects of our Apoftafy from God Alfo the Word reveals unto us a Way to Blelfednefs, wherein God is glorified, wherein all his glorious Excellencies are eminently difplayed, a Way that honours both Law and Lawgiver, alfo a Way that is fure and fafe for us The forfeited and loft Blelfednefs is brought back unto us by the eternal Son of God, who affumed our Nature in a perfonal Union with his divine, and in that Nature which he affumed gave himfelf an Offering and Sacrifice for Sin , and in offering up himfelf a Sacrifice, he gave Glory to the Juftice, Holinefs, and Faithfulnefs of God Yea, the Glory and Honour that is given by the Redeemer to the Law of God, to his rectoral Juftice and Equity, to his Holinefs and Faithfulnefs, is not only equal unto, but greater by far than the Difhonour that is done him by *Adam's* Apoftafy from him, and Rebellion againft

G

him.

him. If it is confidered who he is that gave him
felf a Sacrifice, he is a divine Perfon, one who
thought it no Robbery to be equal with God. The
infinite Dignity and Excellency of his Perfon gave
infinite Worth and Value to his Satisfaction, whereby it bore a juft Proportion to that infinite Evil
and Defert that is in Sin, and was a full Reparation of the Difhonour done to God, his Law, Authority, and Government, by the Entrance of Sin
into the World. Here then we may fee the Holinefs, Juftice, and Faithfulnefs of God fhining
forth in their meridian Luftre and Glory, when
God *fpared not his own Son, but delivered him up
for us all Juftice and Judgment are the Habitation
of his Throne, Mercy and Truth go before his Face*
Judgment is executed upon Sin in the Perfon of the
great Surety, who was fubftitute in the Room of
Sinners, Juftice is fatisfied, and the Law is magnified by him Hence Mercy vents itfelf through
this coftly Chanel, the precious Blood of the Son
of God

As the Way of Peace and Reconciliation to
God, through the Death of his eternal Son, brings
the higheft Glory to God, fo it lays a folid Foundation for true Peace, Quiet, and Reft to the Confcience of the convinced Sinner Therefore it is
a Way not only honourable for God, but fafe for
us. Here the Sinner, convinced of Guilt and Sin,
may fee that the God whom he has offended, whofe
Law he has broken, may, notwithftanding of his
fpotlefs Purity, his deep Hatred of Sin, his inexorable Juftice and Righteoufnefs, and his untainted
Faithfulnefs pledged in the Threatning of the Law,
n   .ly pardon and forgive Sin without Prejudice to his Juftice and other Attributes, but alfo that
he is *juft* even *in juftifying them that believe,* Rom.
iii.

iii. 26.　Here a Sinner may see a beautiful Reconciliation of seemingly inconsistent Attributes, *Mercy and Truth are met together*: All this gives Ground for a Song, even for an eternal new Song, *Psalm* xcviii. 1. *O sing unto the Lord a new Song, for he hath done marvellous Things. The Lord hath made known his Salvation, his Righteousness hath he openly shewed in the Sight of the Heathen,* that is, in the Sight of the Nations, yea, in the Sight of the whole rational World; the Death of the Son of God being a publick Evidence of his Justice, Holiness and Faithfulness before the whole World, to the Admiration of Angels, and to the Confusion and Terror of Devils, that, through this glorious Chanel of the Death of Christ, the Love, Mercy, and Grace of God might flow down upon Men for their eternal Salvation.

Upon this Foundation and Bottom, the Atonement made for Sin in the Death of the Son of God, whereby the highest Glory is given unto God, *Peace is proclaimed on Earth, and Goodwill towards Men;* Christ is preached in his Person and Offices as the *Salvation of God to the Ends of the Earth,* as the Foundation and Ground of our Access to God, and Acceptance in his Sight, as the great Ordinance of God for Righteousness unto our Justification, and as the Fountain-Head and Spring of all Sanctification. In the Gospel we are told, that Peace with God, the Pardon of Sin, the Adoption of Children, Conformity to the Image of God, Grace here, and Glory hereafter, are all to be found in the Lord Jesus Christ. If it is inquired how we may be interested in the Blessedness that is in Christ, the Gospel informs us, that it is through Faith in the Lord Jesus Christ, *Jo.* iii. 36. *He that believeth on the Son of God hath everlasting Life, and he that believeth not the Son, shall not see Life, but the Wrath*

of

of God abideth on him. Every Unbeliever is under the Curfe, and all that believe, and only they, are interefted in Chrift, and in all that Bleffednefs that is in him; for *he that believeth hath everlafting Life.* Hence all that believe are not only juftified, but fanctified alfo; the Image of God loft in the firft *Adam* is reftored unto them, a Principle of Purity and Holinefs is implanted within them, which inclines to purfue after Conformity to the whole commanding Will of God. They, and they only, return to their Allegiance and Duty to God, for they fee the exceeding Evil that is in Sin, and the Contrariety that is in it unto the Authority and Holinefs of God, not only in the Glafs of the righteous and holy Law of God, but alfo in the Sufferings and Death of the Son of God. A Sight of Sin in his Death makes them lothe and abhor it, and forrow and mourn for it as the greateft Evil, they forrow and mourn for Sin with a fatisfying Reft on the Atonement that is made by Chrift, and they turn from it as the worft of Evils, they become zealous of good Works, and they evidence the Sincerity, Reality, and Truth of their Faith, in Duties of Obedience both to the firft and fecond Tables of the Law: To this they are daily influenced, from the Authority, Love, Grace and Kindnefs of God in Chrift, and that they may glorify him in their Bodies and Spirits which are his. If it is faid, great is the Corruption and Depravation of our Nature, and that there is not only an Inability to believe, but a natural Enmity in us againft the Way of Salvation through Chrift, then that Faith whereby we are united to Chrift, together with the Renovation of our Natures, and the Sanctification of our Perfons, are all of them promifed Bleffings: Hence the Promife is, *Thy People fhall*

be

be willing in the Day of thy Power, Pfalm cx. 3.
The holy Spirit is promifed as *Floods on the dry
Ground*, and then *one fhall fay*, *I am the Lord's*,
Ifa xliv 3, 4, 5. The *new Heart* and the *new Spirit* are promifed, with all fanctifying Grace, *Ezek.*
xxxvi. 25, 26, 27 And, in the laft Place, the greateft Security is given to all that believe, for the full
Enjoyment of all the Bleffednefs that is promifed.
Though they are in the Midft of Snares, Dangers
and Temptations, they fhall not, nay, they cannot
lofe their Bleffednefs, they cannot fall totally nor
finally away, they have his Word for it, that they
fhall be *kept by the Power of God through Faith unto
Salvation*, 1 Pet 1 5. Yea, they have his Oath
likeways, *Wherein God, willing to fhew more abundant-
ly unto the Heirs of Promife the Immutability of his
Counfel, confirmed it by an Oath, That by two immutable Things, in which it was impoffible for God to lie,
they might have ftrong Confolation, who have fled for
Refuge to lay Hold on the Hope fet before them*, Heb.
vi. 17, 18. This great Security is given them, not
to encourage or indulge them in Sloth, but to quicken and incite them to the Ufe of all appointed
Means, to animate them under Difficulties, to for-
tify them againft Temptations, to embolden them
againft all the Oppofition they may meet with from
Satan or his Inftruments in the Way of their Duty, and to give them the fatisfying Hope of a Glory to be revealed hereafter; as alfo to let them fee
that their Standing for Bleffednefs is upon a more
excellent and better Foundation and Bottom than
Adam's was when in a State of Innocence, even
upon the Bottom of the unchangeable Love of God,
the everlafting Covenant of Grace, and the daily
Mediation of the Lord Jefus. But, not to infift on
this large and extenfive Subject, every Thing in
the

the Way of Salvation and Bleſſedneſs through
Chriſt proclaims, that it is a Device that honours
God, and that it is ſafe and ſuitable for us. If
Men in their Oppoſition to it ſhould ſearch into
the Bottom of Hell for Weapons to fight againſt
it, no Weapon that is formed againſt it ſhall proſ-
per: All the Schemes that are ſet up in Oppoſition to the Goſpel bear a Stamp and Impreſs of
the Father of Lies upon them; they are inconſiſtent
with themſelves, and they fly in the Face of all the
moral Perfections and Excellencies of God, and
can never afford Quiet or Reſt to an awakened Conſcience. I conclude this Head with obſerving, that,
though Men ſhould deſpiſe his Perſon, his Word
and his Grace, yet the Deſigns of infinite Wiſdom and Love, in the Incarnation, Obedience and
Death of the Son of God, ſhall not, yea, they
cannot be diſappointed . The utmoſt Efforts of the
Gates of Hell cannot prevail againſt the Rock of
Iſrael, and therefore, though we ſhould preach
Chriſt crucified a *Stumbling-Block* to ſome, and *Fooliſhneſs* to others, yet *unto all that believe he is*, and he
will be *the Wiſdom and Power of God*

4thly If it is ſo, that Bleſſedneſs is only to be
found in Chriſt; hence ſee, that all that are without a ſaving Intereſt in Chriſt are under the Curſe.
It is in him that Men have Redemption from the
Curſe, in him they are juſtified, ſanctified and eternally ſaved , if you are out of Chriſt, you are under the Curſe of the broken Law, you are under the Wrath of God, God is angry with you e-
very Day, ye are curſed in your common Bleſſings, *Deut.* xxviii 16. *Curſed ſhalt thou be in the
City, curſed ſhalt thou be in the Field, curſed ſhall le
thy Basket and thy Store; curſed ſhalt thou be when
thou goeſt out, and curſed ſhalt thou be when thou*
comeſt

comeſt in. The Plowing of the Wicked is Sin; all that are out of Chriſt, their beſt Works are abominable in the Sight of God, though they may in ſome Caſes be profitable to themſelves, and very uſeful to others.

Hence, *5thly.* See the Excellency of Chriſt. *Men ſhall be bleſſed in him,* all Bleſſedneſs is to be found in him · He is *Immanuel, God with us, fairer than the Sons of Men,* all *Grace is poured into his Lips, God hath bleſſed him for ever,* that Men may be bleſſed in him Behold him in the glorious Fulneſs of his Perſon ! All the rich Treaſures of Grace and Glory are in him, he is *full of Grace and Truth,* the glorious Conduit of all ſpiritual Bleſſings to Men. Who can declare what is in his Perſon ? What Tongue can tell, what Heart can conceive the unſearchable Riches that are in him ? All the Glory of God is in the Perſon of Chriſt, and all the Glory of Heaven is in him . He is the Bleſſedneſs and Glory of the Church triumphant, and the Confidence and Joy of the Church militant, he is the Object of the Wonder, Admiration and Praiſe of the Redeemed from amongſt Men, and of all the holy Angels through Eternity. Behold him in the Fulneſs of Merit that is in his Death ! An offended God is atoned, awful Juſtice is ſatisfied, in his Death he trode upon Sin and *Satan,* he *triumphed over Principalities and Powers,* he *deſtroyed him that had the Power of Death, that is the Devil,* he brings back the Bleſſing unto us, by bruiſing the Head of the Serpent, and ſpoiling the mighty Powers of Darkneſs, and none but he was Match for them. Is he not then matchleſs and incomparable ? May we hot ſay of him, *There is none like unto the God of Jeſurun, who rideth upon the Heaven in thy Help, and in his Excellency on the Sky ? The eternal God is thy Refuge, he hath thurſt out the Enemy from before thee,*

Deut.

Deut. xxiii. 26, 27. To conclude this Head, you may obferve that Chrift has all fpititual Bleffings for every one of you. *Ifaac* had but one fpiritual Bleffing to give, but Chrift has all fpiritual Bleffings to give *Ifaac's* Bleffing was confined to *Jacob*, he could not beftow the very fame Bleffing on *Efau* , but Chrift beftows all fpiritual Bleffings upon every one that comes unto him, and there is Room in him for you all, he will not put any away that come unto him.

6thly. If it is fo, that Men are bleffed in Chrift, hence fee that all that believe have nothing in themfelves wherein to glory *Let him that glorieth, glory in the Lord* According to the Tenor of the firft Covenant, Man was to work for Life, to do for Life, his own Obedience gave him a Right and Title to eternal Life; but Matters are now otherways ftated in the new Covenant, all fpiritual Bleffings whatfoever are the free Gift of God through Chrift : That Righteoufnefs, whereby we are juftified, is the free Gift of God through Chrift, Faith and Repentance unto Life, the Renovation of our Natures, the Adoption of Children, and Perfeverance unto the End, are all the free Gift of God through Chrift In a Word, eternal Life is the free Gift of God through Jefus Chrift our Lord *Where is Boafting then? It is excluded*, there is no Room for it in the new Covenant Why, in ourfelves we are Enemies and Rebels, but in Chrift Peace and Reconciliation is given · In ourfelves we are guilty, under the Curfe and Wrath of God, but in him *we have Redemption through his Blood, even the Forgivenefs of Sin, according to the Riches of his Grace :* In ourfelves we are dead, but in him we have Life ; for he is *the Refurrection and the Life* In ourfelves we are dark and blind, but in him we have Light and Sight , he is Light to them that fit

in Darkneſs, and he opens the Eyes of the Blind :
In ourſelves we are wretched, miſerable and naked ;
but he is Gold tried in the Fire to inrich the Poor,
and a Covering for the Naked : In a Word, in
ourſelves we are loſt, but in him we have Salvation , for he is *the God of Salvation :* Therefore all
the Ranſomed and Redeemed of the Lord muſt
needs ſay, *Not unto us, not unto us, but unto thy Name
be the Glory* ; yea, they ſhall through Eternity caſt
down their Crowns before him, and cry with a loud
Voice, *Salvation unto our God who ſitteth upon the
Throne, and unto the Lamb,* Rev. vii. 10.

7thly. Hence ſee the adorable Condeſcendence of
the Lord Jeſus, in ſtooping to be the Conduit of all
ſpiritual Bleſſings unto Men. How great is his Condeſcendence, if we conſider, 1. Who he is in whom
Men are bleſſed ? He is *the Son of God* ; this is the
perſonal Character of this glorious divine Perſon ;
he is *the Son,* by eternal, ineffable and incomprehen-
ſible Generation ; for, *Who can declare his Generation ?* He is the ſame in Subſtance with the Father,
*the Brightneſs of his Glory, and the expreſs Image of
his Perſon,* equal with him in Power and in Glory.
Is it not wonderful Condeſcendence, that he whoſe
Name is *Jehovah,* who is infinitely bleſſed in himſelf,
and who ſtands not in the leaſt Need of any of his
Creatures, ſhould ſtoop to be the Conduit of all ſpiritual Bleſſings to Men ? Eſpecially when it is con-
ſidered, 2. To whom it is that he is the Conduit of
ſpiritual Bleſſings . They are Men that have rebelled, Men who have broken his Law, and have
trampled under Foot his Authority, and thereby
have brought themſelves under his Curſe, and are
obnoxious unto his Sin-revenging Juſtice. Yea,
conſider, 3. How it is that he becomes the Conduit
of all ſpiritual Bleſſings unto Men : It is by aſ-

H   ſuming

fuming our Nature into a perfonal Union with his divine That the great God fhould become Man, that Men might be bleffed in him, is amazing Condefcendence . *The Word was made Flefh, and dwelt amongft us* , he was made Flefh, by affuming our Nature into a perfonal Union with his divine , and tho' here there is no Confufion of the two Natures, yet the human Nature had never any diftinct Subfiftence of itfelf, but from the Moment of his Incarnation did always fubfift in a perfonal Union with the divine Nature, and will do fo through Eternity And this is one Reafon, amongft others, why all *Images* and *Pictures* of the human Nature of the Son of God may be juftly reckoned an Affront upon his Perfon, and an Indignity done to the great God our Saviour : But more of this afterwards.   And, in the *laft* Place, as he affumed our Nature, fo he fuffered unto Death, that he might be the Conduit of fpiritual and eternal Bleffednefs unto Men.   That the Son of God fhould become Man, is wonderful Condefcendence , that he fhould be a fuffering Man, is greater, but that he fhould be made a Curfe, that we might be bleffed, and that he fhould die, that we might have Life, is moft wonderful · Yet all this was needful, nothing lefs could bring the Bleffing unto us.

I proceed now to a *fecond* Ufe of the Doctrine, which may be of *Lamentation.*   And here may we not lament over the Contempt that the World cafts upon Chrift ? *He was defpifed and rejected of Men* when he appeared in Perfon upon Earth , *He came unto his own, but his own received him not* · He was afterwards rejected by the Bulk and Body of the *Jewifh* Nation, when the Gofpel was firft preached to them by his Apoftles, and therefore *Wrath came*

upon

upon them to the uttermoſt : He was alſo rejected and deſpiſed by the great Pretenders to Wiſdom among the *Gentiles,* 1 Cor. 1. 23 *We preach Chriſt crucified, unto the* Jews *a Stumbling-Block, and unto the* Greeks *Fooliſhneſs.* He has been a *Stone of Stumbling,* and *Rock of Offence,* in all Ages and Generations : And how much is he deſpiſed in the Age wherein we live ? His Perſon is undervalued, his Grace is abuſed, his Word is ridiculed, and his Spirit is reproached O what Ingratitude is there in the Contempt that Men caſt upon him, if we conſider that it is he who brings the Bleſſing to Men, yea, he himſelf is the great Bleſſing that is given unto us ! O how great Wickedneſs is there in it ! When he is deſpiſed, all the Grace, all the Love, and all the Mercy of God is ſlighted . Yea, O what Injury do Men unto themſelves, when they reject him in whom alone Bleſſedneſs is to be found ! *He that ſinneth againſt him, wrongeth his own Soul.* When Chriſt is deſpiſed, Life is deſpiſed, Salvation from Sin and Wrath is deſpiſed , Death, upon the Matter, is preferred to Life, and the Curſe is preferred to the Bleſſing. O what Folly, yea, Madneſs, is here ! If Men reject Chriſt, there is not another Way to obtain Bleſſedneſs , for there is no other Saviour, there is no other Redeemer : Therefore all that deſpiſe him muſt periſh.

But, ſince this is the heinous Guilt and Sin of the Age in which we live, I muſt give you ſome particular Inſtances of the Contempt that is caſt upon him in whom Men are bleſſed. And here I lay the Charge of deſpiſing the Son of God, our exalted and glorious Redemer, againſt the following Perſons.

1ſt. He is deſpiſed by all ſuch as caſt off and reject that Revelation which God makes of his

Mind to Men in his written Word, or who do not believe that the Scriptures are the Word of God. There are too many in this degenerate Age, who have been baptized in the Name of Christ, and yet have laid aside the Bible · Some of them not only reckon it altogether useless, but even hurtful; and, instead of regarding it as the Word of the living God, reproach and revile it. But, having spoken to this on a former Head, I shall not enlarge upon it now : Only, all such as despise revealed Religion would know, that, since they reckon the manifold Wisdom of God Foolishness, and that Christ died in vain, they are *treasuring up Wrath unto themselves against the Day of Wrath, and the Revelation of the righteous Judgment of God.* It will be no Apology for them, that they have formed their Principles according to their depraved and blinded Judgments; nay, it will be their *Condemnation, that Light is come into the World,* and that *they have loved Darkness rather than Light,* John iii. 19.

2dly. He in whom Men are blessed is despised by the blasphemous *Socinians,* who refuse that Christ had any Existence before his Birth of the Virgin *Mary,* and who affirm that he was only a Prophet to teach, and not a Priest to satisfy the Justice of God for Sin, and that the principal End and Design of his Death was to confirm his Doctrine; and that he lived and died chiefly to give a Pattern and Example of Patience in suffering, of Obedience to God, and Resignation to his Will. It is a strong Evidence of the Corruption and Depravation of Man's Nature, when such who profess to own divine Revelation, do, after such a bold and daring Manner, attempt to overthrow the very first Foundation of the Christian Faith. Our blessed Lord, the faithful and true Witness, testi-

fies

fies concerning himſelf, *John* viii. 58. *Before* Abraham *was, I am.* He who is a *Child born* unto us, and a *Son given* unto us, is the *Mighty God,* the *Everlaſting Father,* or *Father of Eternity,* Iſa ix. 6. He who, according to *Micah*'s Prophecy, was to be born in *Bethlehem,* his *Goings forth have been of old, even from everlaſting,* Micah v. 2. There is no Doubt that in his Life and Death he is the greateſt and beſt Pattern of Obedience and Reſignation unto the Will of God · But was this the principal End and Deſign of his Life and Death, to teach us the Will of God, and to confirm his Doctrine by his Sufferings, or to give us a Pattern of Patience in Suffering, and of Reſignation to the Will of God? Nay, if Men will not ſhut their Eyes againſt the plain Teſtimony of God in his own Word, it is evident that the principal End and Deſign of the Manifeſtation of the Son of God in the Fleſh, was to make an Atonement for Sin, to ſatisfy the Juſtice of God, to bring in an everlaſting Righteouſneſs for our Juſtification in the Sight of God, and to give his own Life as the Price of our Redemption from Sin and Wrath, that God might be honoured and glorified in our Salvation ; hence it is ſaid, that *he was wounded for our Tranſgreſſions,* and *the Chaſtiſement of our Peace was upon him,* Iſa. liii. 5. *He made his Soul an Offering for Sin,* Iſa. liii. 10 *He was made Sin for us,* 2 Cor. v 21. *He once ſuffered for Sins, the Juſt for the Unjuſt,* 1 Pet. iii 18. He was made *a Curſe for us,* Gal. iii. 13. His Subſtitution in the Room of Sinners, his ſuffering in their Stead, his making a proper Atonement for their Sins, cannot be expreſſed in ſtronger and clearer Terms, than in theſe and the like Words of the Spirit of God. I ſhall only obſerve upon this Head, that when Chriſt is only

preached

preached as a **Pattern** of **Morality**, when the main
End and Defign of his Obedience and Death is
overlooked, or but flightly touched at, true Sanctification and Holinefs can never be obtained, if
the Foundation and Spring of Holinefs is neglec-
ted, you have an empty Shadow without the Subftance, you have the fpecious Name of Morality
and Virtue, and that is all. If Men reject the A-
tonement made by the Son of God, and will not
be obliged to the Merit of his Death for Redemption from Sin and Wrath, they defpife the Bleffings both of Juftification and Sanctification, and
confequently of eternal Salvation, that flow through
this coftly Chanel.

3*dly.* Chrift is defpifed by the wicked *Arians*, who
deny his true and proper Deity. The ancient *A-
rians* owned that he had a Being before the Creation of the World, and that by him God created
the World, but would not allow him to be co-eter-
nal and co effential with the Father, they denied
that he was the fame in Subftance, equal in Power
and Glory with the Father. Our modern Refiners
upon the *Arian* Scheme pretend to fpeak more ho-
nourably of him than their Predeceffors did, yet
they will not allow him to be the *fupreme*, the
felf exiftent, and the *independent God*, and truly, if
he is not felf exiftent and independent, he is not
God, but a mere Creature : But his Name is *Jehovah*, that is, the *felf exiftent* and *independent Being*,
he is *the Lord of Hofts, the whole Earth is full of
his Glory* The Seraphims cover their Faces with
their Wings before him, and cry one to another,
Holy, holy, holy is Jehovah Tzebaoth, *the whole Earth
is full of his Glory*, Ifa vi 3. *Thefe Things faid E-*
faias *when he faw his Glory, and fpake of him*, John
xii. 41. He is *Alpha and Omega, the Beginning and*

the

the *Ending, which is, and which was, and which is to come, the Almighty,* Rev. 1. 8. He *is the First and the Last,* and *besides* him *there is no God,* Rev. i. 11,——17. with *Isa* xliv. 6. His absolute Eternity, Self-existence and supreme Deity, cannot be expressed in plainer Terms · And, if he were not the supreme God, his Satisfaction could have born no Proportion to the Indignity and Dishonour that is done unto God by Sin, it would not have had Merit, Worth, or Value in it to make an Atonement for Sin · But he is *Jehovah, God over all blessed for ever,* and therefore our sure and all-sufficient Help is in his great Name

4*thly* He in whom Men are blessed is despised by the Popish Church. The whole Doctrine of Popery is levelled against the Offices, the Word, and Grace of the Lord Jesus Christ: That universal Headship that the Pope of *Rome* claims to himself over the House of God, is an Evidence that he is that *Antichrist,* who, *as God, sitteth in the Temple of God, opposing and exalting himself above every Thing that is called God,* 2 Thess. ii 4 Their Doctrines concerning the Imperfection of the holy Scriptures, the Authority and Necessity of unwritten Traditions, as also the Infallibility their Church claims to herself, and that blind Subjection that is required from all her Members to her Decrees and Canons, are all so many Evidences that their Church is antichristian. Their Doctrines concerning the Merit of good Works, concerning Penance for Sin in this Life, and a Purgatory after this Life, are opposite to that only and abundant Merit that is in the Death of Christ, to the Fulness of Virtue and Efficacy that is in the Satisfaction he gave to the Law and Justice of God, and contrary to the Freedom of Grace manifested in the Justification of a Sinner

ner before God, on the Account of the Righteoufnefs of Chrift imputed and received by Faith a-
lone. If our Perfons are accepted, either in Whole
or in Part, on the Account of any good Works
done by us ; if any Thing done by us by be reckoned in the leaft fatisfactory for Sin, then the
Doctrine of Juftification and Salvation by the free
Grace of God is quite overturned, for, *if by Grace,
then it is no more of Works, otherways Grace is no
more Grace*, Rom. xi. 6. But I fhall not now infift on thefe Things, I only obferve at the Time,
that the Popifh Doctrine concerning *Images* or *Pictures* of the Lord Jefus is highly difhonourable to
him. I have already noticed, that all *Pictures* of
Chrift are an Indignity unto his divine Perfon. Some
of you, it is like, may fay, May we not have a Picture
of the human Body of Chrift, to bring him to our
Remembrance, as we remember our abfent or deceaft
Friends by their Pictures? But, is there not a vaft
Difference betwixt that Remembrance you ought to
have of Chrift, and the Remembrance you may have
of any abfent or deceaft Friend? Ought you to have
any Remembrance of Chrift but what is religious?
that is, Ought you to have any Remembrance of
him but what includes fupreme Love to his Perfon, Confidence and Truft in him for fpiritual and
eternal Bleffednefs, and alfo Gratitude and Thank-
fulnefs to him for what he has done and fuffered?
This is what you will readily acknowledge, if you
are confiftent with your Chriftian Profeffion. But
you will fay, May we not have a Picture of him to
excite to this religious Remembrance, though we
do not worfhip the Picture? If you think fo, then
you and the Papifts are agreed in this Point: They
exprefly refufe that they worfhip Images or Pictures; they are not fo mad as to affirm that there

is

is any Divinity or Virtue in them, for which they
ought to be reverenced or adored Nay, fay they,
" We make Ufe of Images or Pictures of Chrift
" to affift us in our Devotions, to excite in us a
" more lively Remembrance of him, and to raife
" our Affections unto him " See the Bifhop of
Condom's Expofition of the Doctrine of the Catho-
lick Church, *Sect* 5

But an *Image* or *Picture* of Chrift, for religiou
Ends and Purpofes, is the Idolatry forbidden in
the fecond Command The firft Command directs
us to the Object of Worfhip, namely, *JEHO-
VAH* the true God. who is one God in three Perfons , the fecond Command directs us to the Means
of Worfhip, namely, all fuch Ordinances as he has
appointed in his Word The firft Command forbids us to worfhip any other but the true God , and
the fecond Command forbids us to worfhip the true
God by Images, or any other Way not appointed
in his Word It expresly forbids all Images or Pictures of any Thing in Heaven or in Earth, as af-
fifting or exciting Means of our Devotion, and that
becaufe God is a *jealous* God Therefore all Images and Pictures of Chrift, for exciting a religious
Remembrance of him, are an Abomination in the
Sight of God. If you inquire where it is that
you may fee Chrift, I anfwer, Chrift is fet before
you, crucified, in the Word and in the Sacraments ;
thefe are the Ordinances of his own Inftitution
and Appointment . And, if ever you get a faving
Sight of Chrift, it is only in his own Ordinances
that you can fee him , for it is not with the Eye of
Senfe, but with the Eye of Faith, that a crucified
Chrift is feen, 2 *Cor.* v. 7———16. His own Inftitutions are the only as well as the moft fufficient
Means for giving us the faving Knowledge of him,

I   and

and for exciting our Love to him, and our Confidence and Trust in him, therefore all Images and Pictures of Christ are only an imaginary Christ, and a gross Delusion. Let me then advise you to be concerned to get a spiritual View of the Glory that is in a crucified Christ, as he is set before you in the Ordinances of the Gospel. If Men lose once a spiritual Sense of the Things of God, and spiritual Views of Christ in his Person and Sufferings, they are ready to substitute in the Room thereof *Images*, *Pictures*, or *Paintings* of Christ, to gratify their carnal Senses, and this is the true Origin and Spring of all that Idolatry and Superstition that for so long a Time has been the Sin and Plague of the Christian World

5*thly* All carnal Representations of Christ and his Sufferings, for a profane or common Use, are a high Contempt of the Person, Death, and Mediation of the Lord Jesus. If it is an Abomination in the Church of *Rome* to frame Images or Pictures of him for a religious Use, is no less an Abomination to carry about a *pretended Picture* of Christ in his Sufferings, to expose it as common Shew for Money, under a Pretence of shewing a fine Piece of Paint, this is a most profane Prostituting of the sacred Mysteries of our holy Christian Religion. I am bold to warn you against such an abominable Practice; it is, with a Witness, a *trampling under Foot the Son of God*, and *a counting the Blood of the Covenant, wherewith we are sanctified, an unholy or common Thing.*

6*thly*. Christ is despised by them who do not believe on him, or who receive not the Testimony that is given in the Word concerning him. All who do not receive Christ into their Hearts, who do not submit unto his Government, and who do not study Conformity to him in their Lives, despise

ſpiſe him. The Charge, as it is now laid, is the epidemick Sin of this Generation, it is the Sin of this Generation, it is the Sin of this Congregation. Have we not Reaſon to ſay, *Who hath believed our Report? To whom is the Arm of the Lord revealed?* You have enjoyed the Word of the Goſpel for a conſiderable Time, but ſome are more hardned under the Means of Grace, and others are altogether indifferent and unconcerned about the Bleſſing that the Word of the Goſpel brings unto them, they prefer the World, then Trade, or their Merchandiſe, to Chriſt and the Bleſſedneſs that is to be found in him, like thoſe mentioned, *Matth.* xxii 5. Some deceive themſelves with a preſumptuous Hope and Confidence in themſelves, and others are wearied of the Goſpel, they lothe the Doctrines and plain Truths of the Goſpel, as the *Iſraelites* did the Manna in the Wilderneſs. Too many give up themſelves to open Profanity and Wickedneſs, while others content themſelves with an external Profeſſion, and an outward Attendance upon the Ordinances of the Goſpel. Know, that if you do not receive Chriſt into your Hearts, if you do not receive the Teſtimony of God in his Word concerning his Son, if you do not embrace him in his Perſon and Offices, as he is offered to you in the Word and Promiſes of the Goſpel, you deſpiſe and reject him, and if you deſpiſe and reject him, you reject the Bleſſing, you prefer Death to Life, you prefer Deſtruction and Miſery to eternal Felicity and Bleſſedneſs. And, for a Concluſion to this Head, may I not ask at you, What ails you at Chriſt? *He is altogether lovely, he is fairer than the Sons of Men, a Name is given unto him above every Name, that Men may be bleſſed in him.* What ails you at the Way of Salvation through Chriſt?

Is

Is it not a Way that honours and glorifies God, and a Way that is safe for you? What ails you at the Righteousness of Christ? Is not all your own as filthy Rags? Can you present any Thing that you can call your own before a holy God, as the Ground of your Acceptance in his Sight? Is not the Righteousness of Christ a sufficient, as well as the only Ground for the Justification of a Sinner before God? What ails you at the Government of Christ? Is not his *Yoke easy*, and his *Burden light? His Commandments are not grievous* All the Commands of the moral Law are the Commands of a God in Christ unto his People, and that Obedience unto them which springs from Faith, and is influenced by the Love of Christ, is both Pleasantness and Peace, for Wisdom's *Ways are Pleasantness, and all her Paths are Peace*, Prov iii 17

I proceed to a *third* Use of the Doctrine, and it is by Way of *Exhortation*. If it is so, that Blessedness is to be found in Christ, then I exhort you all, and every one, to come to him for the Blessing. I shall offer a few Things by Way of Motive. And, 2. A Word by Way of Direction unto you. And, to move you to come unto him for the Blessing, consider, 1st. All that Blessedness that is to be found in Christ is offered unto you In the Word of the Gospel that we preach unto you, all the Blessings of the new Covenant are brought unto your Door, they are spread before you, *Thus saith the Lord, Incline your Ear, and come unto me, hear, and your Souls shall live, and I will make an everlasting Covenant with you, even the sure Mercies of* David, Isa. lv 3 God doth earnestly call and invite you to come and partake in the Blessedness that is to be found in Christ, his awful Authority is interpofed, commanding you to come unto him for the Bleffing, *This is his Commandment, that we fhould believe on the Name of his Son Jefus Chrift,* 1 John III. 23

2*d*. Confider to whom it is that the Bleffing is offered My Text tells you that it is unto Men; for *Men fhall be bleffed in him.* God comes as a God of Bleffings in his Chrift to finful and rebellious Men, *Unto you O Men, I call, and my Voice is to the Sons of Men,* Prov VIII. 4.

3*ly* Confider what is the Bleffing that is offered unto you It is no lefs than God himfelf, he gives himfelf in Chrift unto you, *I will be your God, and you fhall be my People.* And with himfelf he gives Salvation and Deliverance from Sin and Wrath, and the eternal and beatifick Vifion of himfelf in Glory, all this is offered unto you : What would you have more, or what can you defire more?

4*thly* Confider the Worth and Excellency of the Bleffings wherewith Men are bleffed in Chrift · They are moft excellent, and moft valuable, if they are compared with all other Things, they will be found to excel them all (1.) The Bleffings that are to be found in Chrift are *fubftantial* Bleffings. All Things in this World are at beft but a Shadow, a *vain Shew,* Pfal XXXIX 6. But the Bleffings that are to be found in Chrift are a fubftantial Portion and Inheritance, they that inherit them, *the it Subftance,* Prov. VIII 21. They are fubftantial Food to the Soul, *Eat ye that which is good,* Ifa lv 2. Hence (2) the Bleffings to be found in Chrift are *Soul fatisfying* Bleffings, they afford abundant Satisfaction The World, and the beft Things in it, can never fatisfy the Defires and Expectations of the Soul, but all fuch as are bleffed

fed in Chrift, are fatisfied with his *abundant Grace*, with the *Goodnefs of his Houfe, even of his holy Place*, Pfalm lxv. 4. They are *fatisfied as with Marrow and Fatnefs*, Pfalm lxiii. 5. (3.) The Bleffings that are to be found in Chrift are fure and certain; they are called the *fure Mercies of David, Ifa* lv. 3 All other Things are uncertain; *Riches take Wings and fly away*, one may be rich to-day, and poor to-morrow, you have every Day Inftances of the Uncertainty of all Things in this World · But fuch as are bleffed in Chrift can never be deprived of their Bleffednefs, the Bleffings wherewith they are bleffed are in a fure Hand, they are kept by the Lord Jefus Yea, he himfelf is their Bleffednefs, therefore, take from the Believer what you will, you can never take his Portion from him, for his God is his Portion : Whatever the Believer may lofe, he can never lofe his Treafure, Chrift is his Treafure, *Who fhall feparate us from the Love of Chrift?* Rom. viii 35. (4.) The Bleffings that are to be found in Chrift are *eternal*, 2 Cor iv 18 If a Man fhould enjoy all the good Things that this World can afford, Death deprives him of them all, it makes a Separation betwixt us and every Thing in Time, but the Bleffings that are to be found in Chrift go through Death with the Believer · Yea, the full Enjoyment of that Bleffednefs which is promifed unto him, is in that *better Country*, the *heavenly*, which lies beyond the Line of Time

5thly. Confider all the Bleffings that are in Chrift are freely given You have nothing but Poverty and Mifery, but the good Things that are treafured up in Chrift, are given out freely to wretched and miferable Men · Pardon of Sin is the free Gift of God, eternal Life is the free Gift of God, all the

Bleffings

Bleſſings purchaſed by Chriſt are Bleſſings of Grace unto you, you may have them *without Money and without Price*, Iſa lv. 1. *Whoſoever will, let him take the Water of Life freely*, Revel. xxii. 17. Finally, if you are not bleſſed in Chriſt, you muſt remain under the Curſe, and under the Wrath of God, you ſhall die under the Curſe and you muſt needs ly under the Wrath of God for ever. Whatever you may think of it now, you ſhall know in a little, to your woful Experience, that the Threatnings of God's Word are not mere *Scarcrows*, and that the Wrath of a Sin-revenging God is not a Matter of Jeſt *It is a fearful Thing to fall into the Hands of the living God.*

I ſhall conclude this Head with a few Words by Way of Advice unto you If you would be bleſſed in Chriſt, 1ſt Seriouſly conſider your miſerable State in the firſt *Adam*, and that, while you are in a natural State and Condition, you are under the Curſe and under the Wrath of God Atheiſm lies at the Root of all the more open, or more ſecret and hidden Contempt that there is, amongſt Men, of Chriſt, and the Way of Bleſſedneſs through him, it is the Spring of the Indifferency and Careleſneſs that is amongſt the moſt Part of the Hearers of the Goſpel about their eternal Salvation. Did Men really believe that they are by Nature under the Curſe and Wrath of God, did they believe the Juſtice and Holineſs of God, and the Deſert of every Sin, they would readily value and prize the Revelation and Offer of Bleſſedneſs that is made unto Men through the Lord Jeſus Chriſt. 2dly See your Inability to come unto Chriſt for the Bleſſing Some reckon it an eaſier Matter to believe than to practiſe; ſuch, I am ſure, are Strangers both to ſaving Faith and ſound Practice. Saving

Faith

Faith in Chriſt is above the Power of Nature, it is the Fruit of the *exceeding Greatneſs of divine* **Power**, it is the Effect of that *mighty Power which wrought in Chriſt when he was raiſed from the Dead*, Eph. i. 19, 20. And without Faith there can be no Soundneſs in Practice. It is the firſt Principle of any acceptable Obedience unto God, either in the Duties of the firſt or ſecond Table of the Law, for *without Faith it is impoſſible to pleaſe God*, Heb xi 6. If ever you come to the Lord Jeſus for the Bleſſing, you muſt be convinced of your Unbelief; and a thorough Conviction of Unbelief is the ſpecial Work of the holy Spirit, *John* xvi 8. If you are convinced of your Unbelief, you will not only ſee your Inability to believe, but alſo the Enmity that is in your Heart againſt the Way of Salvation through Chriſt, *Rom.* viii. 7. 3*dly* Wait carefully upon the Ordinances of the Lord's Inſtitution and Appointment *Faith comes by Hearing, and Hearing by the Word of God.* The Bleſſing is promiſed in his own Ordinances, and it is in them that you may expect to find the Bleſſing, *Exod* xx 24 *In all Places where I record my Name, I will come unto thee, and I will bleſs thee* In the *laſt* Place, Pray for the Bleſſing from him. Prayer is a ſpecial Mean of his own Inſtitution and Appointment for obtaining the Bleſſing : All the Bleſſings of the Purchaſe of Chriſt are freely promiſed and freely given, the Grace of Faith, as we obſerved before, whereby we are intereſted in the Bleſſedneſs that is to be found in Chriſt, is likeways a promiſed Bleſſing And this may encourage you to look, to wait and pray for the Spirit of Faith, and if you are ſeeking the Spirit of Faith, under a Senſe and Feeling of your Unbelief, ye are in the Way to obtain it.

I pro-

I proceed to the *laft* Ufe of this Doctrine, and it is in a Word to fuch as are Partakers of that Bleffednefs that is in Chrift. And here I fhall, in the *firft* Place, give fome *Characters* of them. 2. Offer fome Things for their *Confolation* and Encouragement. And, 3 conclude with a few Words by Way of *Advice* unto them.

In the *firft* Place, I fhall give you a few *Characters* of them that are bleffed in Chrift.

1ft If you are bleffed in him, ye have feen yourfelves under Sin, and under the Curfe and Wrath of God by Nature, the Spirit of God has convinced you both of Sin and Mifery You have feen the Sin of your Nature, and of your Way; you have feen yourfelves Sinners in the firft *Adam*, and that you are *Tranfgreffors from the very Womb*; ye have feen that your Life has been one continued Series and Tract of Rebellion againft God; you have feen Sin in its exceeding Sinfulnefs, you have feen it in its Contrariety unto the holy Nature of God, and confequently that you are loathfom and vile before him; ye have feen Sin in its Contrariety unto the Authority of God expreffed in his Law, and confequently that you are guilty before him, and that you are not only obnoxious unto everlafting Wrath, but alfo that you deferve nothing but Wrath, and that he is righteous, juft and holy, tho' he fhould condemn you, you have feen that all your Duties are as an unclean Thing, that all your own Righteoufneffes are as filthy Rags, and that you can do nothing at all for your own Help and Recovery from that Mifery and Ruin that Sin has brought you under, and that, if you are faved, your Salvation muft be by the free Grace of God alone through Jefus Chrift. In a Word, every convinced Sinner, who has come unto the Lord Jefus for the Bleffing, fees the Evil of Sin,

K and

and also the high Desert of it ; all Confidence in himself is beat down, his lofty Looks are humbled, the Haughtiness of his Heart is made low, he lothes himself before the Lord for his Iniquities and his Abominations, *Isa.* ii. 12——17. *Ezek* xxxvi. 31.

2dly. If you are blessed in Christ, you have a spiritual Inbeing in him, through the Faith of the Operation of God. Many of you are joined to the Lord Jesus only by an outward Profession , you are baptized in the Name of Christ, you attend upon his Ordinances, you have some common Knowledge of the Principles of Religion, and make an outward Subjection unto Christ : But, if these are the only Ligaments and Bonds wherewith ye are joined unto him, ye have no Part as yet in the Blessing, ye are Strangers unto him, ye are amongst the Branches that shall be taken away as withered and useless, who are gathered in the End and cast into the Fire, and are burned, *John* xv. 2——6. If you have any real and spiritual Inbeing in Christ, the Spirit of the Lord has taken the *Face of Covering from off you*, he has, by the Means of the Word of the Gospel, *shined into your Hearts, and given unto you the Light of the Knowledge of the Glory of God in the Face of Jesus*, 2 Cor iv 6. You have got a Discovery of Christ in the Glory of his Person, and in the Suitableness of his Offices, as a meet Saviour and Redeemer for you , and your Souls have ecchoed back to the Gospel-Revelation of Christ, *In the Lord have I Righteousness and Strength I count it a faithful Saying, and worthy of all Acceptation, that Christ came to save Sinners, of whom I am the Chief* In a Word, you approve of the whole Plan of Salvation thro' Christ, as a Device full of infinite Wisdom and Love, as a Device

vice that honours and glorifies God, and that is
suitable and safe for you, you rest upon the Person
and Mediation of Jesus Christ for Salvation from
Sin in its Guilt and Filth, and also in its Power
and Being; you rest upon him for Deliverance from
the Wrath to come, for Acceptance in the Sight
of God, for a Right and Title to eternal Glory,
and for the actual Fruition and Enjoyment of whatever is contained in the everlasting Covenant.

3*dly*. If you are blessed in Christ, you will esteem
him highly yourselves, and it will be your Desire
that he may be exalted and honoured by others:
I say, you will esteem him yourselves. If he is
despised by them that believe not, if he is a Stone
of Stumbling and a Rock of Offence unto them,
yet *unto them that believe he is precious*, 1 Pet ii.
7 They prefer and esteem him above all other
Persons and Things whatsoever. Likeways, it
will be your Desire that he may be exalted and honoured in the Congregation and Place where you
live, and you will readily lay out yourselves, in
the several Stations in which you are placed, to
honour and glorify his Name, you will desire that
he may be exalted in the Land wherein you live,
yea, you cannot but cry out with the Psalmist, in
the Words following our Text, Blessed be his glorious Name for ever, and *let the whole Earth be filled with his Glory, Amen, and Amen.*

4*thly* If you are blessed in him, then you will
study Conformity to his Image. It is one of the
distinguishing Characters of all that are blessed in
him, that they are *conformed to his Image*, Rom viii.
29 And this is no small Part of that Blessedness
wherewith Men are blessed in Christ, as you heard.
All that are blessed in him, they are renewed in
the whole Man after the Image of God, *Eph.* iv. 23,

24.

24. They are made *Partakees of the divine Nature*, 2 Pet. i. 4. They have an inward Principle of Purity and Holiness implanted in them, and it is their Endeavour daily to die unto Sin, and to live unto Righteousness, to advance in Sanctification and Holiness, till the Top-Stone is set upon the Work in Glory. If you are conformed unto the Image of Christ, then you will love the whole Law of God, because of its Purity and Holiness, you will hate every false Way, because of its Contrariety to the Holiness and Authority of God, indwelling Sin will be your daily Burden, you will maintain a daily Conflict and Fight against it, you will make Christ your Pattern and Example, you will daily pursue after Conformity to your holy Head, and you will thirst after Deliverance from the Inbeing of Sin, and after that consummate and complete Sanctification and Holiness, which, according to his Promise, you shall shortly attain unto, for he will *present* all his Members *unto himself a glorious Church, not having Spot or Wrinkle, or any such Thing, but holy and without Blemish*, Eph. v 27.

I proceed, in the *second* Place, unto a Word of *Consolation* and Encouragement unto all that are indeed blessed in Christ, and particularly to you who can lay Claim to the Characters just now given. Whatever discouraging Providences you may be tried with, whatever Difficulties you may be under, whatever your Afflictions or Troubles may be, yet you have Ground for strong Consolation. For,

In the *first* Place, If you are blessed in Christ, your Blessedness is well secured unto you. Your great New Covenant Head is Trustee for you, he is not only intrusted with all the Concerns of his Father's Honour and Glory, but also with all that concerns you for Time and Eternity, neither Devils

vils nor Men can pluck you out of his Hand, *John* x. 28 *I give unto Them eternal Life, and they shall never perish, neither shall any pluck them out of my Hand.* The first *Adam* lost the Stock of Blessedness that was put into his Hand, and thereby ruined himself and all his Posterity, but the second *Adam is the mighty God*, what his Father put into his Hands shall be surely and safely kept, and what you have committed unto him, he is *able to keep against that Day*, viz the Day of his glorious Appearance, *2 Tim* 1 12.

2ly If you are blessed in him, you are blessed in any Thing that you have If you have but little in the World, there is a Blessing in it, *A little that a righteous Man hath, is better than the Riches of many wicked.* There is a Blessing in all your Losses, and in all your Crosses, whatever cross Winds of Providence may blow in your Face, they are designed for your Good, whatever Losses you may meet with, they are for your Good, for *all Things shall work together for Good to them that love God*, Rom viii 28

3ly If you are blessed in Christ, you can never be accursed. *Satan* and his Instruments may curse and revile you, but they cannot hurt you, if they malign and revile you, reckon the Reproach of Christ your Crown and your Glory · *If you are reproached for the Name of Christ, happy are you; for the Spirit of glory and of God resteth upon you*, 1 Pet. iv 14 You are safely sheltered and covered from the Curse of the Law, and from the Sin-revenging Justice of God, under his Shadow who is *the Lord our Righteousness* The Curse of the Law can never take Hold on you, it is a Hand-Writing that is cancelled and blotted out, for *there is no Condemnation to them that are in Christ.* In a Word, you have

have Ground for that holy Gloriation and Boaft of Faith, *Who ſhall lay any Thing to the Charge of God's Elect? It is God that juſtifieth: Who is he that condemneth? It is Chriſt that died, yea rather, that is riſen again, who is even at the Right-Hand of God, who alſo maketh Interceſſion for us*, Rom. viii. 33. 34.

4thly. If you are bleſſed in Chriſt, you ſhall be bleſſed in your Death; *Bleſſed are the Dead that die in the Lord*, Rev. xiv. 13. You muſt die as well as others, but Death will be a Bleſſing unto you: Death is diſarmed of its Sting, and is a Friend unto all them that are in Chriſt, it is a Meſſenger ſent to bring them to the Poſſeſſion of that perfect and complete Bleſſedneſs that is reſerved for them. Are you bleſſed in Chriſt? Then Death will put a Period to all your Doubts and Fears, to all your Temptations and Trials; it will ſet you free from all the Remains of Sin, it will bring you unto the immediate Enjoyment of God himſelf, who is your everlaſting Glory and Bleſſedneſs Hence,

In the *fifth* Place, You ſhall be bleſſed after Death. The Souls of Believers are at their Death made perfect in Holineſs, and they paſs immediately into Glory, you ſhall then paſs into the immediate Fruition and Enjoyment of God, you ſhall ſee him as he is, you ſhall be with him where he is, and ſhall behold his Glory, *John* xvii 24 You ſhall paſs into the immediate Worſhip and Service of God, for *there his Servants ſhall ſerve him*, Rev. xxii. 3. You ſhall paſs into an everlaſting Freedom from all Sin, all Sorrow, and all Trouble: *God ſhall wipe away all Tears from your Eyes, and there ſhall be no more Death, neither Sorrow, nor Crying, neither ſhall there be any more Pain*, Rev. xxi. 4.

6thly. You ſhall be bleſſed at the Day of Chriſt's glorious Appearance. He who ſuffered and died, and

and who rofe by his own Power from the Dead,
and who is now fet down on the Right-Hand of the
Majefty on High, will come again from Heaven to
Earth with Power and great Glory: *Surely*, fays
he, *I come quickly*, Rev. xxii. 20, The Day of
his Coming will be a terrible Day to his Enemies,
and to the Enemies of his Church and People: It
will be the Day of his righteous Vengeance on *Satan*, and on all the wicked and ungodly · But it
will be a Day of Bleſſings unto you that are interefted in him, you fhall then be raifed up in Glory,
your *vile Bodies* fhall then be *changed*, and fhall be
faſhioned like unto his glorious Body, your glorious
Head, in whom you are bleſſed, will openly acknowledge and own you as his, before his Father,
and before the holy Angels, yea, before the Devils,
and before all the wicked and ungodly World;
he will in like Manner openly acquit you from e-
very Accufation and Charge that Law and Juftice
may give in againſt you, and from all the Reproaches that *Satan* or his Inftruments may throw
upon you. You are now juftified and pardoned;
but then the Sentence fhall be publifhed and declared before all the World. *Every Tongue that
rifeth in Judgment againſt you ſhall be condemned.*
Then will he fay unto you, *Come, ye bleſſed of my
Father, inherit the Kingdom prepared for you from the
Foundation of the World*, Matth. xxiv. 34.

I conclude this Subject with a few Words by
Way of *Advice* to fuch as are Partakers in the
Bleſſedneſs that is to be found in Chrift.

And, in the *firſt* Place, be concerned to honour
him in whom ye are bleſſed. He is a glorious and
honourable Perfon, yea, he is infinitely excellent
and glorious: A Name is given him which is a-
bove every Name that is named, both in this

World,

World, and in that which is to come You are
under the ſtrongeſt Obligations to honour him, he
humbled himſelf, he vailed the Glory of his
divine Perſon, and made himſelf of no Reputation
for a Time, that you might be bleſſed in him.
Should you not then lay out yourſelves to honour
and glorify him? If you inquire what Way you
ought to glorify him? I anſwer, Be concerned for
his declarative Honour and Glory in the World,
appear for him in the ſeveral Stations in which
you are placed, be neither aſhamed to own his
deſpiſed Members, nor to confeſs any of his inju-
red Truths, beware of grieving his Spirit, and ſtu-
dy univerſal Obedience to his Law, let your E-
ſteem of his Perſon increaſe and grow the more that
you ſee him undervalued and deſpiſed I know
not if in any Period, ſince the Dawning of Reformation-Light in *Scotland*, more Contempt has been
caſt upon the Perſon, upon the Offices, upon the
Word and the Spirit of Chriſt, than in the Age
wherein we live. Is not that bleſſed Book, the Bible, the Object of the Scorn and Ridicule of many?
Is not his Perſon rejected, and his Grace deſpiſed?
Are not the ſpecial Operations of his bleſſed Spirit
reviled? But, if he is a Stone of Stumbling, and
a Rock of Offence unto others, let him be more
precious in your Eyes, let your Love to him grow,
for he is worthy to be loved, he is infinitely glorious, and altogether lovely. And, if you can do
no more for him, be affected with the Diſhonours
that are done unto him; mourn in ſecret for the
Diſhonours that are done him in *Scotland*, and in
the Place and Congregation where you live.

2*dly* If you are among thoſe who are bleſſed in
him, then live upon him who is the inexhauſtible
Treaſure-Houſe of all ſpiritual Bleſſings. Let all
your

your Hopes and Expectations centre in him: Truſt him with what concerns you for Time and E-ternity: Make Uſe of that Fulneſs of Grace that dwells in his Perſon; he has new Bleſſings to give you every Day; he *giveth liberally, and upbraideth not.*

3*dly.* See that you *glory in his holy Name.* You have Ground for a holy Boaſt and Gloriation in your bleſſed and glorious Head, glory in him as your Strength for every Duty, and under every Difficul-ty; glory in him as your juſtifying Righteouſneſs, under whoſe Shadow you are ſheltered and ſaved from the vindictive Wrath of God, and in whom you have Acceſs with the Boldneſs of Faith into the Holieſt of all. In a Word, glory in him as the God of your Salvation, he will be your All and your Glory through Eternity: *Let him that glorieth, glory in the Lord,* 1 Cor. 1 31.

4*thly.* Be concerned for others, that they may be bleſſed in him. Come with your Families unto him for the Bleſſing, bring your Children and Servants unto him, that he may bleſs them, pray for the Congregation wherein you live, that many in it may be bleſſed in him, pray for a Bleſſing on your Neighbours, yea, *bleſs them that perſecute you, and pray for them that deſpitefully uſe you.*

Finally, Give Glory to him in whom you are bleſſed · Bleſs his holy Name, all and every one in *all Nations,* who are bleſſed in him, *ſhall call him bleſſed* When he bleſſeth us, he makes us bleſſed, he communicates his Bleſſings unto us: But he is infinitely bleſſed in himſelf, he can receive no Ad-dition to his Bleſſedneſs, and therefore, when you are called to bleſs him, and to give Glory unto him, you are called to declare his Glory, to acknow-

L   ledge

ledge what he is, and what he has done for you :
And who is fufficient for this Work and Exercife ?
For who can fhew forth his Praife ? Who can declare his Glory ? Yet you ought to mint at it ; it
is what you ought to endeavour to do. Are you
bleffed in him ? O then give Glory to him, and
blefs him, acknowledge with Heart and Tongue
that he is infinitely bleffed in himfelf, and that your
Goodnefs cannot extend unto him. Give Glory to
him, by declaring his glorious Excellencies and
Perfections · Blefs him, by acknowledging yourfelves Debtors to his fovereign and free Love, and
his rich and abundant Mercy and Grace : And
though you have much Reafon to complain that
you have neither Hearts nor Tongues for this fpiritual Exercife, yet the Time is coming, when you
fhall, without a jarring Note, or miftuned Heart,
join the heavenly Quirifters, who cry out with a
loud Voice, *Worthy is the Lamb that was flain, to
receive Power, and Riches, and Wifdom, and Strength,
and Honour, and Glory, and Bleffing And let every
Creature which is in Heaven, and on the Earth, fay,
Bleffing, and Honour, and Glory, and Power be unto him
that fitteth upon the Throne, and to the Lamb for ever
and ever,* Rev. v. 12, 13.

F I N I S.

BOOKS *fold by* John Henderson *in* Abernethy.

Bibles of feveral Sorts.
   Watfon's Body of Divinity.
Welfch's Sermons, &c.
Bofton's Fourfold State.
———— on the Covenant.
———— Crook of the Lot.
Marrow of Modern Divinity, with Bofton's Notes.
Rutherford's Letters.
Welwood's Glimpfe of Glory.
Confeffions of Faith, with Scriptures at large.
Durham on the Revelation.
———— on Confcience.
———— on the Commands.
Moncrief's Duty of national Covenanting explained.
———— Glory of Immanuel.
———— Call to the rifing Generation.
Mr. Ralph Erfkine's Faith no Fancy.
———— Gofpel Sonnets.
———— Gathering to Shiloh.
———— Harmony of the divine Attributes.
———— Gradual Conqueft.
———— Little Remnant.
———— King held in the Galleries.
Brown's Life of Faith.
———— Swan's Song.
The Affociate Presbytery's Act and Teftimony.
———— Doctrine of Grace
———— Act for renewing the Covenant.
Acts and Proceedings of the Affociate Synod.
Mr. John Hunter's Sermons.